Borders and Battles

Borders and Battles

A Concise Military History of Modern India

J Francis

Vij Books India Pvt Ltd

New Delhi (India)

First Published in 2019

Published by

Vij Books India Pvt Ltd
(Publishers, Distributors & Importers)
2/19, Ansari Road
Delhi – 110 002
Phones: 91-11-43596460, 91-11-47340674
Fax: 91-11-47340674
e-mail: vijbooks@rediffmail.com
web : www.vijbooks.com

ISBN: 978-93-88161-98-5 (Paperback)

ISBN: 978-93-88161-46-6 (ebook)

Disclaimer:

This facts given in the book are based on the material available in the open sources. Author or the publishers do not claim authenticity of these sources.

Dedication

This Book is dedicated in memory of those lesser known martyrs who sacrificed their lives while guarding the borders of India.

OTHER BOOKS BY THE AUTHOR

1. Short Stories from the History of the Indian Army Since August 1947 - Book 1
2. Short Stories from the History of the Indian Army Since August 1947- Book Two
3. Short Stories from the British Indian Army
4. Bhartiya Sena Ke Itihaas ki Laghu Kathaye (August 1947 Ke Baad)- Bhag 1
5. Bhartiya Sena Ke Itihaas ki Laghu Kathaye (August 1947 Ke Baad)- Bhag 2
6. British Indian Army Ki Laghu Kathaye

CONTENTS

FOREWORD

India's borders have been a colonial legacy of accord and discord. Right from the midnight hour of India's Independence, the country's borders have to a great extent determined the course of India's development. To understand your country's strategic interests, you need to know its borders. Col. Francis has captured the essence of this requirement in vivid and graphic detail in Borders and Battles. His in-depth knowledge of events and places around India's borders is second to none. The author's command over the narrative is amazing. The book's presentation is unique – its style lucid and the presentation of each battle scene highly illustrative. The reader is thus allowed to visualise himself as one of the participants in the various battles described by Col. Francis. The book should be a delight to a historian, a dissertation reference to a scholar; of considerable interest to a diplomat; and a must read for personnel of the Services. Having known Col. Francis over the last couple of years, his discipline and dedication to the cause is clearly reflected in the book. I congratulate him on an excellent book, which is eminently readable.

3 March 2019

Shri M Ganapathi, IFS.

Former Indian Ambassador to Kuwait
and High Commissioner in Mauritius

ABOUT THE BOOK

Lt Gen S Pattabhiraman, PVSM, AVSM, SM, VSM

Former Vice Chief of Army Staff
Coonoor, Nilgiris
December 2018

It is indeed a privilege for me to put down my views after reading yet another of Col Francis's book on India's military history. The book, laid out in sequential chapters along our land frontiers with exceedingly easy to follow maps, sketches and graphics, is yet another factual treatise on what it means for an Indian to feel secure in his/her land of birth, made possible by the supreme sacrifices made by the men and women of the Armed Forces of the nation.

The author has in simple language made it possible to understand the role of the Army in guarding our frontiers. The book indeed is a reference work for anyone wishing to delve deeper and do research on the origin of borders that India inherited at independence, the present status the sacrifices made and the continuing vigil that is required in challenging environment of not so friendly neighbours.

For veterans of generations of those of us who have been a part of this great Army of ours and have seen active service in border areas and wars as described by the author, it is déjà vu and I must compliment my colleague Col J Francis for a great work which helps us reminiscing with fond memories of the time spent in such difficult areas and tense situations, made easy only by the ethos of the Indian Army in discharging one's duty with honour!

Major General SP Kapoor, SM, VSM

Former General Officer Commanding of an Infantry Division
Member State Consumer Commission
Union Territory Chandigarh, Panchkula
December 2018

In his book Borders and Battles, Francis has chartered the emergence of the Indian Nation-State in 1947 through the 'Mangled Mess' of the areas of dominance of over 500 Princely States and the areas ruled by the British as an integrated entity. Francis has very lucidly described not only the variety and history of borders/control lines such as CFL/LOC/LAC etc. across which we face our neighbours and their contentious nature; he takes the reader on the guided tour of the regions through which these lines pass, describing their uniqueness and prominent physical features. The political backdrop and developments, as well as the battles fought which have created or changed the alignment of these control lines, have been very well put across.

For the reader, it is interesting to read how areas that were considered impassable, impregnable and unproductive land-masses till not very long ago, have assumed great strategic importance and how over a period of the last 70 years, India has not only redesigned its border management by raising, arming and equipping its border guarding Central Police/Para Military Forces but have also updated its military potential and strategy.

Reading tales of valour of Indian soldiers, displayed while defending the nation's borders in the wars fought, makes the reader feel the adrenaline rush. The gripping narrative of the book leaves the reader with a deep insight into the uniqueness of territorial limits of the Indian Nation State.

Mr. M.R. Sivaraman, IAS (Retd)

Finance & Planning Secy - Govt of MP
Additional Secy-Ministry of Commerce, Govt of India
Director General-Civil Aviation
Additional Secy-Ministry of Civil Aviation
Union Revenue Secretary
Executive Director-IMF
Advisor-UN Security Council, CTC, Chennai
December 2018

The book Borders and Battles by Col J Francis is a valuable addition to the literature on our military history both by civil and military historians. This is the first time that anyone has attempted a book that brings out the status of our tumultuous borders and the heroic way in which our armed forces both the military and the police have been defending them on several fronts sacrificing their lives.

At the outset, I would recommend it as a compulsory read for everyone who joins the armed forces and also the IAS, IFS and IPS officers who also have to contend with border problems both during conflicts and in times of peace.

Col Francis has delved deep into the military archives to bring out in brief but with succinct details of every battle that was fought in all the conflicts that India has had since its independence in 1947. One does gather an impression that on many occasions India had to contend with an aggressor who caught us unawares and intruded into our territory on all the land borders of India. It is interesting that since time immemorial armies of Alexander to the Pakistanis now wanted to get into India but all of them had to go back defeated and frustrated. This gives a reason for India to contemplate deeply on its strategies to defend its borders. Should we always be defenders or take an aggressive offensive approach whenever we are attacked or at least make it known to our enemies that if at any time our peaceful borders are violated the aggressor may have to pay a heavy price. This becomes more than significant in the context of Pakistan continuing to violate our borders with terrorists trained and armed by them. One or two strikes by the army on terrorist installations have only temporary impact. This should be a regular feature of border defence strategy.

The victims of these periodical wars and conflicts are the people who are living close to the borders. Bullets and shells cannot identify civilians from the forces and invariably civilian property and lives are lost. There has to be a permanent solution to this perennial problem...

In conclusion, I would like to compliment the successful efforts of Col Francis to fill a gap in India's military history and make it available to all.

Lt Gen Milan Naidu, PVSM, AVSM, YSM

Former Vice Chief of the Army Staff
Bhopal
December 2018

The Book "Borders and Battles" authored by Col J Francis is a treatise of the borders of India. It also describes in brief, the battles that were fought by the Indian troops, with the adversaries. It is humanly not possible for anyone to visit the entire stretch of the borders and study its history, even if one has served in the Armed Forces. As such, I feel that this book is a boon to all responsible citizens, and soldiers, alike. At least, one can get a fair idea of the layout of our borders, difficulties faced by us, and most importantly, its implications on the military.

One can easily discern that Col Francis has undertaken painstaking and detailed research for each sector so covered, in the Book. The author has described the battles that have been fought in these remote locations. He has described the manner in which the troops were employed and the results that were achieved, without making his own pronouncements. The balanced view, thus, shuns any pontificating comments on operational and/or strategic aspects. Despite the self-imposed restrictions, Francis has achieved major success in holding the interest and curiosity of both, professionals and laymen alike.

In my view, the Book should be read by all responsible citizens of India, in order to know and understand our security environment. To the young officers and men, it will assist them in knowing the nuances of the past actions fought in an area and help them to devise better / more prudent operational plans when they are so deployed in that Sector.

A Book 'par-excellence'! I strongly recommend the book to be read by all citizens and studied by the members of the uniformed fraternity.

AUTHOR'S NOTE

The contents of this book have been conceived based on my exposure in the fields of human resource development and training of young officers of the Indian and Foreign Armies while serving in the Indian Army. After retirement, during my interactions with young and aspiring candidates of All India Government and Private Sector services, I felt the need for them to acquire more knowledge in the history of Post Independent India, especially the causes and contents of many wars India was forced to fight after 1947. Knowledge of the geography of the battlefields and their impact on warfare is essential for the future bureaucrats and students of military history. The content of this book has been designed to meet these requirements.

I have avoided using terminologies/jargons relating to the Indian Armed Forces in the text. However, I had to use names of organisations such as Division, Brigade, and Battalion etc. Similarly, I have also used the rank structures of the Army with the hope that even those who are not in uniform would know these universally used formations of the armed forces and ranks that are found in the public domain.

The outline maps and sketches are extracted from the public domain without the intension of infringing any copyright, suitably modified to meet the requirement of learning fraternity as a textbook. They are self-explanatory and not to scale. The boundary lines are approximate. The geographical north is towards the top of the maps and sketches. I have visited most of the battlefields included in this book during and after my service with the Indian Army. The names of places are spelt differently in different sources. I have chosen the most common spelling used in those localities.

–Author

ORDER OF THE DAY

Comrades of 50 Parachute Brigade Group,

Time has come when our planning and preparation for the recapture of Jhangar has to be put to test. It is not an easy task but I am confident of success - because our plan is sound and our preparations have been good. More so, because I have complete confidence in you all to do your best to recapture the ground we lost on 24 December and to retrieve the honour of our arms.

The eyes of the world are on us. The hopes and aspirations of our countrymen are based upon our efforts. We must not falter - we must not fail them.

> To every man upon this Earth
> Death cometh soon or late
> And how can man die better
> Than facing fearful odds
> For the ashes of his fathers
> And the temples of his Gods.

So forward friends, fearless we go to Jhangar. India expects everyone to do his duty.

Jai Hind

15 March 1948

Signed

Mohammed Usman

Brigadier

ACKNOWLEDGEMENT

I acknowledge and thank my senior colleagues and distinguished friends for their contributions in making this book a reality. The feedback about the book I have received from some of them is the result of their deliberate reading of my drafts and my subsequent interaction with them. I am grateful for their time and effort. Thanks are due in large measures to Brigadier PK Vij, the publisher and my guide.

My family has been a constant source of inspiration.

–Author

ABBREVIATIONS/GLOSSARY

AGPL	Actual Ground Position Line
APC	Armoured Personal Carriers.
AR	Assam Rifles
Battalion	About 1000 all ranks of Army
BOP	Border Out Posts
Brigade	Three Battalions
BSF	Border Security Force
Capt	Captain
CFL	Ceasefire Line
COAS	Chief of the Army Staff
Company	About 150 all ranks of Army
Corps	Three Divisions
CRPF	Central reserve Police
DCB	Ditch Cum Bund
Division	Three Brigades
IB	International Border
ITBP	Indo Tibetan Border Police
J&K	Jammu & Kashmir
JAT	Name of an Infantry Battalion

La	Mountain Pass
LAC	Line of Actual Control
LI	Light Infantry
LOC	Line of Control
Lt Col	Lieutenant Colonel
2 Madras	Name of an Infantry Battalion
2 Mahar	Name of an Infantry Battalion
MVC	Maha Vir Chakra
NEFA	North east Frontier Agency
PARA	Parachute
PLA	Peoples Liberation Army
POK	Pakistani Occupied Kashmir
2 Punjab	Name of an Infantry Battalion
PVC	Param Vir Chakra
2 Raj Rif	Name of an Infantry Battalion
SM	Sena Medal
SSB	Sahastra Seema Bal
VrC	Vir Chakra

Note: Non-military readers may find the use of capital letters in this Book different from convention. For example, the word 'company' is a common noun and written in lower case. However, when referring to a particular company, the word 'Company' is written in Title case. The names of places are spelled differently in different sources. I have chosen the most common spelling used in those localities.

INTRODUCTION

ORIGIN OF INDIA'S BORDERS

The Indian subcontinent comprised the land mass bounded by the Himalayas in the north, Arakanese in the east, Hindukush in the west and the Indian Ocean in the south. It was ruled by many kings and queens belonging to different dynasties. There were numerous dynastic kingdoms spread over thousands of years in the subcontinent. The British came to trade with Indians in 1608 AD. They found the subcontinent fragmented. The conditions were ripe for the British to take advantage of the prevailing political situations. They exploited it to their advantage and became the masters of the subcontinent between 1757 and 1947; mostly with the help of natives. The history of this period is well recorded and published.

While consolidating their gains and extending their frontiers towards northwest and northeast, the British realised that there was no demarcated border with the neighbours. They found that in the remote areas there was no concept of international borders. The boundaries existed were more for tax collection than sovereignty. Tribal chiefs and monarchs collected taxes as far as their power centres would allow. Traditional borders were vague. India had many nations within the state and many states within the nation. By 1899, the British proposed a border with China, but no written agreement could be made until 1914 (that too only with Tibet). The evolution of the British border in north-western India was a long and complicated process. It was mostly achieved by frontier campaigns. Most borders had been settled on paper but not always demarcated on the ground. When the British left India in 1947, the borders with China/Tibet remained vague and ambiguous.

During the last forty years of British rule over India, many formations and units of the British Indian Army were sent to foreign countries to participate in World Wars I and II on behalf of the British. There, Indians witnessed all-round development taking place in society under the democratic form of governance. They were exposed to industrial advancement, good quality of life and the modern way of warfighting. When they returned to India after the wars, they experienced the spirit of Indian nationalism taking centre stage over colonial rule in the Indian society. This changed their mindset. Their patriotic fervour was not hidden to the British. With the commissioning of a large number of Indians as officers in the British Indian Army and their improved fighting qualities comparable to the British, it became apparent to the British rulers that they would not enjoy the loyalty of Indian officers and men if and when they are employed against the nationalistic interest of the Indians. They realised that their days of rule over Indian subcontinent were at an end.

The two World Wars had ravaged the economy of Britain and British India. The combination of changed mindset in the rank and file of British Indian Army, the patriotic fervour of the Indians, and the declining economy in Britain had made the departure of British from India inevitable. The British could not depart from India leaving behind British India as one intact nation due to political, societal and religious complexities. It had to be divided. Events leading to the freedom of British India and the partition of India into India and Pakistan are out of the purview of this book.

In March 1947, Lord Mountbatten arrived as the last viceroy of India with a mandate to transfer the governance of British India to Indians before June 1948. The new Viceroy had decided to do his job well before the deadline that was given to him. Sir Cyril Radcliffe, an eminent legal luminary from England, was assigned the task of dividing British India into two nations, India and Pakistan, in three segments based on the principle of Two Nation Theory expounded by Mr Jinnah. He arrived in India in June 1947. He was assisted by two teams of Indian Judges comprising Justices Mehar Chand Mahajan, Teja Singh, Din Mohammad and Muhammad Munir for the western boundary and Justices CC Biswas, BK Mukerji, Abu Saleh Mohamed Akram and SA Rahman for the eastern

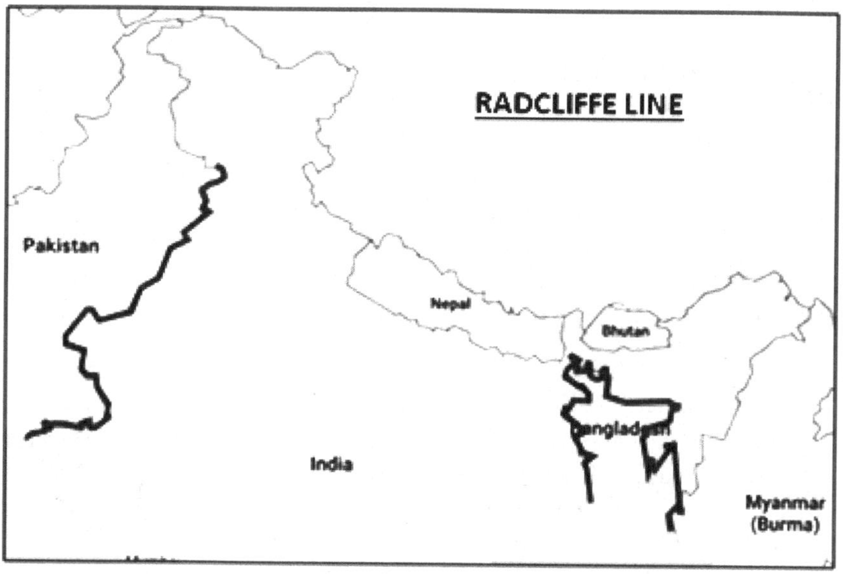

boundary. The division had to be completed before 15 August 1947. The task was a gigantic one; to divide 450,000 square kms of territories, where more than 88 million people of different religious faith and speaking different languages lived. The time given to them was just five weeks. Notwithstanding the constraints, the demarcation plan was finalised and submitted to the Viceroy on 12 August 1947. Some of the factors which were kept in mind by the partition committee while drawing the partition line were, minimum separation of farmers from their fields, relocation of affected population and maximum use of natural boundaries, roads, water courses and irrigation system to demarcate the dividing line.

British India was divided into the Union of India and the Islamic Republic of Pakistan. Primarily, the States of Punjab and Bengal were partitioned. Pre-existing borders of the other states were left unaltered. The Princely States were given the option of joining either of the two new independent nations or continue to remain independent. Most of the Princely States joined India or Pakistan. Mr. Jawaharlal Nehru became the first Prime Minister of India on 15 August 1947 with Lord Louis Mountbatten as the Governor General. Just a day earlier, Lord Mountbatten was present in Karachi to install Mr. Muhammad Ali Jinnah as the first Governor General of Pakistan. Neither the first Prime Minister of India nor the Governor General of Pakistan knew the exact boundary of their respective nations on the day of their independence. It was disclosed to both governments on 17 August 1947, presumably to avoid the anticipated bloodshed on the Independence Day celebrations of both nations.

The alignment of the boundary line between the two newly born nations was named as the Radcliffe Line. Sir Radcliffe left India two days before the announcement of the alignment of the border between India and Pakistan. He refused to take his fee which was fixed at Rupees 40,000. His views on the partition were published later in Sunday Tribune. It said, "I had no alternative; the time at my disposal was so short that I could not do a better job of it. Given the same period, I would do the same thing. However, if I had two to three years, I might have improved on what I did."

Jammu & Kashmir (J&K) was a Muslim majority Princely State ruled by Hindu Maharaja. The Maharaja of J&K had entered into a standstill agreement with Pakistan between 12 and 15 August 1947. However, Pakistan attacked J&K across the border with the militias and Razakars in October 1947. Not being able to repulse the onslaught of the attack, the Maharaja of J&K declared the accession of J&K with India on 26 October. On 27 October Indian Army entered into J&K and saved approximately two third of the State. The balance one-third was occupied by Pakistan and continues to be under their illegal occupation.

The Princely State of Hyderabad had a Hindu majority which was ruled by a Muslim Nizam. Majority of the people of Hyderabad rebelled against the continued rule of the Nizam when rest of India surrounding Hyderabad became secular and democratic. Moreover, the attempts made by the ruling Nizam to raise a Muslim Army and Air Force with the help of Pakistan was opposed by the people of Hyderabad. In support of the demands of the people of Hyderabad, the Indian Army was ordered to secure Hyderabad. This was achieved; the Nizam of Hyderabad surrendered and a Treaty of Accession was signed on 24 November 1947. With that, Hyderabad merged with the Union of India.

Junagarh was a Princely State that had declared its accession with Pakistan on 13 September 1947. The Hindu majority people of Junagarh revolted against the Muslim ruler and the state administration collapsed. A plebiscite was held in December. As per the wishes of its people, Junagarh joined with Independent India.

The Radcliffe Line between India and West and East Pakistan became the International Border (IB) between the two countries. In the west, it begins from the shores of the Arabian Sea at the southern tip of Sir Creek. The boundary lies between the Indian states of Gujarat, Rajasthan and Punjab and the Pakistani provinces of Sind and Punjab. In the east, the Radcliffe line was drawn dividing the State of Bengal into West Bengal and East Pakistan. In the east, the IB originates from the shores of the Bay of Bengal surrounding East Pakistan with West Bengal to the west and the north and north-eastern states and Myanmar in the east. *(On the eve of East Pakistan becoming Bangladesh in 1971, the Radcliffe line as IB remained unaltered.)*

When the British ruled the Indian subcontinent, the Durand Line marked the boundary with Afghanistan. This became the boundary between Pakistan and Afghanistan after 14 August 1947. The boundary between India and J&K remained unaltered. In the case of Tibet/China, India inherited a contentious border. Aksai Chin is the northeastern part of Ladakh in J&K. The Government of British India took many initiatives between 1865 and 1900 to mark the boundary with China. This gave birth to Johnson Line and McCartney McDonald Line in Aksai Chin. These lines represent different territorial claims.

In 1914, a borderline known as the McMahon Line was proposed under the Simla Accord between British India and Tibet. China participated in the deliberations but refused to sign the Accord stating that Tibet did not have the locus standi to enter into an accord of this nature with India. The McMahon Line is approximately 1,150 kms long; starting from the east of Bhutan to Myanmar (Burma) along the northern limits of NEFA/Arunachal Pradesh. After China annexed Tibet, China claimed the entire Aksai Chin and 65,000 square kms of Arunachal Pradesh south of the McMahon Line as their territory. Burma was a colony of British and was part of British India until 1 April 1937 (when it became a directly administered colony of the British). On 4 January 1948, Burma became an independent country. The pre-existing border between India and Burma became IB. Mostly it is well marked. There are no major territorial disputes between the two countries.

Representatives of India and China met many times after 1947 to settle border disputes. However, they could not arrive at any mutually acceptable solution. The annexation of Tibet by China in 1950 and the fleeing of the 14th Dalai Lama to India in 1959 (where he established a Government of Tibet in Exile) worsened relations between India and China. Although China recognized various boundary lines between the two countries which pre-existed 1947, by 1956 they had surreptitiously occupied the Indian Territory in Aksai Chin and constructed National Highway G219 linking Tibet with Xinjiang Region through Aksai Chin.

With the division of J&K into J&K and POK in 1948, the India-China border begins from the trijunction of India, POK and China borders near Indira Col. From there, the boundary line runs through the Karakoram Ranges in the north and east of Daulat Beg Oldi and turns to the south cutting across the Pangong Tso Lake east of Chushul to Nepal passing through the northern limits of Himachal Pradesh and Uttarakhand. The pre-existing Nepal-India boundary, which runs along the west, south and east of Nepal, is 1,580 kilometers long. From the east of Nepal, the boundary line runs to the north of Sikkim and then to Bhutan. The India Bhutan border is 669 km long and well settled. From the eastern end of Bhutan, the boundary with China runs across Arunachal Pradesh north of Thagla Ridge roughly following the alignment of the McMahon Line to Geiling and Kibithu to Myanmar. The IB with Myanmar remained unaltered and well settled. The IB with Bangladesh was drawn by the Radcliffe Committee between India and erstwhile East Pakistan in 1947.

India's international border areas have different physical features, terrain and climatic conditions. It ranges from salt marshes, deserts with shifting sand dunes, rich plains with perennial rivers, low hills, thick forest, dense jungles, barren high altitude mountains, rocky deserts to glaciated areas. These varying geophysical characters demand a different approach to border protection and warfighting with complex logistic support.

Since Independence, India has fought four wars against Pakistan and one against China. In addition, there have been many skirmishes. Consequent to these wars, the status of the border between India, Pakistan and China have remained unsettled. They have been given different names such as Ceasefire Line, Line of Control, Line of Actual Control, and Actual Ground Position Line. There are a plethora of issues between India and her two largest neighbours - most relate to J&K. The conflict in J&K, which began soon after Independence, has in a sense never ended. Although actual military operations of First Kashmir War lasted a little over a year, the problem that gave birth to the conflict remains unresolved. Incidents of infiltration, skirmishes and unprovoked firing continue to this day. It has claimed tens of thousands of lives of soldiers as well as civilians on both sides of the border. In spite of several attempts made to resolve the crisis through bilateral negotiation and third-party mediation, the J&K problem remains unresolved. China's ambivalent attitude towards a settled border with India caused a major war and many skirmishes. The India-China border remains disputed.

India shares around 15,000 kilometre-long land borders with six different countries; Pakistan, China, Nepal, Bhutan, Bangladesh and Myanmar. *(The notional India Afghanistan border of 106 kms long is with POK).* These six international borders are guarded by different paramilitary forces during peace time. The India-Pakistan and India-Bangladesh settled International Borders are guarded by the Border Security Forces (BSF). The India-China border is guarded by the Indo-Tibetan Border Police (ITBP); a specialized mountain police force raised in 1962. Borders with Sikkim and Arunachal Pradesh are guarded by the Sikkim and Arunachal Scouts. Both the India-Nepal and India-Bhutan borders are guarded by the Sashastra Seema Bal (SSB), while the India-Myanmar border is guarded by the Assam Rifles (AR). The LOC and AGPL are manned by the Army.

This book provides an overview of India's borders and battles fought at various places along the border to readers who seek to study the history of post-independent India. The technique of war-fighting including aspects of planning and logistics support during the war, though important, has been left out of this book for brevity. The book begins at Sir Creek in Gujarat. From there, readers will travel along the IB, LOC, AGPL and LAC to the border trijunction of India, Myanmar and Bangladesh via the Rann of Kutch, deserts of Rajasthan, the plains of Punjab, low and high altitude mountains of J&K, Nepal and Bhutan borders, Sikkim, Arunachal Pradesh, the jungles of Myanmar and Bangladesh.

THE WARS IN BRIEF

Since Independence, the Indian Army was called upon to fight five wars; four times against the Pakistani Armed Forces and once against the Peoples Liberation Army of China when their armed forces crossed into Indian Territory. Pakistan's repeated attempt to capture J&K and the illegitimate claims of China over a vast Indian Territory consequent to China annexing Tibet was the causes of these wars. The IB drawn by the Partition Committee headed by Sir Radcliffe between India and West and East Pakistan was least contentious. So were the pre-existing borders with Nepal, Bhutan and Burma.

FIRST KASHMIR WAR/FIRST INDO-PAKISTAN WAR

Pakistan got its independence on 14 August 1947. Against the expectations of Pakistani leaders, the Princely State of J&K did not opt to join Pakistan. J&K had entered into a Standstill Agreement with Pakistan and decided to remain independent. Muslims living close to the western borders of J&K with newly created Pakistan rebelled against this decision of Maharaja. It resulted in large-scale communal violence and anarchy in Punch Tract (west and south of Pir Panjal Ranges) and Muzaffarabad areas. The J&K State Army units stationed in Gilgit revolted against the Governor and took over the control of the region. By 20 October 1947, forces comprising rebel militias of J&K, deserted officers and men from J&K State Forces and Pashtun Tribes of Pakistan led by the Pakistani Army personnel crossed the border into the Princely State of J&K in violation of Stand Still Agreement made previously.

The First Kashmir War started on or about 20 October 1947. Pakistan had named this operation as Operation Gulmarg. The infiltrators had occupied Muzaffarabad, Uri and Baramulla and advanced towards Srinagar. They were to capture the airport and the city. Loyal J&K State Forces were few in number and thinly spread from Punch in the west to Ladakh in the east. They could not defend their territory against the attackers who infiltrated into the State simultaneously from the plains of Jammu at Chamb, Punch Valley, Kashmir Valley and Kargil areas in large numbers.

Maharaja Hari Singh of J&K decided to join India under the provisions of Indian Independence Act 1947. Accordingly, the Instrument of Accession was signed by him on 26 October 1947. With this, the Pak-J&K border became India-Pakistan Border and the First Kashmir War became the First Indo-Pakistan War. By then the Pakistani-led forces were pillaging Baramulla and heading for Srinagar. On 27 October 1947, the Indian Army landed at the Srinagar Airport. They were tasked with saving Srinagar from the raiders and evicting the invaders from the territory already occupied by them inside J&K.

Pakistan had been planning to launch Operation Gulmarg even before 20 October. While most of the infiltrators were familiar with the terrain in J&K, for the Indian Army J&K was new territory. The Indian Army had been preoccupied with the security of refugees in Punjab. Indian leaders could not have anticipated fighting a war against Pak-led Forces in J&K within two months of Independence. With the accession of J&K, the Indian Army had to be moved in haste to prevent the capital city of Srinagar from falling into the hands of invaders. They were hurriedly airlifted from New Delhi on 27 October in Dakota aircrafts; some of which were hired from civil aviation.

Notwithstanding many challenges faced by the Indian Army units in J&K such as lack of information about the enemy and terrain, non-availability of maps, cold weather and inadequate transport, the young Indian Army fought its first and the longest war for over 14 months from 27 October 47 to 31 December 48. By the end of the war, the Indian Army had saved nearly two-thirds of J&K from Pakistan. Pakistan had occupied the rest of J&K and retained under their control when ceasefire was declared with the help of the UNO.

This was followed by the Karachi Agreement of 1949 signed by both countries. It called for a cessation of hostilities and withdrawal of all tribesmen and Pakistani nationals from J&K. India was asked to progressively reduce its forces to the minimum level required for keeping law and order. It also laid down principles that India should follow in administering law and order. India was to conduct plebiscite under the supervision of UN Representative. Pakistan did not withdraw her Army and other Pakistani nationals from their occupied area.

The area retained by Pakistani invaders at the end of the war is known as Pakistani Occupied Kashmir (POK). The boundary-line between India and POK, named as the Ceasefire Line (CFL), began from Burejal Village west of Akhnoor in the south and followed a northerly course west of Palanwala, Naushera, Punch, Uri, and Tithwal, then along the Kisanganga River towards Gurez, Kargil and beyond up to a point at GR NJ 9842, south of Siachen Glacier. The area between GR NJ 9842 and Chinese border in the north could neither be surveyed nor demarcated. A mention was made in Karachi Agreement that beyond Point GR NJ 9842 the boundary will be towards the Glacier in the north. The major outcome of this War was the division of J&K State into J&K and POK. The contentious CFL replaced the IB starting from Burejal to GR NJ 9842.

1962 CHINESE AGGRESSION

India inherited an unsettled Chinese border from the British. The attempts made by the British during their rule over India to demarcate the border with Tibet did not succeed. Attempts made by India after Independence failed to convince the Chinese who in the meantime had annexed Tibet and claimed a vast territory in NEFA and Aksai Chin in Ladakh as part of Tibet. The Chinese ignored pre-existing borderlines such as the Johnson Line, McCartney McDonald Line and McMahon line. India's support to the Tibetan people including the Dalai Lama antagonised the Chinese Government. Any Indian attempt to occupy the border areas within her own territory was perceived as an aggression against China.

The Peoples Liberation Army (PLA) of China crossed the traditional borders in Ladakh in October 1962 and advanced up to their claim lines brushing aside the feeble opposition offered by Indian Army units deployed in penny packets in Daulat Beg Oldi Sector. In the south, a well-contested defensive battle was fought by the Indian Army at Chushul and the PLA was .prevented from capturing Chushul complex including the airfield there. In NEFA, the PLA advanced up to Bomdila after crossing from Thag La and Bum La in the west. In Walong Sector in the Lohit River Valley of NEFA in the east, the Indian Army opposed the advance of PLA and prevented them from advancing beyond Walong when the PLA declared a ceasefire. The PLA withdrew from the captured Indian Territory from NEFA and Ladakh. It was a one-sided war started by China. They swept through NEFA up to Bomdila and Walong and captured some defended localities in the north and east of Chushul. Of their own accord, the PLA withdrew back to their starting point. Overall, the 1962 war was won by China.

After the war was lost, India adopted a realistic expansion policy for the Armed Forces to face future threats. The India-China border remains disputed; therefore the boundary is known as the Line of Actual Control (LAC).

1965 INDO-PAKISTAN WAR

After the First Indo-Pakistan War in 1947-48, Pakistan was busy increasing the size and composition of her armed forces. This was done through weapons received from the western countries in the guise of keeping the communist forces away from Pakistan. By 1965, Pakistan had acquired a large quantity of weapons and equipment including tanks and long-range artillery guns from the USA. As against this, the Indian Army had to fight a war with weapons and equipment of World War II vintage against an overwhelmingly large PLA. In 1965, the Indian Army was still in the process of recovering from the trauma of reverses suffered in 1962.

Pakistan had been claiming a vast area of Greater Rann of Kutch in Gujarat contiguous to their territory in the Sind Province based on a century-old border dispute. Many meetings were held between the representatives of the two counties but no solution could be found to resolve the dispute. In April 1965, Pakistani Rangers crossed the International Border and occupied the ruins of Kanjarkot Fort. The Indian Central Reserve Police Force (CRPF) established a Border Post near Kanjarkot and named it Sardar Post. The Pakistan Army crossed the IB and attacked Sardar Post. Although they established a foothold, they did not capture Sardar Post. Later they attacked other defended localities at Sera Bet and Biar Bet held by Indian Army and CRPF using tanks supplied by USA and captured the two localities.

Due to logistical constraints, India did not react to the Pakistan aggression with adequate forces in the Rann of Kutch. India raised objections in international forums of the use of aided weapons by Pakistan Army as it was meant to be used against Communist forces. Simultaneously, India planned to launch a counter-offensive on Pakistan at more vulnerable areas in the north. This did not happen as the Pakistani foray ended with the intervention of international community to prevent a large-scale all-out war. A tribunal under the UNO processed the territorial claims of Pakistan and awarded 10% of their claim. From subsequent events, it became evident that the attack launched by Pakistan in the least expected area of Gujarat was a ruse to facilitate the offensive of Pakistan in J&K later.

Just four months later in August, Pakistan launched Operation Gibraltar in J&K and Ladakh. It was a repeat of 1947 infiltration operation. The task assigned to the infiltrators was to foment an uprising by the local people against J&K Government and enlist their support for the annexation of J&K by the Pakistan Army later. It did not succeed. The Indian Army adopted counter-measures against Pakistan infiltrators and captured or killed most of them. The Indian Army also attacked on Haji Pir Pass inside POK and captured it successfully. The loss of Haji Pir Bulge along with the pass posed threat to the major communication centres of POK.

Reacting to the loss of Haji Pir Bulge, Pakistan Army attacked in Chamb Sector and threatened to capture the strategically important Indian town of Akhnoor and the only Bridge across River Chenab there. If Pakistan had succeeded in capturing Akhnoor, it would have cut off the Punch Tract west of Pir Panjal Ranges from the rest of India. Against this offensive, India launched a major counteroffensive in J&K, Punjab and Rajasthan and threatened Lahore, Sialkot and the Green Belt of Sind. A ceasefire was enforced. At the end of the war, India had captured more territory than Pakistan and destroyed a large number of Patton and other tanks supplied by the USA.

After the war, a meeting between Alexei Kosygin, President of USSR, Lal Bahadur Shastri, Prime Minister of India and Ayub Khan, President of Pakistan was held at Tashkent from 4 to 10 January 1966. At the end of the meeting, the Tashkent Agreement was signed. According to the agreement, areas captured by both countries during the war were returned. Hence there was no change in the alignment of the IB/CFL after 1965 Indo-Pakistan War.

1971 INDO-PAKISTAN WAR

In the sixties and early seventies, East Pakistan witnessed a large-scale civil war launched by the Bengali Muslims demanding their rightful place in the governance of Pakistan. With the help of India, the freedom fighters of East Pakistan raised a liberation army known as Mukti Bahini and engaged Pakistan Army in hit and run raids. The war between Pakistan Army and Mukti Bahini was heading for a disastrous end for Pakistan. To divert the Indian resources which were assisting Mukti Bahini in the east, Pakistan attacked across the Indian border in the west in J&K, Punjab and Rajasthan on 3 December 1971 employing Air Force and Army mechanised formations. The Indian Armed Forces contained the offensive and launched a riposte in Pakistan's most vulnerable sectors in the west. The war in the east ended with the surrender of Pakistan Army on 16 December 1971. With that, the war in the west also came to an end. During this war, a large chunk of POK territory was captured by the Indian Army in Ladakh. India lost some territory in Chamb Sector. Pakistan had lost its eastern wing and in its place, a new nation came into being called Bangladesh.

After the declaration of ceasefire, a meeting was held between Indira Gandhi, Prime Minister of India and ZA Bhutto, President of Pakistan on 2 July 1972 at Simla and an agreement was signed. It was agreed that both sides would resolve their differences through bilateral negotiations in future, thus ending the role of UNO in the peace process in J&K. The IB remained unaltered with the withdrawal of troops to their respective territory. The CFL was renamed as LOC. Its alignment had changed according to the area captured by both sides in 1971 War in J&K which was not returned. The start point of LOC shifted from Burejal to the bed of Munawar Tawi River. The LOC was redrawn in Kargil and Shyok Valley with the inclusion of Turtuk with India.

1984 OCCUPATION OF SALTORO RIDGE, SIACHEN

The LOC beyond GR NJ 9842 and the Chinese Border in the north in Ladakh could not be demarcated. Hence, these areas were left unoccupied. However, in the absence of demarcation in the Siachen Glacier area, Pakistan took advantage of ambiguity in the alignment of LOC beyond GR NJ 9842 and their activities indicated a mala fide intention of occupying the Siachen Glacier that rightfully belonged to India. India decided to pre-empt and occupy the dominating heights of the three prominent passes across Saltoro Ridge which was the gateway to the Glacier from the west. Operation Meghdoot was launched by the Indian Army on 13 April 1984 and the shoulders of the three passes were occupied just in time. After the Indian Army had occupied the posts, it was discovered that Pakistan indeed had a plan to occupy these areas. All subsequent attempts made by Pakistan to capture the passes were frustrated. India is in possession of this vital piece of territory.

Beyond GR NJ 9842, the boundary joins the trijunction of India, China and POK borders across Siachen Glaciers east of Indira Col. The present alignment between GR NJ 9842 and Indira Col is known as the Actual Ground Position Line (AGPL). The AGPL runs across the edge of the Saltoro Ridge, starting from GR NJ 9842, passing through Gyong La,

Bilafond La and Sia La, then on to Indira Col. These passes (La) are located at the heights in excess of 7,000 meters.

1999 KARGIL WAR

Kargil is strategically important due to its location. The LOC in this Sector is within the range of Pakistani artillery guns deployed close to the LOC. NH1 which is the life line of Ladakh passes through Kargil town. It runs nearly parallel to LOC for 160 kms. Since the construction of NH1 in 1958, Pakistani Army has made many attempts to disrupt the traffic on the NH1.

The LOC in this sector passes through rugged high-altitude areas of above 14,000 feet. There are many rocky mountain peaks which dominates vast surrounding areas. The harsh terrain, low temperature and fast wind adds to the woe of difficult living conditions. The troop density on the Indian side was inadequate to prevent infiltration by a determined enemy, especially during winter. Due to heavy snowfall the troops activities get reduced to bare minimum. During late ninety's, troops from Kargil Sector were deployed in counter insurgency role in Kashmir valley. As a result, the LOC in Kargil sector remained porous.

Kargil Sector was guarded by two Indian brigades. On the POK side, large number of SSG, Army and Northern light infantry units are deployed. During the winter of 1968/69, a combined Pakistani Force of nearly 5000, who were specifically trained for this operation code named as Badr had infiltrated across the LOC into Indian territory and occupied about 500 square kms including some of the dominating features from Dras to Batalik sub sector. They had created defense works and laid mine fields. The localities were stocked for a prolonged battle. Indian Army came to know of the Pakistani occupation of their territory in May 1999 when one of their patrol was captured and killed by the occupants.

Initially, the units responsible for the protection of the LOC made many unsuccessful attempts to evict the infiltrators. Once the Pakistanis strength and disposition became clearer, Indian Army concentrated a force of more than 20,000 and launched Operation Vijay. The ground dictated that Tololing be cleared of the enemy first. Accordingly, Tololing, Tiger Hill and Point 4875 in the Dras Sub Sector and Juber Hill, Point 4812, Khalubar and Point 5203 in Batalik Sub Sector were captured over a period of two months in June-July 1999 and regained control over the NH1. Indian Air Force provided effective support.

The Indian operations involved attacking the well-fortified defences at high altitude which dominated the surrounding areas, thus making it difficult to approach unobtrusively. Both air attack and artillery fire were least effective against the well concealed enemy point targets. Each enemy locality was isolated and captured with numerical superiority and firepower. Indian Army had planned and divided the infiltrators held localities and cut off from their withdrawal route.

Pakistanis were evicted from the Indian Territory. Both sides suffered heavy casualty. Pakistan came under international pressure and withdrew behind the LOC.

THE BATTLES

Chapter 1

GUJARAT

SIR CREEK

The 3,323 kilometre-long IB between India and Pakistan begins in the west at the southern tip of Sir Creek. It is located at the western boundary of Gujarat in India and the eastern boundary of Sind in Pakistan. A creek is a narrow inlet of the sea or a lake into the land. There are many creeks on the Gujarat's southern coast of Arabian Sea. The important ones located east of Indus River Delta are Kori Creek in India, Sir Creek on the border between India and Pakistan and Kalhar Creek in the Sind Province of Pakistan. Sir Creek, originally known as Ban Ganga, is about 96 kms long with its width varying according to the tide and season. During the monsoon season, the banks become unidentifiable.

The ownership of Sir Creek was disputed between the Princely State of Kutch and Sind Province even before the partition of India. After Sind became part of Pakistan, Pakistan claimed the entire Sir Creek as theirs with the boundary line running along the Eastern Bank of Sir Creek (marked as 'Green Line' in the map below). This was supported by the Para 9 of Bombay Government Resolution of 1914 which was signed by the then Government Representative of Sind and Maharaja of Kutch.

However, India's stand is that boundary is along the line joining the midpoints of Sir Creek (marked in dotted line in the middle of Sir Creek in the map below) which is also found in Para 10 of the same 1914 Resolution. India's claim is also supported by the International Convention based on Thalweg Doctrine which is applicable to navigational channels the world over. Boundary pillars were installed in 1924 along the line joining the mid-points of Sir Creek.

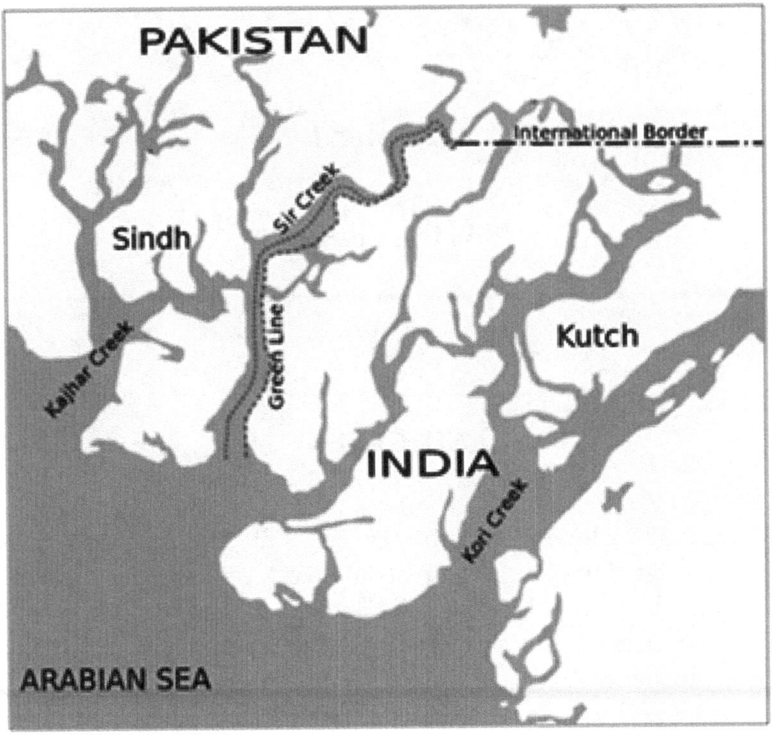

Creeks on the Gujarat Coast

(Photo Courtesy: By Nichalp at English Wikipedia)

Many rounds of talks were held between the representatives of India and Pakistan. The conflicting claim by both sides has territorial and economic implications; hence both countries are reluctant to give up their century-old claims. In the absence of clearly identifiable boundary markers at the Sir Creek, security forces from both countries arrest each other's fishermen who languish in jails for prolonged periods in both countries. They are exchanged periodically at Wagah Border near Amritsar, far away from their home. Invariably they don't get their boats back and are deprived of their livelihood. Unless this boundary dispute is resolved, maritime boundary between the two countries cannot be finalised and demarcated.

In August 1999, a Pakistani Air Force Atlantique aircraft flew over Sir Creek. (Later Pakistan claimed that it was carrying 16 naval officers and men on board.) It crossed into Indian Airspace in violation of 1999 Indo-Pakistan Agreement. Two Indian Air Force MIG 21 fighter aircrafts were scrambled and attempted to chase the Pakistani Atlantique. Following international protocols, the aircraft was contacted and asked to land. However, it neither changed its course nor landed as was asked. When the attempt to force land failed, one of the Indian MIG fighters fired an air to air missile and shot down the Atlantique. The debris on the ground was found on both sides of the border close to Sir Creek. Pakistan had organised a visit of a few foreign diplomats to the scene of shooting down of the Atlantique. They opined that the Pakistani aircraft may have violated the airspace. It was the Pakistan Navy's biggest combat-related casualty since the Indo-Pakistani War of 1971. Besides the destruction of the aircraft, 16 naval personnel including five officers travelling in the Atlantique were killed.

Pakistan reacted by reinforcing their border area with additional naval units armed with surface-to-air missiles. On the day following the incidence, Pakistani anti-aircraft units attempted to shoot down one of the Indian MIG 21 aircraft while it was flying within Indian Air space. The Pakistani missile failed to hit the Indian aircraft and the fighter returned to its base safely. Following these incidences, armed forces of both countries were put on high alert. Pakistan had approached the International Court of Justice for compensation for the loss of Atlantique. This was rejected by the Court.

At present, ownership of Sir Creek and the exact alignment of IB in the area remain contentious.

RANN OF KUTCH

Border and Claim Line

From the northern end of Sir Creek, the Indo-Pakistan borderline takes a right turn towards the east up to a point near the border town of Lakpat. From there, it turns due north for about 100 kms and turns to the east through the marshy desert and crosses Shakoor Lake. The lake extends to 300 square kms of which more than two-thirds is on the Indian side of the border. From the eastern shore of the Lake, it touches a point north of the ruins of Kanjarkot Fort. Kanjarkot Fort was a small ancient fort which is in ruins and marked on the map on the Indian side of the Indo-Pakistan IB. From there, the border runs due east dividing the Great Rann of Kutch between India and Pakistan.

The Rann of Kutch is a sparsely populated salt desert with low sand dunes and patches of high ground known as Bet that become islands during the rainy season. According to mythology, the River Saraswati which originated in the Himalayas drained into the Arabian Sea through the Rann of Kutch. The River doesn't exist anymore. Due to geographical changes many salt lakes and creeks had formed and are still found in this region. The Little Rann of Kutch is in the south-east and south of Kutch. The Great Rann of Kutch is in the north and northeast covering an area of over 18,000 square Kms.

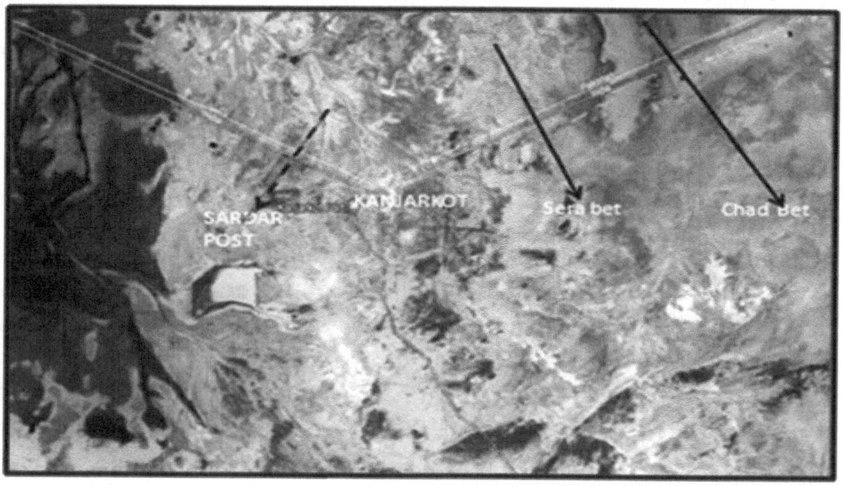

Kanjarkot

The Little Rann is exclusively located in the state of Gujarat. The Great Rann is spread between Gujarat in India and Sind Province in Pakistan roughly aligned with the 34th Parallel at the southern edge of Thar Desert. It gets flooded during the monsoon season making it impassable by vehicles. There are a few villages in the northern area of Great Rann. Khavda is the largest population centre in the Greater Rann which is about 67 kms from Bhuj. The Rann of Kutch on the Indian side is unfit for any military operations, whereas on the Pakistani side in the north, limited military operations can be undertaken.

Salt marsh

The Great Rann on the Indian side becomes a huge water body and marshy islands in the rainy season and salt dunes and sandy desert in the dry season. This four-in-one terrain is a wasteland with acute shortage of potable water. Except in some areas in the northern fringes of the Rann, movement of vehicles away from the existing roads is extremely restricted. Bhuj is the HQ of Kutch district. It is located about 110 kms from Kanjarkot and linked by Gujarat State Highway SH 45. Bhuj is connected by rail with the rest of India.

The Rann area is unproductive; hence no major economic activities take place. It had no road capable of taking sustained vehicular traffic all through the year. After the partition of British India, very little attention was paid to demarcate the boundary line in the area of Great Rann of Kutch. During the Indo-Pakistan border negotiations in 1960, both sides made their claims and counterclaims of the territory and boundary lines on the ground. Having failed to find any solution, both countries had decided to hold further discussions later. Until then, both countries had agreed to maintain status quo. India's CRPF and Special Reserve Police Force (SRPF) were responsible for patrolling the border. They had five companies deployed; two companies each at Vigakot and Chhad Bet and a company at Karim Shahi. This force was inadequate to make their presence felt over this vast undeveloped area.

Since independence, Pakistan has created better connectivity to the IB in their side of the border which is in close proximity to their major cantonments such as Karachi, Hyderabad and Badin. In 1965, the Indus Rangers were guarding their side of the border. Two more battalions were located at Hyderabad and Chhor. One company was guarding the border north and east of Kanjarkot. Rahim Ki Bazar area had a larger presence of Rangers.

The Radcliffe Line which divides the Great Rann between India and Pakistan was not marked on the ground accurately across the Greater Rann; hence it remained contentious. The border dispute between the Princely State of Gujarat and the Kingdom of Sind dates back to the first decade in 20th Century. It remained disputed when British India was divided in 1947. Pakistan had claimed a large chunk of 9,100 square kms from the Great Rann of Kutch. In 1956 for the first time after Independence, Pakistanis attempted to establish a post at Chhad Bet about 8 kms inside the Indian Territory and the Indian Army had to chase them back into their territory. Thereafter, an Army Post was established there which was later replaced with SRP Company. During the Chinese aggression in 1962, 1 Maratha LI was moved to Bhuj with the responsibility of protecting the Indo-Pakistan Border as a precautionary measure.

In 1965, the Indian Army was still recovering from the trauma of 1962 Chinese aggression. The Army was on an expansion mode to increase the strength and modernize the weapons and equipment. Pakistan, who harboured the ambition of annexing Kashmir to her fold, continued increasing her war-fighting potential beyond their defensive requirements. She received large quantity of modern weapons including tanks, machine guns, artillery, anti-tank weapons and communication equipment from USA under Military Assistance Program, primarily meant to defend against Communist aggression.

In the month of January 1965, the CRPF personnel who went to patrol the border area near Kanjarkot noticed vehicle tread marks coming from the Pakistani side of the Border into Indian Territory up to Kanjarkot about two kms south of the boundary line. The track was visible for roughly over 20 kms stretch parallel to the Border. This was reported to the higher authorities and a protest was launched. Later in February, Kanjarkot was occupied by Rangers surreptitiously and freshly dug trenches were seen in the vicinity. Another protest note was handed over across the Border asking them to vacate Kanjarkot. Pakistan Rangers refused to vacate. Indian Sector commander's proposed meeting of the Surveyor Generals of both countries to resolve the issue, it did not materialise. Pakistan contented that Kanjarkot was in their territory and it had been in occupation by the Rangers for quite some time.

To prevent further ingression, 2 CRPF Battalion was ordered to establish a company post in the vicinity of Kanjarkot inside Indian Territory. This was established by March 1965 and was named as Sardar Post after the great statesman of Gujarat, Sardar Vallabhbhai Patel. A few army personnel, medium machine guns and 3-inch mortars were added to the post. They also intensified the patrolling of the area. Patrols reported increased military activities on the Pakistani side of the border.

Seeing the resolve of India to assert her claim, Pakistan mobilized her armed forces and moved them closer to the border. Large-size force was staged up towards Hyderabad, Badin, Rahim ki Bazar and Diplo. Having failed in her effort to evict the intruder peacefully and suspecting Pakistan's offensive intention of moving the army formation closer to the border, 31 Indian Army Brigade, located at Ahmadabad, was moved to Bhuj. The CRPF had strengthened the Sardar Post and other posts at Vigokot southeast of Sardar Post, Chhad Bet and Karimshahi. Major Karnail Singh was the commander of Sardar Post. In anticipation of an imminent attack on Sardar Post, he followed a system to conceal the main location of his trenches to the potential attackers. The forward Platoons were vacated from their trenches at night, leaving behind a listening post and occupied night positions in depth areas. Sardar Post deployed machine guns in the flanks to bring down maximum fire on attackers when they would be most vulnerable. The Post was strengthened with a total of three companies along with an officer, JCOs and a few men of 1 Mahar Infantry Battalion of the Army. Major Karnail Singh ensured that if they were attacked in any of his main positions, the enemy will be interfered effectively from more than one positions.

Around 3 AM on 9 April 1965, Pakistan Army launched an attack on Sardar Post with artillery fire followed by infantry crossing the border with three regular army battalions which was later identified as 8 Frontier Force, 18 Punjab and 6 Baluch. They advanced towards Sardar Post and Vigokot. When they reached the vicinity of forward platoon locality of Sardar Post, fire from the depth platoons and the machine guns from the flanks and mortar fire devastated the attackers. One of the attacking Pakistani companies lost their direction and fired at their own men assaulting from a different direction causing large-scale casualty to their own troops. With their overwhelming artillery fire and large manpower, the enemy was able to occupy one of the forward platoons. Pakistani artillery continued firing on the forward platoon locality which was occupied by their own troops causing more casualty on them. Brave Major Karnail Singh, Company Commander of Sardar Post made an attempt to retake the forward platoon from the enemy. However, he was unsuccessful. In the ensuing fight, he was captured and taken prisoner along with a few more CRPF personnel.

The remaining two Platoons held their ground when the day broke. During the day, for reasons best known to the Pakistanis, they withdrew from the position they had captured earlier. Ironically, the CRPF Platoons occupying the depth locality were unaware of the disastrous consequences suffered by the attacking Pakistanis in the locality ahead of them. In the absence of their Company Commander who was captured by the Pakistanis earlier, they started withdrawing from Sardar Post.

Having learned about the situation at Sardar Post, Brigadier SSM Pahlajani Commander 31 Infantry Brigade took off from Bhuj in a small reconnaissance aircraft with his Staff Officer Capt KS Puntambekar travelling in another aircraft following him. Having flown over the Sardar

Post area during twilight hours, the Brigade Commander decided to control the situation by reoccupying Sardar Post immediately with the CRPF personnel who were in the process of abandoning the Post. The second aircraft in which Capt Puntambekar was travelling landed close to Sardar Post. He was given instructions received from the Commander on radio by the pilot of the aircraft to get down and control the situation at Sardar Post.

Having understood the urgency of the situation, Capt Puntambekar, an officer of 1 Maratha LI, posted as a staff officer at the Brigade HQ, got down from the aircraft and physically stopped the withdrawing CRPF personnel. Realising that the men were unaware of the circumstances, he explained the situation to the men and asked them to return to their defended locality. Convinced that the Pakistanis had not captured Sardar Post and that they were not attacking the post any more, the CRPF men returned to their post along with Capt Puntambekar. He took charge of the Post. Thus the situation was brought under control.

Pakistani troops once again attacked Sardar Post during daylight hours. This was repulsed by the CRPF personnel with accurate fire. Later in the afternoon, 17 Rajputana Rifles (Raj Rif) and 2 Sikh Light Infantry (Sikh LI) took charge of the situation at Vigokot and Sardar Post. A Company of Sikh LI reoccupied Sardar Post which was subsequently relieved by 1 Mahar Battalion. Throughout 10 and 11 April, Pakistanis kept up their intermittent artillery shelling on Sardar Post and Vigokot, but failed to capture any of them.

After Pakistan Army had failed to make any headway in Sardar Post area, they shifted their attention towards Chhad Bet east of Kanjarkot. This Post was held by SRP Battalion. On 10 April Indian Army was directed to take over the responsibility of defending this Sector with additional forces under a newly created formation known as KILO Force. 50 Para Brigade and 31 Infantry Brigade were part of it. Having observed intense activities of mechanized forces opposite Chhad Bet by Pakistan, the General Officer Commanding (GOC) KILO Force asked for more troops including armoured regiment. Due to logistical constraints, this demand was not met and the GOC directed his units to defend the territory without resorting to any offensive actions. Accordingly, by 19 April two companies of 3 Para Battalion reinforced the SRPF posts at Chhad Bet, Sera Bet and Biar Bet areas. Chhad Bet is located 8 kms south of the Border about 30 kms east of Kanjarkot.

On the night of 19 April 1965, Sera Bet, also known as Point 84, came under intense artillery fire. Thereafter, intermittent artillery fire continued. On 23 April, Sera Bet was attacked by the Pakistani infantry during the early hours of the day. B Company of 3 Para opened up with machine guns and 3-inch mortars followed by artillery fire on the attacking Pakistanis. The attack was repulsed. After an hour of pause, Pakistanis once again attacked the Post; this time with their tanks followed by infantry mounted on Armoured Personnel Carriers (APC). The recoilless anti-tank guns from Sera Bet opened up and destroyed three of the advancing tanks. However, against the large-scale tank assault from multiple directions, the attack could not be stalled from the frugally defended localities of Sera Bet with infantry anti-tank weapons. The Company withdrew from there.

The next attack was on Biar Bet which was defended by 'A' Company of 3 Para Battalion along with SRP personnel supported with artillery, RCL Guns and MMGs. On 25 April three Pakistani APCs advanced towards Biar Bet around 1630 hours. The advance was halted with the fire from all the weapons deployed in the defended locality on the enemy. Later, about 10 Pakistani tanks formed up and advanced towards the post. RCL guns and mortars engaged them. The tanks did not assault the Post during the night. Next morning, more number of enemy tanks attacked the Post and the Post was overrun.

It was later learned that Pakistan had attacked Sera Bet and Biar Bet with Pakistani 8 Division which had moved from Karachi with the tanks of 12 Cavalry and 19 Lancers. These formations were equipped with weapons received from western countries which were not meant to be used against India as per the conditions of supply of those weapons. India launched a protest with USA. A large section of Indian population urged the Government to punish Pakistan for this unprovoked aggression in Kutch. The Chief of Army staff General JN Chaudhury recommended to the Government of India that India should launch a counter-offensive on Pakistan across Punjab border in the area of our choosing. This was agreed to by the Government. Having considered the attack on Sera Bet and Biar Bet as aggression against India, India ordered all the three Services to prepare for war against Pakistan. Operation ABLAZE was launched to mobilise the Armed Forces. Accordingly, Indian Army, Navy and Air Force moved their formations to their assigned battle locations. Punjab and Rajasthan Borders were strengthened.

Fearing an all-out war and large-scale destruction, the international community came forward to intervene between India and Pakistan. Mr.

Herald Wilson, the then Prime minister of UK appealed to both countries to stop the war preparations and proposed a ceasefire in Kutch immediately. By 29 April 1965, both countries agreed to the ceasefire proposal. A Tribunal was set up by the United Nations Secretary-General to decide the Pakistani claim of territory in the Greater Rann of Kutch. In its final award in February 1968, 90% of the area claimed by Pakistan was rejected. Only 10% of their claim including Chhad Bet area was given to Pakistan. Both parties, though unhappy with the Award, had agreed to abide by it.

It was an unprovoked aggression by Pakistan with an Army Division and two tank and artillery regiments, armed and equipped with modern weapons and equipment. Military strategists claim that the Pakistan's intention of launching an attack with newly-acquired weapons may have been more than meets the eye. Possibly, it was aimed at drawing out the Indian Army reserve formations from the north to facilitate in their subsequent offensive operations planned by Pakistan to annex Kashmir. Also, Pakistan wanted to battle test the weapon systems received from USA and to test the US reactions to unauthorized use of these weapons against India. In the end, Pakistan Army did capture some of the low value delaying positions held ahead of Indian main defences both at Sardar Post and Chhad Bet, but not the main defended areas. Had they tried to go deeper into Kutch, with the onset of monsoon rains in the middle of May, they would have met the same fate as Germany faced in winter while withdrawing from Russia in World War II.

On the part of India, she was caught unprepared to face a mechanised attack in this sector of Indo-Pakistan border areas where mechanised forces cannot be employed freely and where mobility is restricted due to terrain and climatic conditions. India's reluctance to escalate the battle in this sector in order to retain their capability to give a befitting reply elsewhere in the ground of her own choosing proved to be a strategically guided wisdom that subsequently paid off.

On 19 September 1965 when decisive battles were being fought in Punjab and J&K, the Gujarat border was quiet except a tragic event that took away the life of Mr Balwant Rai Mehta, the then Chief Minister of Gujrat along with seven others including his wife and the pilot of the twin-engine Beechcraft aircraft. The aircraft was heading from Ahmedabad towards Mithapur near Dwarka in the Gulf of Kutch region. A Pakistani F86 Jet Fighter crossed into Indian airspace and shot the aircraft in spite of the fact that pilot of Beechcraft, Jehangir Engineer, gave conventional indication that it was a civilian aircraft and it should not be harmed. The aircraft was destroyed and all eight occupants killed. Recently, the Pakistani fighter pilot, in his book, apologised for shooting a non-military aircraft and killing the civilians on orders from his controller.

1971

The need for centralised border policing was felt after the experiences of the 1965 war. Accordingly, the Border Security Force (BSF) was raised in 1965 under the Border Security Force Act 47 of 1968. In 1971, during the Pakistani Aggression, Kutch Sector was guarded by three of the newly raised BSF Battalions along with a Battalion of Territorial Army. They not only deterred the Pakistani Rangers from crossing the border into Indian Territory, but also captured Chad Bet, Vingi, Baliar, Saro and Virwa which were held by the enemy. Presently the BSF patrols the area including Sir Creek. In the area of Rann of Kutch, BSF uses all-terrain vehicles to patrol the border area.

Present day Sardar Post

Chapter 2

RAJASTHAN

Border Districts-Rajasthan

The IB beyond the districts of Banaskantha and Jalore in Gujarat on the Indian side and Nagarparkar on Pakistan side enter the Thar Desert in Rajasthan with Barmer, Jaisalmer, Bikaner and Sriganganagar districts on the Indian side and Sind Province in Pakistan. The border runs through Thar Desert for about 1,040 kms in one of the most inhospitable terrains of India. The Indus River runs west of Thar Desert in Pakistan. The distance between the IB and green belt in Pakistan is much closer than it is in India.

The Thar Desert offers a host of discomforts to living beings; extreme heat and cold, shifting and permanent sand dunes, blinding dust storm and lack of water and greenery. These anti-human survival characteristics of the desert, combined with very low level economic activities are some of the reasons which inhibit Pakistan from coveting Indian Territory in the Rajasthan sector. The line drawn through Thar Desert by Sir Radcliffe should have been the least contentious border between India and Pakistan. Yet, both in 1965 and 1971, pitched battles were fought along this border.

Typical Desert Terrain

The terrain in Thar Desert varies from plain stony wasteland to shifting sand dunes extending tens of kilometres of ridges like knuckle and fingers of a hand. The stony wasteland offers good cross-country mobility to wheeled and tracked vehicles. In the sand dune areas, gaps in between the sand dunes can be used for limited vehicular traffic. Movement along the fingers of sand dunes is relatively easier than across the fingers.

In the desert, military operations are undertaken to capture objectives such as towns/cities, water sources and important road junctions rather than real estate. Due to extreme heat during the day, operations in the desert are undertaken at night during the cooler hours of summers or during winters. Peak summer months are considered as non-campaigning season in the Thar Desert.

A peculiar phenomenon known as 'temperature inversion' occurs during night in the desert causing extreme discomfort to human beings due to sudden drop in ambient temperature. Another feature of deserts that affect military operations is frequent sandstorms. During a sandstorm, fine sand particles get into weapons and machineries including helicopters which cause moving parts to cease functioning. Sand-proofing of cookhouses and ration-stores are nearly impossible during the storm. Diseases such as diarrhoea and dehydration are the common medical problems in desert. Absence of easily identifiable landmarks both during the day and night affects navigation adversely. In the absence of local resources, everything including water has to be transported from far-off places. The military operation in the desert is truly a nightmare for the logisticians.

BARMER

Barmer is the southernmost border district of Rajasthan. It has 240 kms long IB cutting across in north-south direction through Thar Desert. The green belt opposite Barmer in Pakistan is comparatively closer than other sectors. The border here witnessed fierce battles during the 1965 and 1971 wars against Pakistan.

1965 was a memorable year for both India and Pakistan for several reasons. For the first time since 1948, India faced a military intervention from Pakistan in the Rann of Kutch in April. The outcome of the intrusion was apparently favourable to Pakistan. This added to the misery of Indian Army which was recovering from the trauma of 1962 Chinese Aggression. For Pakistan, the military dictator Colonel Ayub Khan became President. He was elected 'democratically' through a rigged election against Begum Fatima Jinnah who was a popular candidate for presidency. To prove himself as an effective President and a true patriot, Ayub Khan decided to pursue the Pakistan's popular agenda of annexing Kashmir by employing Pakistan Army that was armed with modern weapons.

The limited success in the foray in Kutch in April 1965 encouraged Pakistan Army to launch a large-scale infiltration operation in J&K in

August under the code name Operation Gibraltar. The people of J&K did not support the infiltrators as Pakistan expected. The reaction of the Indian Army to this well known and failed Pakistani strategy of 1947 was quick and fierce. The counter-measures undertaken by the Indian Army against Operation Gibraltar in J&K resulted in the capture of major assets in the Pakistani Occupied Kashmir including the Haji Pir Pass. Operation Gibraltar was a failure and India was well poised to threaten Muzaffarabad.

In order to reduce the Indian pressure in POK and divert Indian resources from J&K, Ayub Khan opened another front in the plain sector by attacking across the CFL in Chamb opposite Akhnoor on 01 Sep 1965. The attack succeeded to a large extent. Akhnoor was threatened by the Pakistani forces which had advanced up to the outskirts of the town.

To force Pakistan Army to recoil in Chamb Sector, India launched a large-scale riposte against Pakistani population centres in Lahore and Sialkot Sectors and towards the green belt of Sind from Barmer. The offensive in Barmer Sector was aimed at preventing the Pakistani Army mechanised forces stationed opposite Barmer from moving to the north against Indian offensive.

Barmer Sector 1965

The IB alignment in Barmer District is north-south up to Gadra City where it turns to the west for some distance before it follows the north-westerly course to form a bulge west of Jaisalmer. Barmer was well connected with the city of Hyderabad in the Sind Province of Pakistan through Munabao, Gadra, Khokrapar and Naya Chor (west of the map) during pre-partition days. By 1965, road and rail communications between the two countries were dismantled in the proximity of IB near Munabao which was prone to large-scale smuggling. The border was guarded by the Rajasthan Armed Constabulary in 1965.

MUNABAO-DALI

1965

Munabao is a small border town and the last Indian Railway Station in this Sector. Across the IB, southeast of Munabao is Pakistani village known as Gadra City. The first Railway Station of Pakistan is Khokhropar. The area is part of the Cholistan Desert which is a barren land with shifting sand dunes. A few roads exist which connect the population centres such as Gadra Road, Gadra City, Dali and Nayachor.

Opposite Barmer Sector, Pakistan had deployed two Infantry and three Ranger battalions. Against this, the Indian 30 Infantry Brigade comprising 3 Guards, 5 Maratha LI and 1 Garhwal Rifle was concentrated at Barmer with a view to launch an offensive in the area of Gadra City. As part of India's riposte, the attack was planned by the Indian Army to destroy the Pakistani forces deployed in and around Gadra City, Dali, Khokropar and Sakarbu area and threaten the population centres in the green belt towards Naya Chor/Umarkot.

On the night of 7/8 September 1965, 30 Brigade crossed the Border south of Munabao and attacked Gadra City after the artillery fire had softened the target areas. By 1300 hours on 08 September, Gadra City was captured and isolated from the west. The enemy gave up fighting and withdrew to the west. Pakistani Air Force was active and strafed the attacking troops and vehicles from early morning. The enemy left behind eight of their dead bodies and large quantity of arms and ammunition. A few prisoners were taken. The withdrawing enemy was intercepted and few more were taken prisoners. The rest escaped. One officer and five men from the Indian side were injured. By midday, Gadra City was in the hands of Indian Army Units.

On 9 September, Pakistani Air Force aircrafts bombed targets along Gadra road and railways in which many goods wagons were destroyed. Indian air support was not available. 5 Maratha LI supported with tanks was tasked to advance to Khokropar via Sakarbu. They contacted Sakarbu. Further advance was contested with heavy enemy air attack. Pakistani air attack and artillery fire had intensified on the ninth and tenth of September as the Indian troops closed in with the green belt. As a result, the advance to Kokropar was called off. The enemy attacked Munabao and captured it on 10 September. Two Indian soldiers were killed and four were wounded in the firing. Many civilian vehicles were destroyed in the enemy air attack. On 13 September Pakistani forces attacked Panchla Post north of Munabao which was held by the men of Rajasthan Armed Constabulary (RAC) and captured it. Attempts made to recapture was not successful.

Khokropar was captured by 5 Maratha LI at first light on 14 September. Raids were launched to disrupt rail communication between Khokropar and Naya Chor on the night of 16 September successfully. Dali is located in the south of Gadra City. It was held by Pakistan army personnel and Rangers. An attack was launched to capture Dali on 18 September from Jessa Ka Par. It was captured successfully during day light hours by 5 Maratha LI and 1 Garhwal Rifles. On 21 September Naupatia, west of Dali was captured. The much wanted Indian Air (Force) support finally materialised on 22 September and destroyed many Pakistani targets including their helicopters and vehicles. When Indian Army was well poised to capture targets in green belt, the ceasefire was declared on the 23 of September. 85 Infantry Brigade joined the battle in the last week of the war. D Squadron of 13 Grenadiers (Camel), 3 Independent Armoured Squadron less two troops provided support to the Infantry units throughout the war.

After the ceasefire was declared, Pakistani Army along with Rangers and dacoits entered into Indian Territory. They attempted to capture Indian Territory and plunder the villages. This was thwarted by timely reaction by the Indian Army units and the enemy was chased back into Pakistan. In the end, India had captured 390 Sq Kms of Pakistani territory at a loss of small area at Munabao Post. Besides territorial gain in Barmer Sector, the aim of preventing the Pakistani Army units moving out of this Sector to the north against the main Indian offensive was fully achieved.

NAYACHOR

1971

This sector was once again activated six years later when Pakistan attacked India in December 1971. By then the border posts were manned by the BSF. The ongoing war in East Pakistan from the middle of 1971 between Pakistan Army and Mukti Bahini duly supported by Indian Army wasn't progressing as per Pakistan's plan. The situation in East Pakistan convinced Pakistani leaders that unless India is distracted away from East Pakistan sooner, they would lose their eastern Wing. Therefore, on 03 and 04 December 1971, Pakistan opened a second front against India in the west with pre-emptive air strikes on all forward Indian airbases close to the IB followed by ground attack across the border in J&K, Punjab and Rajasthan.

The counteroffensive was launched by the Indian Army in Ladakh, J&K, Punjab and Rajasthan. In Rajasthan, the 1965 battlefields of Barmer-Naya Chor were once again chosen for the counteroffensive. On the night of 4/5 December, 11 Infantry Division of Indian Army crossed the border at 1830 hours along three thrust lines from Munabao on both sides of Gadra Road towards Naya Chor clearing the enemy enroute. 17 Grenadiers, a camel battalion, advanced in the north. 10 Sikh and 2 Mahar were part of Central thrust while 18 Madras, 20 Rajput and 15 Kumaon formed part of the southern thrust.

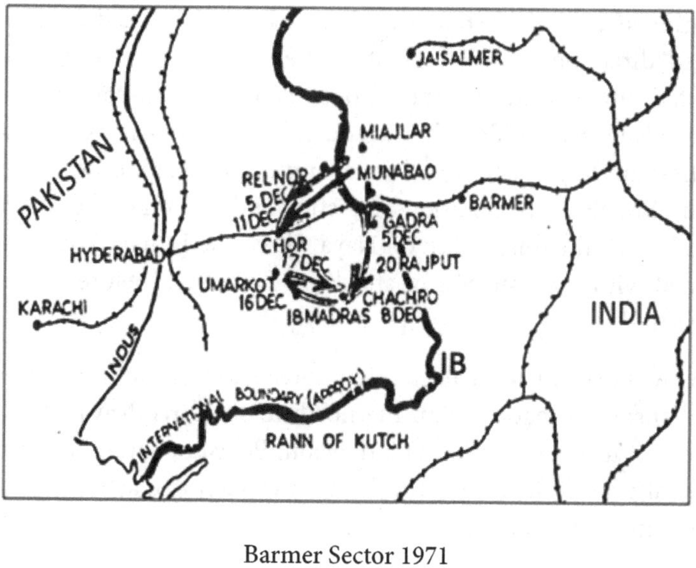

Barmer Sector 1971

The southern Column advanced and captured Gadra City by early morning the next day and it further advanced towards Dali which had witnessed a pitched battle in 1965. Dali was captured by early morning on 7 December. Prior to attack on Chachro, a raid was launched by the desert commandos that facilitated the capture of Chachro by mid-day on 8 December as was planned. An attempt was made to advance towards green belt along Chachro-Umarkot which proved unsuccessful. At this stage, due to difficult terrain conditions, a logistic pause became essential.

The advancing column north of railway line, led by a Camel Battalion, captured Relnor by 6 December. They were poised to progress their operation towards Naya Chor when a patrol reported the arrival of strong reinforcement to guard Naya Chor from the north. Therefore, the column did not advance beyond Relnor.

The central thrust which advanced along the railway line from Munabao to Parbat Ali progressed well in spite of poor road conditions and absence of rolling stocks. A duckboard track was constructed from Munabao to Khokropar. The air-force of both countries was active and caused considerable damage to logistics and disrupted the overall movement. On the morning on 8 December, screen positions at Parbat Ali were contacted after clearing the pockets of resistance enroute. The protective elements were cleared by 11 December. Close reconnaissance revealed that Parbat Ali was held by an enemy battalion with extensive defence works and deep minefields. A deliberate brigade attack was launched from the least expected direction on 13 December after a concentrated artillery fire. Heavy fighting ensued. Pakistani troops launched counter-attacks which were repulsed. By midday, the defenders withdrew leaving behind their casualties and large quantity of arms, ammunition and other stores. Due to unsustainable road conditions, logistic build-up could not take place in time to launch the final attack on Naya Chor. The Indian Army had to be contented with their successful attack on Parbat Ali before the ceasefire was declared.

As was learnt later, Pakistan was forced to thin-out a Division from their offensive formation from the north to reinforce Naya Chor Sector. Consequent to the reduction of a division, Pakistan could not launch the planned attacks in the north. This by itself was a major achievement of the Indian Army in Barmer Sector in 1971.

JAISALMER-LONGEWALA

Jaisalmer, located north of Barmer, is the largest district in terms of area but with the least population density. It has the longest International Border with Pakistan; 464 kms of the Radcliffe Line passes through the Thar Desert in this sector. This district has some of the most difficult terrain with high and long shifting and semi-static sand dunes. The border west of Longewala, Kishangarh and Tanot bulge is closest to the Pakistani green belt. Khairpur, Sukkur and Rahimyar Khan are some of the Pakistani towns opposite Jaisalmer district.

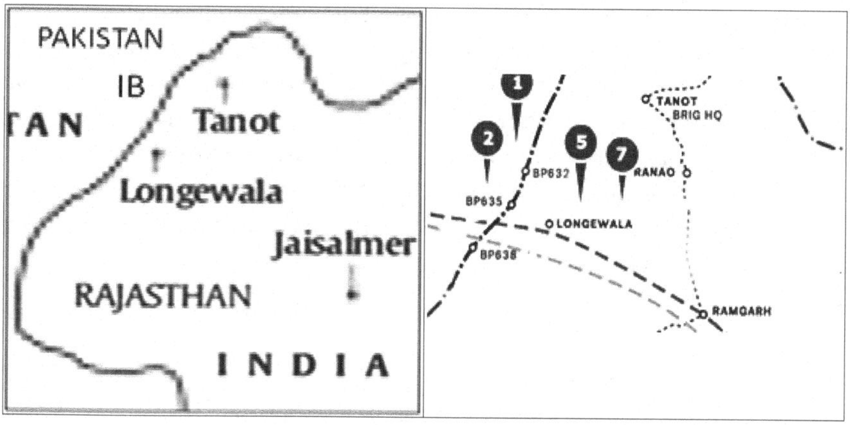

Jaisalmer Longewala

After the air-attacks across the western border in Punjab and Rajasthan on 03 December 71 by Pakistani Air Force, Indian Air Force fighters from forward airbase at Jaisalmer attacked targets across the border on 4 December. This was followed by a ground attack at Islamgarh and the capture of the Pakistani Post.

Longewala had a BSF Post which was reinforced with a company of 23 Punjab a few days before 3 December. Major Kuldeep Singh Chandpuri was the company commander. He had reorganised the defence of the post with his anti-tank weapons and laid a few protective minefields. Patrols were sent up to the IB to monitor the enemy activities across the border. On 5 December, the patrol-leader reported crossing of Pakistani tanks into Indian Territory between Border Pillars No. 635 and 638 west of Longewala. The advancing Pakistani column was estimated to comprise approximately an infantry brigade and a regiment of tanks. Major Chandpuri informed of enemy intrusion to his Battalion Commander who was located 17 kms away. His commanding officer (CO) gave him the option of withdrawing from Longewala if it was beyond the capability of the Company to hold the Post against enemy attack. The CO asked for air-attack on the advancing enemy tanks. Though the demand was accepted, the attack could not be launched as the fighter aircrafts based at Jaisalmer in those days did not have the night-fighting capability.

Enemy progress was very slow. Advancing Pakistani tanks were getting bogged down in the sandy terrain. By early next morning, a few enemy tanks had approached the post at Longewala. However, they did not close in with the post. The enemy tanks were within the range of recoilless anti-tank guns located within Longewala Post. They engaged enemy tanks that were within the range and destroyed two. Other enemy tanks pulled back and were probing around the post. The company from Longewala opened up with every weapon they had on the enemy who came within the range and prevented them from closing in further with the post. Major Chandpuri had decided to stay put and fight it out rather than withdrawing and getting caught by the advancing enemy tanks in the process. It was a sound tactical decision.

Early morning on the 5th of December, an Indian reconnaissance aircraft took off from Jaisalmer and flew over Longewala. The pilot of the aircraft reported the presence of a long column of tanks and vehicles stretching from Longewala to the border. Immediately, Indian Air Force Hunter (fighter) aircrafts took off from Jaisalmer and engaged the enemy tanks and vehicles. Pakistani tanks carrying additional diesel in barrels on top of it exploded by the strafing of the fighters. This lit up the entire battlefield and helped the fighter aircrafts and the anti-tank guns to spot their targets accurately. Pakistanis shelled Longewala Post with long-range artillery guns during the day. In the absence of any opposition in the air, Indian fighters flew over the battlefield at will and destroyed as many as 17 tanks at Longewala and two tanks at Kharotar. 23 more tanks and armoured personnel carriers were damaged. In the meantime, Longewala Post was reinforced. Pakistanis did not assault the Post. Having faced the catastrophe, Pakistanis broke contact and withdrew from Longewala back to the IB towards Gabar.

(Later it was learnt that the Pakistani higher command had planned to capture the road-head at Longewala by the morning of 5 December, advance to Ramgarh by noon and further advance to Jaisalmer by night. In the words of a Pakistani officer, 'Insha Allah we will have breakfast at Longewala, lunch at Ramgarh and dinner at Jaisalmer'. Subsequent events proved that

they neither knew the surface conditions of desert between the border and Longewala nor they realized that they had no air support available to them).

Successful defence of Longewala Post and near destruction of Pakistani mechanised forces planning to advance towards Ramgarh and Jaisalmer is mainly attributable to the Indian Air Force which destroyed bulk of the tanks and deterred the enemy from attacking Longewala Post. The decision taken by the brave Post Commander Major Chandpuri to stay put and fight from his post and organise his company fire power effectively against the enemy, played a vital role in preventing the fall of the post. Otherwise, the Pakistanis may have had their breakfast at Longewala, lunch at Ramgarh and dinner at Jaisalmer. Major Kuldip Singh Chandpuri, the Post Commander of Longewala was decorated with MVC for bravery and the Pakistani Divisional Commander was dismissed from the service.

GANGANAGAR

Ganganagar is the northern most districts of Rajasthan bordering with Punjab in the north and Pakistan in the west. It has an approximately 200 kilometre-long border with Pakistan. Although Ganganagar District lies in the Thar Desert, irrigation from the Gang Canal and Indira Gandhi Nahar Pariyojna has changed a part of this district into one of the largest grain producers of Rajasthan.

IGNP Canal

Throughout the war in 1971, no trans-border military operations took place along this Border. However, just before the war ended, the Border Security Force battalions and a camel battalion of the Indian Army carried out small-scale raids and attacks across the border on Pakistani Border posts of Ghunnewala, Ranal, Rukhanwala, Salamsar and Bijnot and captured about 200 sq kms of Pakistani territories. A week after ceasefire was declared, Pakistani forces had occupied a sand dune inside India near village Nagi. Alpha company of 4 Para battalion counter-attacked against this well-coordinated Pakistani-occupied defended locality and recaptured it with heavy casualties of 20 killed and three times of that wounded.

The terrain and alignment of border in Thar Desert favoured the Indian Army. In both wars, Indian Army units acquitted themselves creditably in spite of lack of exposure to desert warfare and logistic constraints. In the Rajasthan sector, India captured more territory than Pakistan.

Chapter 3

PUNJAB

Bulk of the work of the Partition Committee headed by Sir Radcliffe dividing British India into Union of India and Islamic Republic of Pakistan in 1947 went into dividing the erstwhile Provinces of the Punjab and Bengal. Unlike other border areas, Punjab and Bengal were thickly populated with rivers, canals and road networks connecting the whole of the Punjab and Bengal.

The Indo-Pakistan Border in Punjab runs from west of Fazilka to Bamial village west of Katua. Important towns on the Indian side are Fazilka, Ferozpur, Khem Karan, Bikhiwind, Amritsar and Dera Baba Nanak. Rivers Satluj and Ravi form part of the IB at places. Amritsar and Lahore are nearly equidistant from the IB. The border towns are well connected to the interior towns and cities of Punjab and Rajasthan. The area is fertile and with extensive irrigation system, qualifies to be the richest part of India.

During the partition of India in 1947, this area witnessed a massive upheaval and movement of refugees. Communities that had lived together for hundreds of years became killers of each other in sectarian violence. Millions of Hindus and Sikhs on the one side and Muslims on the other were on the move leaving behind everything they had. Many thousands never made it to their destination. The destruction was unprecedented in human history.

The Punjab Boundary Force comprising about 50 thousand officers and men of Army and Police Force was created. This was too small a force to control a huge migrating population on the move. Armies on both sides tried to bring some orderliness in the chaotic situation prevailing over a vast territory with limited success. However, the hard working people of Punjab slowly rebuilt their beloved land and made it into a prosperous granary of India within two decades. Fazilka, bordering with Rajasthan is the southernmost districts of Punjab along the Indo-Pakistan Border and Pathankot is the northernmost district. In between the two from the south to north are Firozpur, Tarn Taran, Amritsar and Gurdaspur.

Punjab Border Districts

FAZILKA

Fazilka is the southernmost border town of Punjab located 18 kms east of the IB. It is well connected with the interior towns of Punjab and Rajasthan by road and rail networks. Hence it assumes strategic importance for the defence of southern Punjab and northern Rajasthan. Sulaimanke headwork is located at a distance of one and a half kilometres from the IB inside Pakistan opposite Fazilka. The headwork diverts water from the Sutlej River to Pakistan. Fazilka town and Sulaimanke headwork are two important military objectives. The Sutlej River runs nearly parallel to the IB in the west. During the non-rainy season, the riverbed is usually dry and crossable.

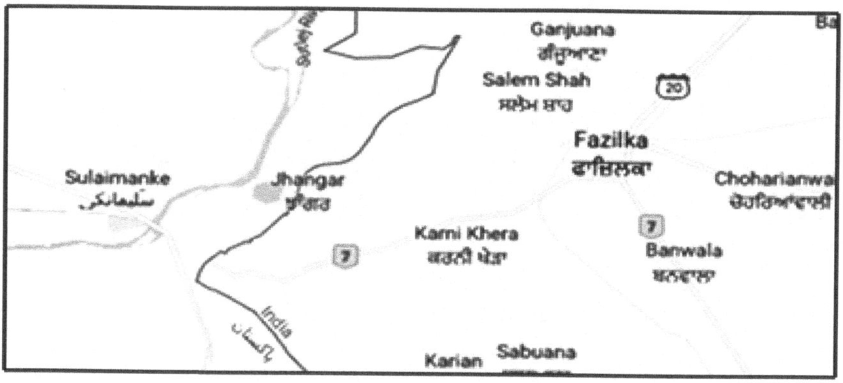

IB, Sutlej River, Fazilka and Sulaimanke Headwork

1965

On 6 September 1965, when an all-out war was underway all along the western Indo-Pakistan Border, the Pakistani artillery opened up on the Indian border-posts held by Punjab Armed Constabulary opposite Sulaimanke Headwork. Indian Army Units that had moved up to the border came under attack on the night of 7/8 September. Pakistan attacked three times; all of which were repulsed. More attacks came in on the 10th and 11th of September. These were also repulsed. A platoon locality which was lost to Pakistan during the attack was recaptured in an immediate counter-attack. Artillery duels continued thereafter till ceasefire was declared on the 23 of September. No territory was lost or gained in Fazilka sector during these battles.

1971

By 1971, based on the experience of 1965 Pakistani attack, it was decided to create an obstacle system between the IB and Fazilka town to prevent Pakistani Army from rushing onto Fazilka town with their mechanised forces in the future wars. The Sabuna Distributary runs parallel to the IB at a distance of about 12 kms west of Fazilka town. The distributary was selected to be converted into an anti-tank obstacle system in the form of ditch-cum-bund (DCB). The DCB was fortified with pillboxes and bunkers. It is 22 kilometres long with many small and large bridges to move across the obstacle by villagers to their fields. Beriwala was the largest bridge. BSF manned the border outposts during peace time. Army units were earmarked to occupy the obstacle system as and when threat was perceived.

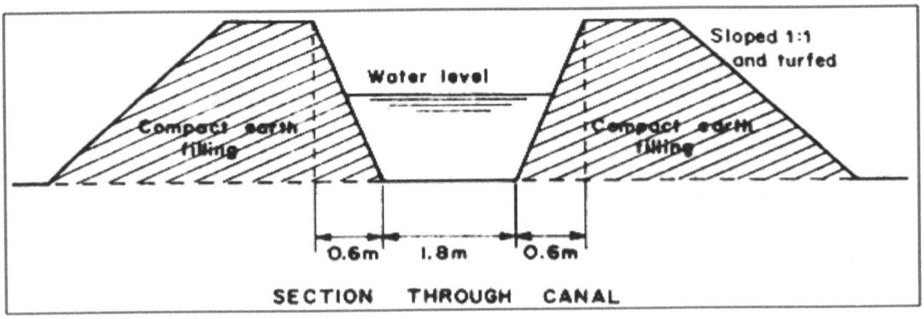

DCB

On the evening of 03 December 1971, Pakistan Army crossed the IB at many places including the area opposite Fazilka. This was preceded by a pre-emptive air attack on all forward airfields of Punjab. At about 1830 hours, the BSF post and covering troops of the battalion holding the defences on Sabuna DCB came under attack. Pakistan Army tanks led the attack followed by Infantry. They overran the BSF Posts and attacked the covering troops ahead of the DCB. After having cleared the forward elements, the tanks contacted the DCB on a broad-front and attacked. The BSF and the covering troops withdrew. While withdrawing, they demolished most of the bridges except Bariwala Bridge.

The attacking Pakistanis found a gap in the defended localities on the DCB in the area of Pakka and occupied it. From there the enemy expanded sideways and captured more bunkers on the DCB including Bariwala Bridge. Through the Bridge, the enemy brought in more troops and captured part of the east bank of Sabuna defences. A counter-attack was launched to recapture the Bariwala Bridge. Although it was not successful, the enemy was contained on the Bridge. The next night, the enemy brought in more forces east of River Sutluj and threatened to attack Fazilka from the north. The second counter-attack was launched on the Bariwala Bridge which once again failed to recapture the Bridge. However, a portion of the Bund north of the Bridge at Gurmukh Khera was recaptured.

In the subsequent counter-attack to recapture the Bariwala Bridge on the night of 5/6 December, Major Narain Singh of 4 Jat led the attack with exemplary courage and bravery. In the words of General Raheel Shariff, the former Chief of Pakistan Army (2013 to 2016), Major Narain Singh was 'fearless with unfaltering, undaunted and unflinching courage'. Raheel Shariff's older brother was commanding the Pakistani Army Company that was defending the captured Bariwala Bridge. He faced the counter-attack launched by Major Narain Singh and his Company. Both Company Commanders died during this Battle.

To neutralize the threat to Fazilka from the north, Indian army crossed the Border at Muzzam, north-west of Fazilka, and captured a Pakistani village on the night of 11/12 December. Further, on the night of 13/14 December, Pakistani Ghazi Post was captured. Pakistanis counter-attacked Ghazi and retook the Post. A fourth and fifth counter-attacks were launched on the Bariwala Bridge on the night of 13/14 and the following night without success till the ceasefire was declared. Major Narain Singh was awarded VrC (Posthumous) for bravery. The CO of 4 Jat, Lt Col RK Suri, Major Sukpal Singh and Subedar Brijinder Singh were also decorated with VrC in this battle.

Fazilka witnessed fierce battle for a full 14 days. The Indian Army defended Fazilka with the life of 189 of their men, including 11 officers and 10 Junior Commissioned Officers. More than 400 were seriously injured. As a mark of respect to those who had laid down their life for the defence of Fazilka, a 'Shaheedon ki Samadhi' memorial was constructed. This memorial is being maintained by the people of Fazilka at Asafwala village. A chowk has been named after Major Narain Singh inside Fazilka Cantonment. Every year on the day of Baisakhi and Vijay Diwas (16 December), melas are organized by civil society and the Army at the Samadhi in memory of the brave Army men whose ashes have been preserved at the site.

FIROZPUR

Ferozpur is the largest cantonment located closest to the Indo-Pakistan Border in Punjab at a distance of about 10 kms from the IB. Kasur is a major communication centre opposite Ferozpur in Pakistan. The Border runs between these two towns along the Satluj River up to a point north of Ferozpur and turns to east and north after crossing Sutluj River. Then it turns to west thus taking a U-turn as shown in the sketch below. The boundary takes a zig-zag line for some distance before it turns south making a small southward bulge and thereafter runs north between Amritsar and Lahore. This eastward Pakistani salient of about 55 square kms of area is known as Sehjra Bulge. Another comparatively smaller bulge of about 45 square kms into Pakistani Territory south of Sehjra Bulge is Hussainiwala Bulge located due west of the city of Ferozpur. The entrance into Sehjra Bulge from the west is through a narrow corridor between Hussainiwala bulge in the south and the southern bulge to the west of Sehjra Bulge in the north.

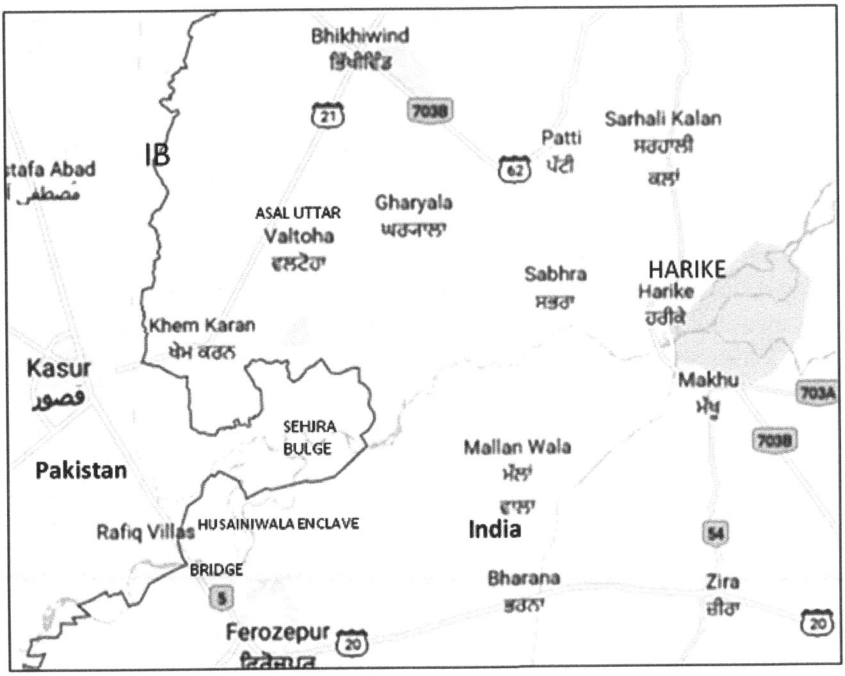

Hussainiwala Enclave, Bridge and Sehjra Bulge

(Harike Barrage to the east, Firozpur in the south)

Harike Barrage near the confluence of Beas and Sutlej Rivers is located in the northeast of Ferozpur. It is a major source of irrigation in Punjab and Rajasthan; thus a strategically important objective for Pakistan. Besides Ferozpur City itself, the road and rail bridge over the Sutlej River is a vital installation. The Hussainiwala Enclave is crisscrossed with rivulets and bunds which have been converted into anti-tank obstacles to prevent the enemy tanks rushing on to the Bridge and Ferozpur town. The location of the National Martyrs Memorial constructed in memory of Indian Freedom Fighters makes every inch of Hussainiwala a holy land. These two Bulges were the scene of fierce battles between India and Pakistan in 1965 and 1971 Wars.

After Pakistani Operation Gibraltar had failed to achieve its aim and Haji Pir Pass was captured by the Indian Army inside POK in 1965,

Pakistan Army crossed the Border and attacked in Chamb Sector, west of Akhnoor. Indian Army mobilised its forces and occupied their designated battle locations all along the Border. Hussainiwala was the operational area of 2 Maratha LI Battalion; one of the oldest Battalions of the Indian Army. They occupied Hussainiwala defences a few days before the commencement of war. Opposite 2 Maratha LI, Pakistan had a high observation tower inside Pakistan which facilitated Pakistani observers to look deep into the defences of Hussainiwala.

To deny Pakistani direct observation, the Commanding Officer of 2 Maratha LI decided to destroy the observation tower. On 7 September 1965, a company of 2 Maratha LI crossed the Border, captured the Pakistani Post and demolished the observation tower. The loss of this observation tower denied Pakistan Army the capability of looking deeper into the Hussainiwala defences. Pakistan reacted violently with heavy artillery fire and airstrikes day and night at Hussainiwala Enclave including the Shaheed Bhagat Singh Samadhi. On the night of 19 September, the Pakistani infantry supported with tanks, attacked Hussainiwala Enclave. 2 Maratha LI lost their Commanding Officer Lt Col Nolan when he was going around the defences and encouraging his men to engage the attacking enemy. The Battalion was rock steady and repulsed the attack. Not being able to make headway, the enemy retreated leaving behind their casualties including four tanks.

Throughout the attack, the Battalion ensured that the Samadhi of Shaheed Bhagat Singh was not desecrated. 2 Maratha LI successfully defended Hussainiwala till the Ceasefire was declared. The Prime Minister of India Sri Lal Bahadur Shastri visited the Battalion at Hussainiwala and appreciated the brave deeds of the officers and men of 2 Maratha LI in defending Hussainiwala successfully against large-scale attack by Pakistan. Citizens of Ferozpur presented a silver replica of Hussainiwala Bridge to show their gratitude to 2 Maratha LI for saving Hussainiwala Bridge and Ferozpur. The Battalion was also presented with the Battle Honour of Hussainiwala 1965 by the President of India.

The border out posts (BOP) was held by the Punjab Armed Police until 1966. After that, the Border Security Forces was created and deployed in the BOPs along the IB. Hussainiwala Bridge was guarded by a company of infantry battalion located at Firozpur. A check-post was functioning at the Border which controlled the foreign tourists, vehicles and load carriers. The bridge was used for international traffic till the evening of 03 December 1971.

1971

Hussainiwala Enclave was once again attacked by the Pakistan Army in December 1971. This time the defence of Hussainiwala including the Bridge over Satluj was in the hands of 15 Punjab (First Patiala). The Battalion was located at Hussainiwala Enclave from February 1971. By November 1971, they had enough and more indications from the ongoing events in East Pakistan that the western Border will be activated any time. It proved to be correct when Pakistani armed forces crossed the western border on 03 December and late in the evening, the entire Hussainiwala Enclave was under enemy attack. Pakistani infantry units supported by tanks attacked from the west along the Ferozpur Highway and the north and south of it. The area was covered with tall dry sarkanda grass that caught fire during attack and detonated the mines. In spite of stiff resistance offered by 15 Punjab, the large-scale attack of Pakistan Army could not be contained before the enemy reached the Memorial in the middle of the Enclave by midnight.

An attempt made by the Indian Army to induct tanks into Hussainiwala Enclave through the Satluj Bridge did not succeed due to enemy interference. To ensure that the Bridge did not fall into the hands of enemy intact, it was partially demolished. This prevented the enemy from crossing the River and contacting Ferozpur.

In other subsectors, a number of Pakistani Posts were captured in a well-planned low-level attacks and gained tactical advantages. At the time of the ceasefire, the Indian Army dominated the Firozpur-Fazilka sectors and no offensive move could take place from the Pakistani side.

SEHJRA BULGE

Sehjra Bulge, a Pakistani enclave surrounded by Indian Territory is located adjacent to Hussainiwala Enclave in the north and northeast. River Sutluj passes through the southern half of the Bulge. Harike Barrage is located to the east of Bulge. Khemkaran is in the northwest, Kasur in Pakistan in the west and Hussainiwala Bulge in the south. Sehjra is the largest village located within the Bulge. The village was well prepared as a fortress and held with a company of Baluch duly supported by Recce and Support elements. Border posts inside Pakistan were held by the Sind Rangers.

When Pakistan was busy in attacking Hussainiwala Enclave and attempting to go for the vital Rail Road Bridge linking Ferozpur across

Sutlej River, India decided to capture the Sehjra Bulge and straighten the borderline. First Battalion of the 5 Gorkha Rifles (1/5 GR) was tasked to capture the village Sehjra while 9 Sikh LI was ordered to capture the Border Posts from the east. 6 Mahar was ordered to isolate Sehjra from the west and cut off the route of withdrawal of the defenders from there. A thorough preparation was done by all three Battalions.

1/5 GR approached Sehjra from the south and attacked the village from the least expected direction at 30 minutes past midnight on 06 December 1971. The Pakistanis were totally surprised. It was well led attack with all the commanders encouraging the assaulting troops from the front. By early morning, all objectives were captured. 6 Mahar had attacked and occupied the Pakistani village of Mahiwala and blocked the route of withdrawal from the Bulge. At the same time 9 Sikh LI attacked and captured the Border Posts of Nagar Amirpur, Mubbuke and Bhukkiwala. By mid-day on the 6th, Pakistani villages of Pattiwala and Mahiwala that were located within the Bulge were also captured and consolidated. All three Battalions reorganized themselves and were ready to face counter-attack from Pakistan Army. Pakistan Army suffered heavy casualty with 30 killed and 65 captured as prisoners along with huge quantity of weapons and ammunition. Subsequent infiltration attempt made by 41 Baluch of Pakistan was thwarted killing another 30 and wounding 15. The successful capture of Sehjra Bulge ensured the safety of Harike Barrage and ruled out any possibility of Pakistani offensive in this Sector.

KHEM KARAN

Khem Karan-Asal Uttar-Bhkkiwind Area

The border from Sehjra Bulge through west of Khem Karan up to Kalra in the north is nearly straight. Khemkaran and Kasur are located at equidistant on either side of the Border. Ichhogil Canal also known as Bambawali–Ravi–Bedian Canal (BRBC/BRB) runs parallel to the Border east of Lahore inside Pakistan from the River Ravi in the north and Sutluj in the south. It is a formidable obstacle to both Infantry and tanks. The canal is 112 feet wide, 30 feet deep with 20 feet of water in it. The western bank of the canal is higher and has many pillboxes and tank ramps made up of cement concrete. There are two aqueducts in the vicinity of Kasur. Another smaller Nala known as Rohi Nala in between BRB and border is a minor obstacle. There were many cluster of villages and clumps of trees between Kasur and the Border which provided good cover from the aerial observation to tanks and vehicles. The area on both sides of the border is cultivated throughout the year with extensive network of irrigation system in place. The IB was guarded by the BSF on the Indian side and Rangers in Pakistan.

On 06 September 1965, a riposte to Pakistani offensive in Chamb-Akhnoor Sector was launched. The Indian Army crossed the border opposite Sialkot, Lahore and Kasur. The southern thrust in Punjab was from Khem Karan towards Kasur. The aim was to contact the east Bank of Ichhogil Canal, destroy the bridges and hold a firm base on the east Bank. The advance commenced after last light on 6 September. Rohi Nala was contacted and cleared against light opposition. Ichhogil Canal was contacted at Theh Pannun by 4 Grenadiers. Further advance towards Ichhogil Canal along the main road drew heavy artillery and machine-gun fire. This was followed by violent counter-attacks with tanks. Pakistani reaction was stronger and quicker than expected. The advance was stalled. Later in the night, Pakistani tank movements were noticed north of Ballawala heading towards the Border.

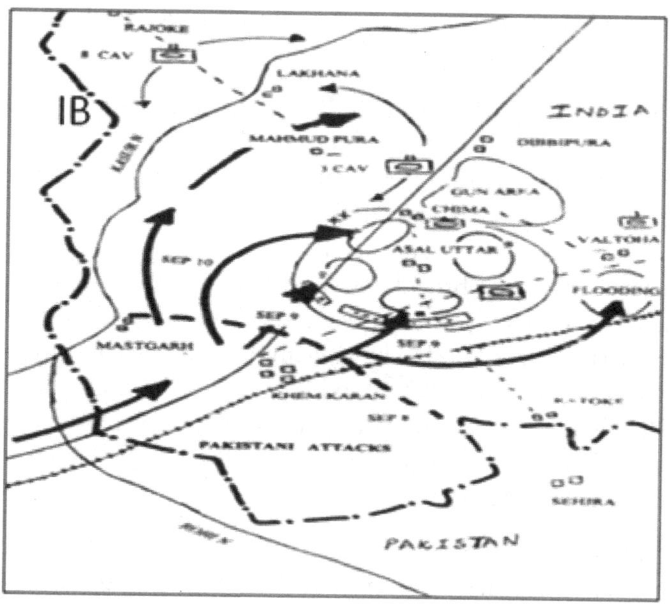

Asal Uttar

By early morning 7 September there were enough indications that Pakistan Army had concentrated a large-sized mechanised force in Kasur Sector beyond the requirement of defending Kasur. This indicated to Indian military leaders of a possible preparation of Pakistan Army for a large-scale mechanised offensive through Khem Karan Sector towards vital targets in the depth areas of Punjab. Therefore the offensive plan made by the Indian Army was abandoned and the troops from the west of the IB were withdrawn. A defended sector was occupied in the areas northeast of Khem Karan in Asal Uttar, Bhkkiwind, Bhura, Kuhna and Chima. The task given to them was to destroy Pakistani mechanised forces and prevent them from capturing the Indian Territory in this Sector. The defended sector comprised four infantry battalion and tank regiments.

On the morning of 8 September, when the defences were still being prepared, Pakistani Forces crossed the IB northwest of Khem Karan with tanks. Own advance elements near the IB engaged the enemy and destroyed two Chaffee tanks. Pakistani intruders withdrew. Once again in the afternoon, Pakistani Patton Tanks attacked 1/9 GR and 4 Grenadiers in the north of Khem Karan and captured part of their defences. Own tanks of 9 Horse contested further move of Pakistani tanks both at Rattoke and Bhikhiwind and destroyed many tanks, thus forcing Pakistani tanks to disengage and withdraw. Having failed to create any major impact on the Indian defences, Pakistanis once again attacked on the night of 8/9 September.

This time the attack was on 18 Rajputana Rifles (Raj Rif) supported by Patton tanks which had night fighting capabilities. The tanks suffered casualty in the minefields. Heavy artillery fire and infantry anti-tank weapons destroyed many enemy tanks and deterred them from advancing further. The attack petered out. Later they withdraw. In the meantime 2 Independent Armoured Brigade under Brigadier Theogaraj was inducted into Khem Karan Sector. On his recommendation, some of the possible enemy tank-runs were flooded by breaching Rohi Nala and Kasur Drain. The attempts made by the enemy to bypass from the north of Asal Uttar and south of Khem Karan inside the defended sector were frustrated by the defenders with their anti-tank weapons and the flooded areas where the enemy tanks got bogged down.

On the night of 9 September the Pakistani infantry came mounted on Armoured Personnel Carriers and launched an attack. The enemy suffered heavy casualty and withdrew. The next morning enemy attacked 4 Grenadiers with tanks. Company Quarter Master Havildar Abdul Hamid and his detachment of jeep mounted anti-tank 106 mm recoilless (RCL) gun took the advantage of limited visibility in the tall sugarcane field and allowed the tanks to approach close to where they were hiding. When the tanks came within the effective range of their gun, Abdul Hameed fired with his RCL gun and destroyed three tanks one after the other from different positions. When he engaged the fourth tank, the enemy shell landed on the Jeep and the gun and the jeep were destroyed. Brave Abdul Hamid was killed along with the driver. For his bravery of very high order and the ultimate sacrifice of his life beyond the call of duty, he was decorated with the India's highest bravery award; Param Vir Chakra.

CQMH Abdul Hamid PVC
(Posthumous)

2 Armoured Brigade with 3 CAV and 8 CAV had created a perfect tank trap in the northwest of Asal Uttar. The enemy tanks fell into the trap in the area of Mahaboobpura and the tanks of 3 and 8 CAV destroyed many of the enemy Patton Tanks. A large number of Pakistani tank crews abandoned their tanks in running condition. Major General Nasir Ahamed, the General Officer Commanding of the Pakistani 1 Armoured Division who landed in a helicopter in Khem Karan Sector along with his staff officers was killed and the helicopter was destroyed. The officers and men of Pakistani 4 Cavalry surrendered on 11 September. With that, Pakistani offensive in Khem Karan Sector ended tragically.

Maj Gen Gurbaksh Singh, GOC 4 Division, Brigadier Theogaraj, Lt Col AS Vaidhya (Later COAS), Lt Col Raghubir Singh, CO 18 Raj Rif, and Lt Col Salim Calib were decorated with Maha Vir Chakra. The Indian plan to recapture Khem Karan was not executed due to the announcement of ceasefire. The near destruction of Pakistani Armoured Division with a loss of more than 80 tanks destroyed or surrendered had a demoralizing effect on Pakistan Army. With the concentration of captured Pakistani tanks a memorial known as Patton Nagar was created. It stands as witness to the bravery of the men of Indian Army. Historians have equated the Battle of Asal Uttar which turned the tide of the 1965 war in favour of India to the Battle of Kursk of World War II.

During 1971 War, Pakistanis made an attempt to capture the border out post at Khem Karan Barrier, which was frustrated.

KALRA-BARKI

The Border from Kalra to Amritsar-Lahore Grand Trunk (GT) Road meanders through the thickly populated and fertile agriculture fields of Punjab with good road network on both sides. On the Pakistani side, the Ichhogil Canal runs 5 to 7 kms west of the IB. Road Bhikhiwind-Kalra-Hudiara-Barki crosses the Border two kms north of Khalra. In between Ichhogil canal and the IB, there are two more canals known as Upper Bhucher Distributary and Hudiara Drain. Village Barki is located half a km east of Ichhogil Canal.

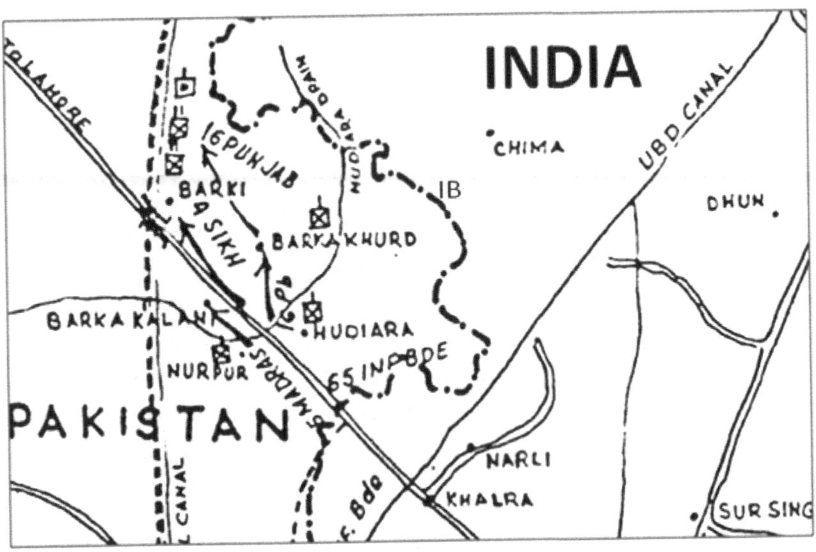

Khalra-Barki

Khalra is a large Indian village located about a km and a half east of the Border. On the Pakistani side of the Border, the first major village along the Khalra-Barki road is Hudiara which is about four kms from the Border. Barki is 10 kms from the IB. Barki village was converted into a strong defended locality to withstand major attacks. There were well camouflaged concrete bunkers inter-connected with tunnels. The village was held by a company of Pakistani regular army troops supported by tanks and anti-tank weapons with minefields covered with defensive artillery fire.

1965

As part of Indian counter-offensive plan in Amritsar Sector, Burki was chosen as one of the objectives across the IB east of Ichhogil Canal. Advance commenced on both sides of the Khalra-Barki Road early morning on 6 September 1965. 17 Rajput heading for Bedian advanced fast brushing aside minor oppositions. The advance came to a halt 500 mtrs short of Bedian Bridge by the heavy volume of enemy artillery and long-range automatic fire from the Ichhogil Canal. 17 Rajput established a firm base there and laid mines on the possible counter-attack approaches. In the north, 4 Sikh had captured the Border Post at Theh, Sarja and Majra along with 6/8 GR. By 1030 hours, advancing forces came under heavy automatic and artillery fire from Hudiara Drain and Nurpur village from north and south of main road. Further advance was considered possible only after clearing Hudiara complex which appeared to be held by two companies of Pakistani regular troops.

The task of capturing Hudiara was given to 5 Guards. The attack was planned for 1330 hours from Nurpur towards Hudiara. After a well contested fight, 5 Guards successfully cut off the Hudiara complex and captured it. The bridge over Hudiara drain was demolished by the withdrawing enemy. This delayed further advance. The engineers constructed a bridge over the Hudiara Drain and the advance and attack on Burki was planned for the next day.

The defence of Barki with Nurpur, Barka Kalan and Barka Khurd forming part of the main defences was held by Pakistani Regular Forces in strength. 4 Sikh and 16 Punjab with tanks and artillery support were tasked to capture Barki Complex. Before the main attack, 9 Madras with the tanks of Central India Horse (CIH) was ordered to capture Barka Kalan. The advance commenced after crossing the newly constructed Bailey bridge and causeway by 1600 hours. After a stiff fight, Barka Kalan was captured by six in the evening on 7 September. The main attack on Barki village was launched by 4 Sikh at 2000 hours on the same day.

Heavy artillery fire was brought down on the village Barki and the enemy gun areas for more than half an hour. When the troops were closing in with the objective, artillery fire was lifted and the tanks of CIH gave close fire support to 4 Sikh. The tanks encountered minefields. This was delaying the advance. To speed up the operation, the Commanding Officer of CIH, Lt Col SC Joshi VrC personally led the tanks through the minefield. When his tank-track was blown off, he got down from the safety of the tank and drove a jeep to continue guiding the tanks. During this process, his jeep was blown off by another mine. The CO was severely injured. Later he succumbed to his injuries. For his devotion to duty and exceptional bravery, he was decorated with a BAR to his VrC which was awarded to him in 1947 War.

The Indian tanks which did not have night-fighting capability provided close fire support to the assaulting infantry troops on that bright moonlit night. This led the Pakistani Army leaders to believe that India had acquired night-fighting capability similar to Pakistan. 4 Sikh entered the village and fought close-quarter battles in the built-up areas. There were concrete pillboxes and bunkers within the village. Each and every bunker was tackled with grenades. The whole village was cleared by 2130 hours.

16 Punjab continued their attack on the Ichhogil canal and captured the East Bank by 2340 hours. The enemy withdrew from Barki leaving behind their casualties and demolished the Bridge over Ichhogil Canal after they had crossed to the west. Pakistanis continued to engage the area of East Bank with artillery and anti-tank weapons.

On the night of 11/12 September, 5 Guards was tasked to capture Jahman, south of Barki. The attack was not successful. The next night, 5 Guards along with 6/8 GR and tanks attacked Jahman once again. The tanks got bogged down in the cultivated fields and the enemy brought down intensive artillery fire. Thus the second attack also failed. A third attempt was made to capture Jahman; this time with 19 Maratha LI and 6/8 GR. The village was captured by 1730 hours on 18 September. More areas including Dholan and Thatti Jaimal Singh were captured by 20 September. The enemy made many attempt to recapture Thatti Jaimal Singh, but did not succeed against the brave men of 19 Maratha LI and their commander Major MA Zaki who held their locality till the end of the War. Pakistan had lost six tanks as against Indian loss of three tanks. Major MA Zaki was decorated with VrC for bravery in the face of the enemy and his devotion to duty. In the area opposite Khalra Sector, the Indian Army captured a vast Pakistani territory between Ichhogil Canal and IB before the ceasefire was declared.

1971

In December 1971, Pakistan launched an attack in the north and south of Amritsar-Lahore GT Road. Due to paucity of troops, Khalra Sector was thinly held by the Indian Army. On the night of 3/4 December, Pakistan crossed the Border on a broad-front and contacted the defences at Chhina Bidi Chand and Narli, north of Khalra and Kalsian south of Khalra by midnight. The BSF was ordered to withdraw from the Border Posts and hold main defences along the Upper Bari Doab Canal (UBDC). By early morning, Chhina Bidi Chand was overrun by the Pakistani Forces. The important bridges over UBDC were demolished. Pakistan's attempt to capture Khalra was frustrated. Attempt made by the Indian Army to recapture Chhina Bidi Chand though successful, could not be held for long as Chhina Bidi Chand was an isolated locality. Pakistan did not make any further advance in this Sector.

AMRITSAR- LAHORE

The IB from Khalra to Dera Baba Nanak (DBN) forms a westward bulge through Attari and Ranian. At Ranian, the IB cuts across River Ravi and meanders on both sides of the River, thus making many enclaves on Indian and Pakistani side of the River. Amritsar and Lahore are located at equal distance from the Border. They are connected by the GT Road through Wagah Border Post. Beyond the Border, at the outskirts of Lahore to the east is the formidable Ichhogil Canal which was constructed to protect Lahore. Other important towns north of Lahore are Narang Mandi and Narowal. Dograi is located on the east bank of Ichhogil Canal and Batapur on the west bank at the outskirts of Lahore. The border was guarded by Punjab Armed Police at the Indian side and by the Rangers on the Pakistani side till 1966.

In the first week of September 1965, Pakistani Forces crossed the CFL in J&K and attacked the Indian Army Posts west of Munawar Tawi River including Chamb. The pressure brought down on Pakistan by the international community to stop her offensive in Akhnoor Sector and withdraw her armed Forces from Indian Territory went unheeded. Pakistan continued her advance towards Akhnoor. Therefore, Indian Army had resorted to limited offensive between DBN and Khalra in Amritsar-Lahore Sector with a view to threatening Lahore by capturing east Bank of Ichhogil Canal along with important road and rail bridges across the canal. Indian Army crossed the IB and advanced along the GT Road on 6 September after overrunning the Border Posts. 3 Jat commanded by Lt Col Desmond Hayde, 15 Dogra under Lt Col Inderjit Singh and 13 Punjab under Lt Col N Chatterjee were on the lead. The Battalions succeeded in capturing their intermediate objectives by 0700 hours. Pakistan Air Force reacted violently and destroyed the support vehicles and reserve ammunitions of the advancing Battalions.

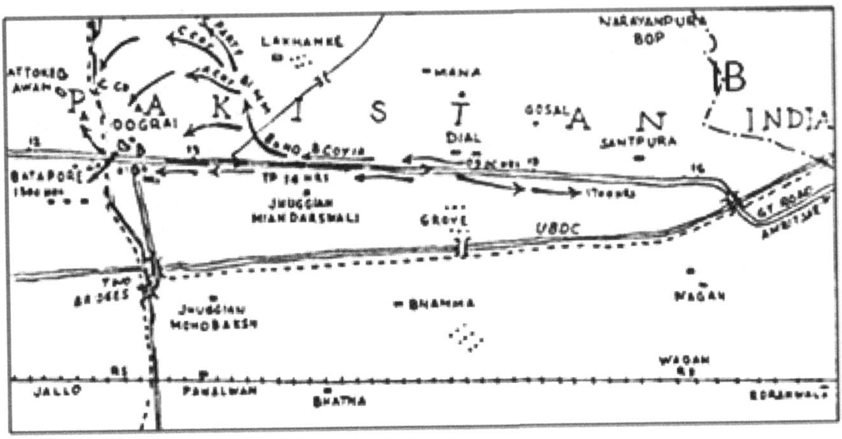

GT Road Amritsar - Lahore

Dograi-Batapur

3 Jat suffered casualties. The Second in Command of the Battalion was killed. The Battalion further advanced and captured the east Bank of Ichhogil Canal and the Bridge over it. The Bridge was partially demolished by the withdrawing Pakistanis. By midday, the Commanding Officer with over two hundred men was at Batapur on the outskirts of Lahore. They encountered enemy counter-attacks with tanks. Air attacks were intensified on the leading elements. Indian Air Support was not available. Therefore, 3 Jat withdrew to the East Bank of Ichhogil canal under pressure. The Battalion reorganised itself and once again crossed over to the West Bank. The communication with their Brigade HQ had broken down. The Brigade HQ did not know that 3 Jat was knocking at the doors of Lahore across Ichhogil Canal. In the absence of direct communication, the Commanding Officer 3 Jat got an order at 1430 hours through an armour squadron tank radio net to withdraw the Battalion to village Gosal-Dial which was east of the Canal. The Battalion withdrew accordingly. The Commanding Officer was wounded during the battle but refused to be evacuated and remained with the Battalion.

Subsequently attempts were made to capture the bridges over the Ichhogil Canal north of GT Road in the area of Basin and Ichhogil Uttar after crossing the IB at Ranian. This was not successful due to strong enemy reaction. Having repulsed the attack, the enemy crossed the IB and captured Ranian and Kakkar which were lightly held. Another attempt was made to capture Jalo Bridge south of the GT Road with no success.

DOGRAI

After the gains made in between the IB and Ichhogil Canal was consolidated, a plan was made to capture the village of Dograi. 3 Jat was chosen for the task as they had passed through the village earlier and were familiar with the area. 13 Punjab was tasked to capture Mile Stone 13 area in the south of Dograi village simultaneously on 21 September. Additional tank and artillery support was provided. In spite of frequent enemy disruption, 13 Punjab with tanks in support captured part of their objective south of Dograi along the GT Road by early morning the next day. Both sides suffered heavy casualties.

Dograi was held strongly with more than a battalion of the enemy in concrete bunkers along with the defence works on the east bank of the Canal. Pakistani tanks were providing defensive fire from the west bank. The Commanding Officer of 3 Jat made his plan and gave out his orders. The attack was to be launched from the northeast. All four Rifle companies were given separate objectives. The Commanding Officer made it clear to all ranks, "reach your stated objective dead or alive but reach, because I certainly will". He further said, "Follow your leaders, shoot at anything that moves or is suspicious, and quickly secure the objective after it is captured." The ultimate result of his advice proved beyond doubt that every word of his orders was well understood by his command and were meticulously executed.

The attack on Dograi village commenced from the forming up place from the northeast of the village at 0150 hours on 22 September. Majors Tyagi, Sandhu, Yadhav and Vatsa were the company commanders. Each member of 'Team 3 Jat' was motivated to capture their objective at all cost. They faced enemy bullets, undertook destruction of bunkers, engaged in hand-to-hand combat and silenced enemy weapons with grenades for over three hours. Dograi was captured by 0530 hours. 3 Jat had done it. The enemy launched four counter-attacks all of which were repulsed with heavy casualty on the enemy.

It took the complete day to clear the enemy from pockets of resistance and secure Dograi. Four officers and more than 50 men sacrificed their life while 151 men and 6 officers were wounded. A large number of the enemy including the Commanding Officer of Pakistani 16 Punjab was taken prisoners. More than 300 enemy dead bodies were accounted for. Dograi was captured after 27 hours of intensive battle by two Infantry Battalions and tanks. It is one of the toughest battles in the history of Indian Army. Lt Col Desmond E Hayde, the Commanding Officer, Major AR Tyagi, 'A' Company Commander and Capt Kapil Singh Thapa were decorated with Maha Vir Chakra. Regrettably, Major Tyagi and Capt Thapa were not alive to receive their awards. In addition, 3 Jat was awarded 4 VrC, 7 Sena Medals, 12 Mention in Dispatches and 11 COAS Commendation Cards. For its exemplary display of courage and determination, the Battalion was awarded the Battle Honour of Dograi, and Theatre Honour of Punjab.

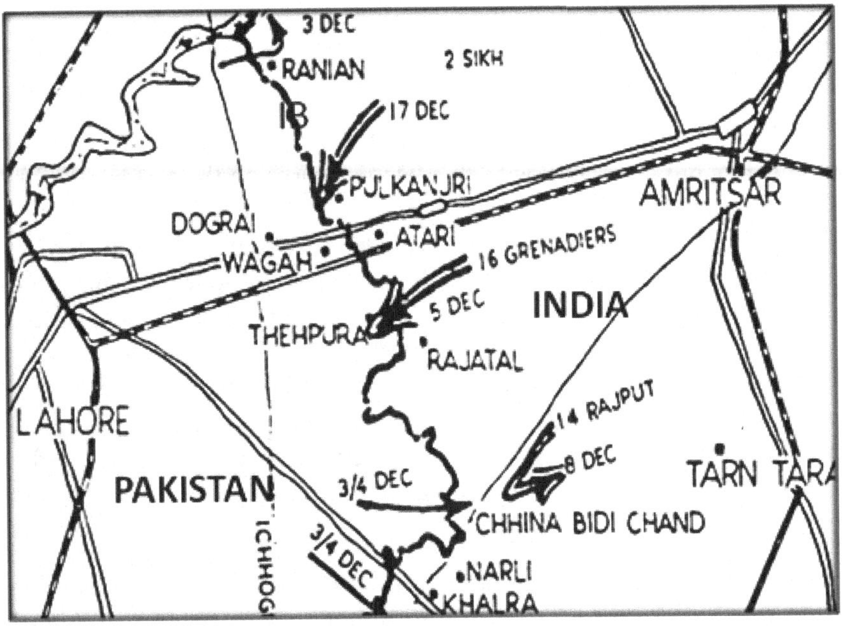

Amritsar -1971

The area along GT road was dormant in the December 1971 Pakistani Aggression. Neither India, which was fully committed in the East Pakistan for the liberation of Bangladesh, nor Pakistan, which was defending Shakhargarh Bulge with everything they had, crossed the Wagah Border.

However, Pakistan attacked the Ranian Post north of GT Road on 3 December. The attack was repulsed by 2 Sikh. Pakistanis attacked Ranian Post five times between 4 and 17 December without any success. Their attempt to capture Shamsher Post was also frustrated. On the other hand, Indian troops captured Pakistani Post at Pulkanjri after crossing a Pakistani minefield. 43 Punjab of Pakistan made many attempts to recapture the Post without success before the ceasefire was announced.

BURJ

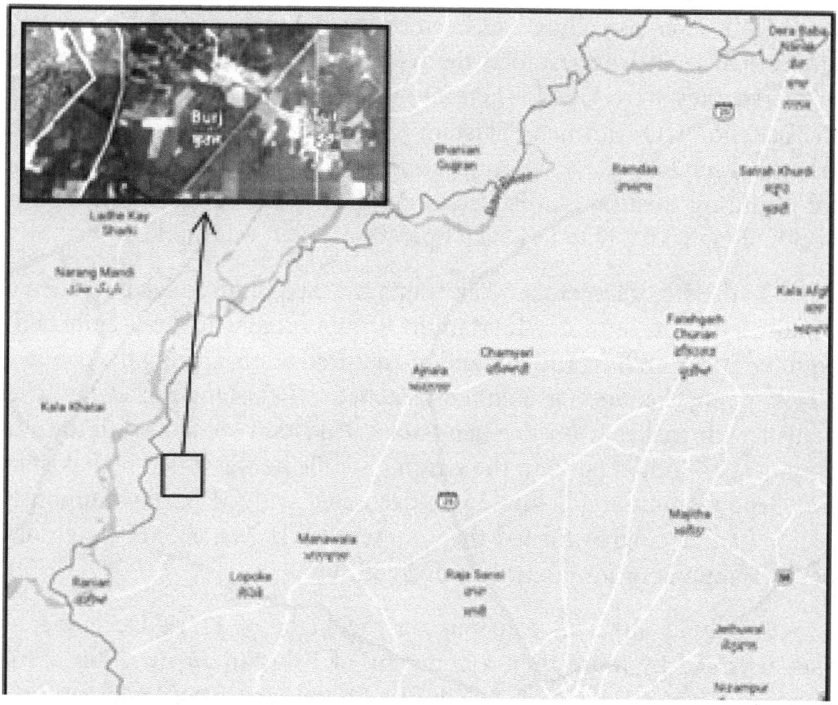

Border areas north of Ranian witnessed many attacks and counter-attacks across the DCB on the Indian side of the Border along Saki Nala in 1971. Both sides had Border Posts manned by BSF/Rangers that were reinforced with the army troops by the last week of November 1971. On the Indian side, the DCB/BOPs in Burj Sub-Sector north of Ranian and west of Ajnala were occupied by the troops of 15 Maratha LI. On the night of 3/4 December, a Pakistan Army unit which was later identified as 43 Baluch Battalion, attacked a portion of DCB in Burj and Tur area and captured it.

Captain Dilip Pandurang Kute of 15 Maratha LI, who was leading a patrol near the IB was cut off from the unit due to enemy advance. He saw enemy movement all around him. His radio-set was not functioning. He decided to withdraw avoiding enemy detection by taking a longer route and return to the unit. While returning he found two Pakistanis near Tur village behind an embankment (bund) detached from their unit. He and his party quietly encircled them in the dark and bounced on them. They were shocked and surrendered without any resistance. He took away their weapons and the map that they were carrying. They were blindfolded and taken to the Battalion HQ. By the time he reached Battalion HQ, it was 0730 hours. Capt Kute was not in communication all these time. The area in which he was patrolling had been overrun by the enemy. Under these circumstances, it was assumed that either the patrol had been captured or worse; they were killed. Therefore when Capt Dilip Kute appeared at the Battalion HQ with two Pakistani prisoners, there was a great sense of relief and jubilation. He was praised for using his presence of mind and for capturing the first two Pakistani prisoners with weapons in Amritsar Sector along with a map in which operational plan was marked.

On the 6th of December, Pakistanis attacked Bindi Aulak but failed to capture it. On the same day 15 Maratha LI supported with tanks launched a counter-attack on Burj and Tur and re-captured them. During the counter-attack, Sepoy Pandurang Salunke snatched a Pakistani rocket launcher loaded with rocket from the hands of a Pakistani soldier while he was aiming at an Indian tank. In the ensuing scuffle he was killed by Pakistani fire. Sepoy Pandurang Salunke was decorated with MVC posthumously. Major Ranbir Singh who led the counter-attack, Major Sher Singh and Sepoy Hanumant More were awarded with VrC.

8 Sikh LI attacked Fatehpur on the night of 11/12 December. It was defended by more than a company of Pakistan Army. After a stiff opposition by the defenders, 8 Sikh LI with the support of tanks captured Fatehpur by midnight. The enemy counter-attacks were repulsed. The Battalion further exploited the initial success and captured a bund junction. Pakistanis counter-attacked bund junction. Seeing the determination of the Pakistanis to recapture their localities and the vulnerability of the counter-attacking enemy troops exposed in the open, Major Tirath Singh, one of the company commanders of 8 Sikh LI, called for artillery fire (DF SOS) on his company position against the enemy who were in the open. His men were well protected inside the bunkers. The enemy took to heels and the counter-attack was defeated. However, Major Tirath Singh who took

calculated risk and was moving from one bunker to another encouraging his men to hold on was mortally wounded. Major Tirath acted 'beyond the call of duty' to hold on to the captured locality and saved the day with his own life. He was decorated with a Vir Chakra.

DERA BABA NANAK

Dera Baba Nanak (DBN) is the northern most border town in Punjab. It is located two kms east of IB at the northern end of Amritsar Sector. It is well connected by road to Gurdaspur, Batala, Beas and Amritsar. There are two enclaves near DBN across Ravi River; one each of India and Pakistan. The Pakistani enclave known as DBN Enclave is the larger of the two and located in the east of Ravi River. This enclave is about two and a half kms deep between the IB and the River. The smaller of the two is inside the Indian Territory, known as Dharm Enclave, and is located in the west of Ravi River. DBN Enclave is connected with mainland Pakistan across Ravi River with a bridge. Both sides had prepared their enclaves with defence oriented bunds/bunkers and concrete pillboxes where the army units could quickly occupy defences when required. The enclave is dotted with marshy patches of land covered with tall sarkanda grass, cultivated fields and nalas. On the Pakistani side of the enclave is the famous Gurudwara of Guru Nanak Dev located at Kartarpur.

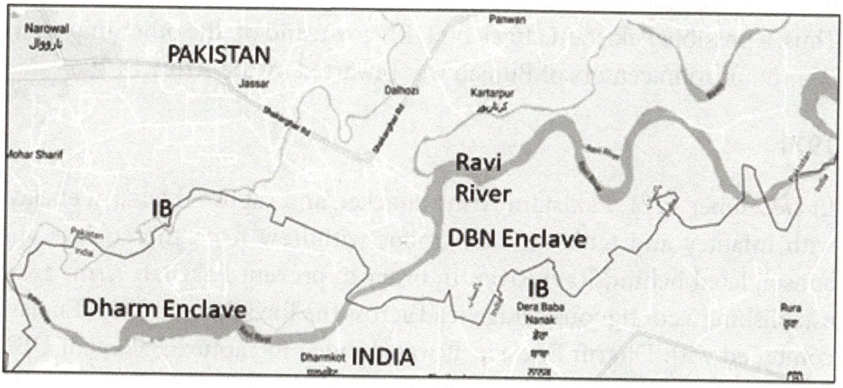

Indian and Pakistani Enclaves across Ravi River

1965

DBN witnessed well contested battles in 1965 and 1971. In September 1965, when the entire Amritsar Sector was activated in the south and Shakargarh Sector in the north, it was decided to capture and eliminate DBN Enclave. Accordingly, 2 Madras and 1/5 GR were tasked to attack across the IB and capture the Pakistani DBN enclave and the bridge connecting it with the mainland Pakistan. Attack was launched on the night of 5/6 September at 0400 hours. After a tough fight, the objectives were captured by early morning. Before the captured positions could be consolidated, enemy launched counter-attacks on the captured localities. This lasted the whole of next day.

To overcome this critical situation, 3 Raj Rif was ordered to attack on the next night through the area captured by the other two Battalions during the previous night and capture the east bank of DBN Bridge. The Battalion played a trick on the enemy by advancing in their vehicles through sarkanda grass with full head lights on in a broad-front at 0200 hours on 07 September. The enemy fell prey to the ruse and ran away from their localities presuming that they were being enveloped by large number of Indian tanks. They left behind their heavy weapons and stores and withdrew from the enclave through the bridge. A portion of the bridge was demolished by the withdrawing enemy. Thereafter, till the ceasefire was declared, DBN Enclave remained in the hands of the Indian Army. Thus, a possible Pakistani attack on DBN town and on the other important communication centers of Punjab was thwarted by the Army in 1965.

1971

In December 1971, Pakistani Army attacked and captured Dharm enclave with infantry and tanks. Indian troops withdrew from the enclave and consolidated behind Ravi River. In order to prevent Pakistan Army from establishing a contiguous bridgehead across the Ravi River in DBN Enclave combined with Dharm Enclave, it was decided to capture Pakistani DBN Enclave. Attack was launched with four battalions and tanks under the overall command of Brigadier K Gowri Shankar.

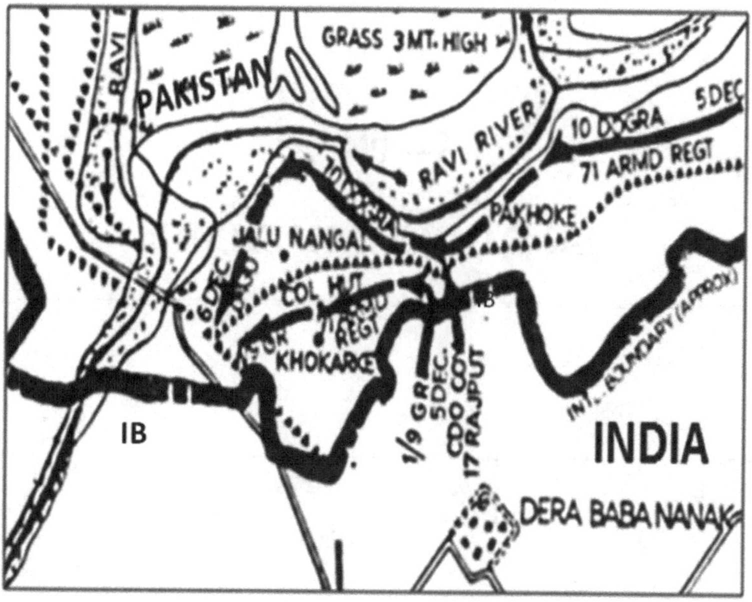

DBN in 1971-Plan of Attack

According to the plan, 4/8 GR crossed the border at Metla a few kms east of DBN and secured a firm base for 10 Dogra and the tanks. The attack was to commence during the night 5/6 December. 10 Dogra took more time than was expected to commence their attack. In the meantime 1/9 GR was ordered to attack the objective. Ultimately both 10 Dogra and 1/9 GR captured their objective after a tough fight. The battle progressed with systematic bunker bursting along the bund with multidirectional attacks supported by concentrated artillery fire. Finally, 17 Rajput joined the battle and recaptured the Dharm Enclave through DBN Enclave. Pakistanis counter-attacked on the nights of 6/7 and 7/8 December. The counter-attacks were repulsed. Pakistan Army units retreated to the west of Ravi River through the Bridge. Pakistanis destroyed the first pier of the Bridge during their retreat.

With that, both enclaves were in the hands of Indian Army and the threat from this Sector to Punjab was eliminated. The battle ended with 26 Pakistanis taken as prisoners and 34 killed. Indian casualty was 10 killed and 32 wounded. The brigade commander was awarded with MVC for a successful operation conducted by him.

Chapter 4

JAMMU AND KASHMIR

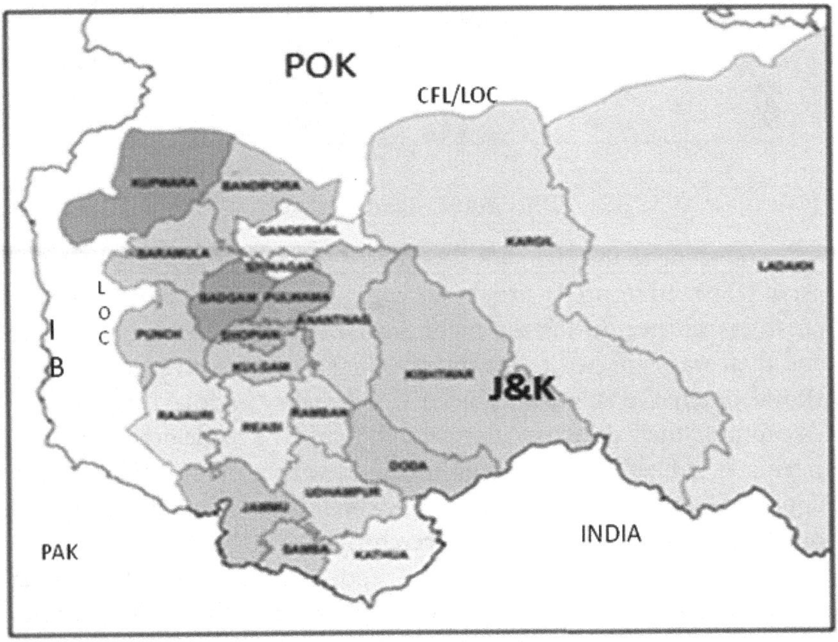

The state of J&K comprises the plains and semi-mountainous low hilly regions of Jammu, the Punch Tract west of Pir Panjal Ranges, the Kashmir Valley including the mountainous Tithwal and Gurez Region, the northern Region of Gilgit, Baltistan, the rocky desert of Ladakh, the glaciated regions of Siachen and cold desert of Aksai Chin. Geographically, it was one of the large kingdoms in the Indian Sub-Continent when British ruled this part of the world. Due to its salubrious climate and natural beauty, it was an attractive region for many foreign invaders. The rulers could not integrate J&K as one homogenous kingdom due to lingual, religious and cultural diversity, harsh terrain, vast distances, lack of means of communication and absence of adequate law and order enforcing agency/security forces commensurate to the vastness of the territory of the kingdom. Three major religions - Hinduism, Islam and Buddhism - were practised in this kingdom. The original inhabitants were Hindus. Muslims were either converts or those who came along with various invaders and settled down in the valley. Ladakh was influenced by Tibetan culture.

In 1947, J&K was a Muslim majority independent state with Hindu rulers. The northern region of Gilgit and Baltistan was administered and protected by the British directly. While partitioning the British India, the British gave the option to J&K either to join India or Pakistan or remain independent. Maharaja Hari Singh was in dilemma and the future of the people of J&K was uncertain. When British India was divided in August 1947, J&K remained an independent kingdom; but not for a long. In a little over two months after British had handed over the power to India and Pakistan, Pakistan sent raiders across the border to annex J&K. This situation forced the King of J&K to seek help and merge with India on 26 October 1947. J&K joined India when it was under attack. Along with the beauty and diversity, J&K brought unrest and unsettled borders to India. Besides Pakistan, J&K had borders with Afghanistan and China. All of them were contentious.

The Indian Army landed in Srinagar airfield for the first time on 27 October 1947. After many battles, mostly fought close to the present LOC for 14 months, both countries nearly ran out of options and agreed to a ceasefire in J&K organised with the intervention of UNO. While majority of J&K became part of Independent India, smaller parts in the west and north remained occupied by Pakistan. The boundary of the divided J&K and POK was known as CFL, which was later converted into LOC after 1971 Indo-Pakistan War.

SHAKARGARH SECTOR

Shakargarh Bulge

Shakargarh Bulge is the largest Pakistani territorial projection surrounded by Indian Territory on three sides in the plains. Opposite this Pakistani enclave is the Indian State of Punjab and J&K. It brings Pakistani Territory closer to the Pathankot-Jammu Highway which was the only major and shortest link to J&K from the rest of India. To the north of this bulge is Jammu and Akhnoor including Chicken Neck and in the south is Amritsar and Lahore. Pathankot is located to the east of the bulge. The Radcliffe Boundary line ends west of Kathua near the Border village of Bamial west of Pathankot.

At the periphery of the Bulge are the Indian villages/towns of Dera Baba Nanak in the south, Bamial in the east and Ramgarh in the north. Pakistani towns and large villages inside the Bulge are Shakargarh, Zafarwal, Narowal and Sialkot. Rivers Chenab, Ravi and many distributaries of these rivers flow through the bulge. The area is dotted with villages and small towns surrounded with cultivated fields, roads and canal networks. Pakistan has strengthened most of the rivers, canals, ditches and bunds

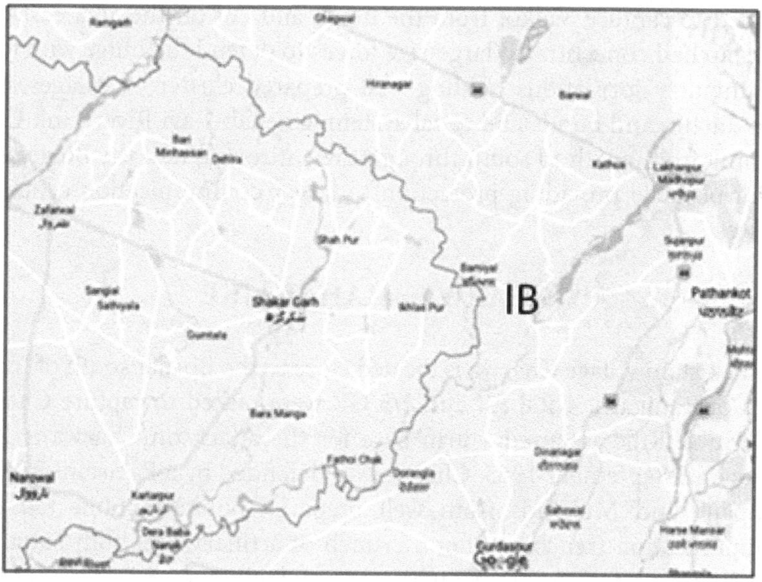

Ramgarh-Kathua-Bamial-Dera Baba Nanak

inside the bulge with pillboxes and bunkers and converted them into anti-tank obstacles.

1965

Shakargarh Bulge was the scene of some of the toughest tank and Infantry battles in 1965 and 1971 Wars. Besides Shakargarh, names such as Nainakot, Chawinda, Charwa, Maharajke, Jasso Ran, Phillora and Bada Pind (Basantar) are synonymous with decisive battles of the two wars. The 1965 war was started by Pakistan with the arrogance of possessing modern war-fighting machinery given by the USA. By September 1965, Pakistan, after a small gain in the Rann of Kutch and failure in Operation Gibraltar to foment crisis in J&K, opened a new front in Chamb/Akhnoor Sector to reduce the pressure from the counter-measures taken by the Indian Army to Operation Gibraltar. In return, India decided to attack in more sensitive sectors across the borders in J&K, Punjab and Rajasthan. One such sector chosen for offensive was Shakargarh Bulge.

Sialkot is a major road and rail communication centre from where logistic support was being provided to the entire Shakargarh and Chamb Sectors. Hence the capture of Sialkot assumed greater importance to the elimination of the Bulge. Tactically, capturing the Bulge from east to west would have been costly and time-consuming option. Therefore it was decided to capture Sialkot from the north and cut off the area east of it. Pakistan had concentrated large-size forces to defend the Bulge with tanks and infantry formations holding well prepared cluster of villages, anti-tank ditches and bunds and canal system. Chenab-Ravi River Link Canal running from north to south through the entire width of the Bulge was a major obstacle providing protection to larger communication centres in the west.

CHARWA - MAHARAJKE

The Pakistani village Charwa is located close to the Border south of Indian town of Ramgarh. 4 Raj Rif and 2/5 GR were tasked to capture Charwa. 6 Garhwal Rifles secured a firm base for the attack on Charwa at 2030 hours on 5 September 1965. Charwa was defended by a Pakistani infantry company and Mujahids from well prepared bunkers connected with communication trenches. After a crunch of artillery fire, both battalions launched the attack from the outskirts at 2300 hours on 5 September 65. 4 Raj Rif was on the right of the village and 2/5 GR was on the left. By 0300 hours, the outskirts on both sides of the villages were captured. Having isolated the village the Raj Rif and Gorkhas entered the built up area of the village. Simultaneously the road behind the village was cut off.

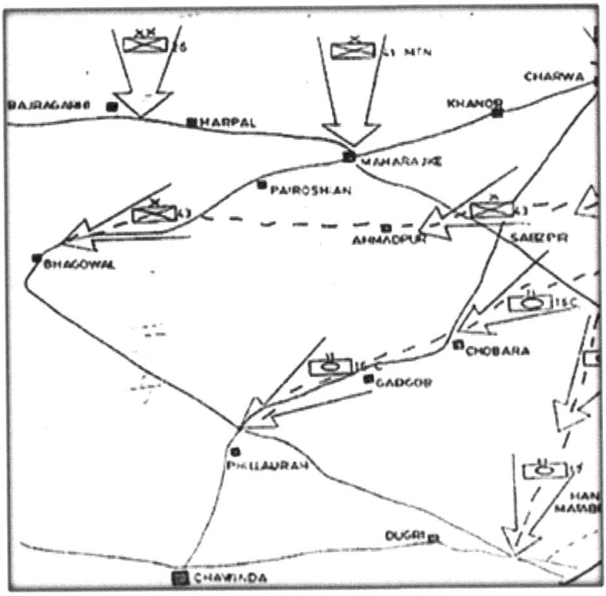

Charwa-Maharajke-Phillora-Chawinda Area

The battle for the capture of Village itself was tough. Pakistanis were firing from hideouts in the houses and underground tunnels. It forced the attackers to fight for every inch of their territory with blood and sweat. The school building was the largest complex added with strong defence works. It had underground storage facilities and tunnels. It was blasted with anti-tank recoilless guns. The Battalions captured large number of vehicles, arms, ammunition including mines still in their factory packs and other military stores and ration including live chickens. The village was ultimately cleared of all pockets of resistance on 09 September. Pakistanis suffered large casualties compared to the attackers.

Maharajke, located west of Charwa, was attacked on the night of 7/8 September 1965 with 4 Madras providing a secured firm base inside Pakistan. After crossing the Border, 3 Madras and 9 Kumaon passed through the firm base and attacked the right half of the village at 2300 hours. By 0130 hours, the right half of the village was captured against light opposition and the road Pagowal-Sialkot was blocked. At 0300 hours, 4 Madras after having provided firm base to 3 Madras and 9 Kumaon attacked the left half of the village Maharajke. When the Battalion closed in with the enemy from the left, the defenders opened up with artillery and Medium Machine guns on 4 Madras. Due to concentrated heavy firing from close quarters, the unit suffered heavy casualties and, the momentum of attack was petering out.

At this critical stage, Lt Col HL Mehta the commanding officer of the Battalion, rushed forward to the leading company and rallied the men personally with the Battalion war cry. His presence electrified the men and they responded to the call of their brave commanding officer and moved forward resuming the attack on the objective with greater vigour. 4 Madras captured their objective. But the Commanding officer was killed by the enemy fire. He saved the day with his own life. For his exceptional bravery beyond the call of duty and outstanding leadership which led the Battalion to victory, Lt Col HL Mehta was decorated with a Maha Vir Chakra. The enemy reacted violently to the loss of Maharajke. Many counter-attacks were launched which were successfully repulsed.

BAJRAGARH

5/4 GR was tasked to capture the border village of Anula and later 2/1 GR and 8 J&K Rifles to attack Bajragarh. 5/4 GR crossed the border after last light and captured Anula successfully. Similarly Bajragarh was captured before 0530 hours on 8 September against light opposition.

Having secured a safe enclave inside Pakistan territory from Charwa in the east to Wains in the west, the next move was to isolate and capture Sialkot and paralyse the logistics support to Pakistan Army in Chamb and Shakargarh Sectors. As a prelude to the main attack on Sialkot, it was planned to advance towards Phillora and Chawinda from the secured areas between Charwa and Maharajke, and then attack Sialkot from the east. Mechanized forces combined with infantry advanced towards Phillora. Pakistani tanks contested the advance in the area north of Phillora near Gadgore. Indian tanks engaged them and destroyed eight tanks. Before further advance was made, additional tank units were inducted in to this sector.

PHILLORA

Phillora is located north of Chawinda between rail track and road leading to Sialkot. It was an important enemy locality for the defence of Sialkot town. Phillora was defended with infantry and a tank regiment with screens and strong points thrown all around the village. The area between Sialkot and Phillora had series of minefields. A regiment of Pakistani tanks was deployed in between the minefields.

The attack on Phillora was planned for 10 September. Indian 4 and 16 Cavalry Regiments grouped with Lorried infantry attacked Phillora from the most difficult approach. Intense tank-to-tank battles took place. It lasted for the next two days in the north and northwest of Phillora. Indian Army used a total of five tank regiments against two of the Pakistanis. After having perceived the quantum of tanks being used by the Indian Army, Pakistan had switched tank regiments from Chamb and Khem Karan Sectors. Subsequently, this area witnessed the largest tank-to-tank battle in 1965 War.

Indian 4 and 17 Horse provided protection to the attacking Infantry from the area of Libbe. 16 CAV engaged Pakistani 11 Cavalry Regiment defending Phillora. In a series of tank battles, 11 CAV was decimated by the Indian 16 Cavalry Regiment. Not being able to withstand the onslaught of Indian attackers, the defenders withdrew to Chawinda in the south. A major tank-to-tank engagement took place between 17 Horse and the attacking Pakistani tanks in the north west of Phillora in the sugar cane fields at close ranges. The battle lasted for 45 minutes in which Pakistan had lost 28 tanks against the loss of one tank of 17 Horse.

5/9 GR and 5 Jat attacked and captured Phillora in the afternoon and by 1530 hours the village was in the hands of the attackers. Thereafter, defence of Phillora was reorganized and small pockets of enemy were cleared. The enemy aircraft's continued to strafe the targets throughout the day. On the 12th of September, in the area southwest of Phillora Indian tanks contested the advance of enemy tanks and forced them to retreat.

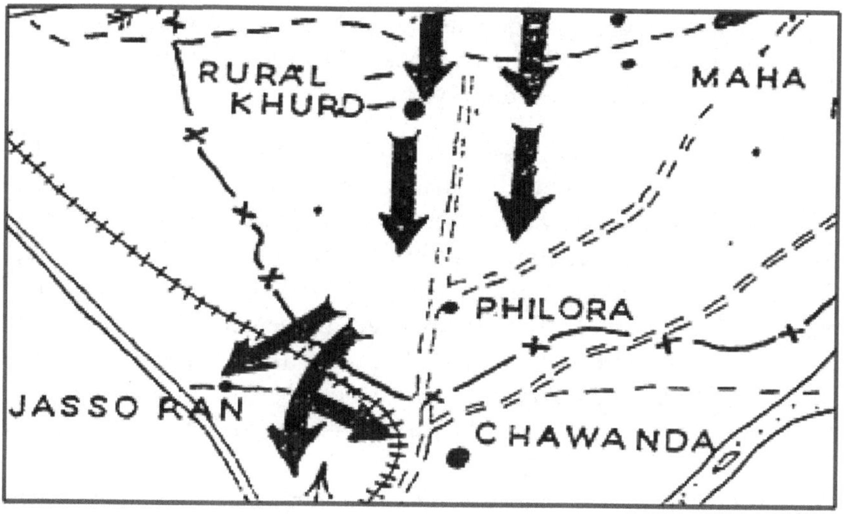

Phillora-Chawinda-Jassoran

On 14 September Chawinda was attacked with tanks and infantry from the north and northwest. The defenders' Patton tanks opposed the attackers and enemy was fighting an organized battle in the area of Kalewali and Alhar. Both villages were captured. 18 of enemy tanks and many anti-tank guns were destroyed. The enemy counter-attacked and recaptured Kalewali but only for a short while. The village was once again captured on the night of 14 September. The next day Khananwali village was captured and the railway line Chawinda-Sialkot was cut off. Alhar was occupied by 4 Raj Rif. Having consolidated north of Chawinda, the attack on Chawinda was planned for night 17/18 September.

CHAWINDA

Chawinda is a major communication hub east of Sialkot with good road and rail connectivity. The roads converge here from all four directions. Capturing Chawinda was vital to the reduction of Sialkot. As a prelude to the attack on Chawinda, village Jassoran, which is located on the Sialkot Road between Chawinda and Badiana in the west, was attacked. By the end of the day on 16th, Jassoran and the area around it were captured by 8 Garhwal Rifles duly supported by 4 and 17 Horse. 28 of the enemy tanks including Patton tanks were destroyed.

After the capture of Jassoran, a combined force of 8 Garhwal and 17 Horse was ordered to capture Butur-Dogarandi and isolate Chawinda from Pasrur in the south. The valiant Commanding Officer of 17 Horse Lt Col AB Tarapore, fighting continuously for five days and injured, led the attack from his command tank and attacked on Butur-Dogarandi and destroyed many more enemy tanks. In the thick of an engagement at close range, the command tank was shot and burst into flames. The Commanding Officer was killed. Lt Col AB Tarapore was decorated with the India's highest bravery award in war; Param Vir Chakra, for his exceptional bravery of very high order and sacrifice of his life. Between 11 and 16 September, 17 Horse under the command of Lt Col Tarapore had destroyed nearly sixty enemy tanks and captured Phillora, Wazirwali, Jassoran and Butur Dograndi.

Lt Col A B Tarapore, PVC (Posthumous)

Along with 17 Horse, 8 Garhwal Rifle, under the command of Lt Col JE Jhirad, launched the attack on Butur Dogarandi. At 1230 hours, while leading the Battalion in an assault, the Commanding Officer was mortally wounded by the enemy fire. Immediately the Second-in-Command, Major Abdul Rafey Khan took over the command and continued the assault on the enemy. The objective was captured by late evening. During the night the enemy launched three counter-attacks which were defeated. On the 17th morning before the Battalion was asked to pull back for another attack, the enemy tanks once again approached the locality held by 8 Garhwal. Rifleman Balwant Singh Bhist, who was armed with rocket launcher, moved close to the enemy tank without being detected by the enemy and when he closed in within the range of his rocket launcher, he fired the rocket at the enemy tank and destroyed it. Being very close to the enemy, he could not extricate himself and came under enemy fire and was killed.

In the meantime, the enemy had reinforced this sector and made 8 Garhwali's position untenable. The Battalion was asked to withdraw to a firm base. In the face of the enemy onslaught, the withdrawal became a challenge. In spite of the adverse circumstances, Major Abdul Rafey Khan exhibited a high level of professionalism and brought his men to safety by systematic withdrawal. In the process, he was killed by the enemy fire. For his bravery of very high order, he was decorated with a VrC posthumously. Notwithstanding the heavy casualties including the Commanding Officer and Second-in-Command, the Garhwalis fought well and stood firm against great odds. The battalion was awarded with the Battle Honour of Butur Dograndi for the outstanding contribution made by all ranks of the Battalion.

By 17 September, all the tactically important targets around Chawinda were secured. An attack on Chawinda was planned for 18/19 September. 6 Maratha LI which launched the attack in spite of heavy enemy tank, artillery and automatic fire from the village, captured their objective by 0410 hours. Other battalions faced the enemy tanks being used as pillboxes and found the going impossible against heavy opposition. The attackers had to fall back to Jassoran. Two Companies of 6 Maratha LI which had captured the Railway Station at Chawinda was ordered to withdraw with 4 Horse providing protection. Chawinda was with the Pakistanis when the ceasefire was declared.

TILAKPUR

Tilakpur and Muhadipur are two Pakistani villages located on the road Sialkot-Chaprar, midway from the Border and Sialkot. 1 Madras and 10 Mahar were ordered to capture these villages. 5/11 GR was tasked to provide flank protection to the attacking Battalions. They crossed the border on the night of 18/19 September 65 and secured the area for the attack on Tilakpur and Muhadipur. 1 Madras and 10 Mahar headed for Tilakpur and Muhadipur respectively and attacked their objectives from the least expected directions at 2230 hours. The enemy was surprised and their reaction initially was sluggish. However, they regained their posture and offered stiff resistance. The opposition was overcome and by 0300 hours both objectives were captured. Subsequently, the enemy counter-attacks were repulsed. On the night of 22/23 September, the enemy once again counter-attacked both Tilakpur and Muhadipur. With the Indian artillery pouring shells on the enemy, the attack was repulsed. The Pakistanis suffered heavily and withdrew.

On 23 September, ceasefire orders were received. Suspecting the possibility of Pakistani last-minute attempt to recapture their lost territory in Shakargarh Sector, Indian Army Units remained prepared to face any contingency. They were correct in their assessment. Pakistani forces made a desperate attempt in the village of Alhar northwest of Phillora. The enemy's attempt to capture the village and the railway station was frustrated with heavy casualty to the attacker. Both Indian and Pakistani artillery fired the entire left over ammunition till the last minute at 0330 hours on 23 September when the ceasefire became effective in Shakargarh Sector.

In this sector, Indian Army captured nearly 500 square kms of Pakistani territories including the village of Phillora. More importantly, the offensive operations undertaken in this sector had forced the Pakistanis to abandon their offensive designs both in Chamb and Khem Karan Sectors. Indian Army had destroyed more than double the number of enemy modern tanks vis-à-vis their own tanks. Killed, wounded and captured personnel were nearly the same on both sides except officers killed in the Indian Army was proportionately higher.

1971

Pakistan opened up the Western Front on 03 December 1971 by attacking across the IB and CFL. All was quiet till 5 December in Shakargarh Sector before Pakistan crossed the border in Punch, Chamb and Jaisalmer Sectors.

India decided to prevent any deep penetration into Indian Territory by immobilising the Pakistani reserve formations wherever they were located. India achieved this by launching a riposte in Shakargarh bulge and in Barmer Sector. The advance into Shakargarh bulge was aimed at containing the large Pakistani reserve formations deployed in and around Sialkot Sector. Shakargarh and areas east of it up to the Border was held with Pakistan Army mobile teams comprising tanks, reconnaissance and support elements and Rangers. Pakistanis had converted the natural obstacles such as rivers and nalas into anti-tank bunds with bunkers at regular interval in this sector. Extensive minefields were laid extending thousands of meters at many places.

Shakargarh itself was defended with a mix of regular army troops and para-military forces. The Indian Army units crossed the Border into Shakargarh Bulge from Thakurpur in the east and from Ramgarh in the north. Nainakot was the first major objective captured by the Indian Army. 6 Maratha LI was part of the attacking force. The Company Commander, Major Salunke was decorated with VrC for bravery and successful capture of one of the largest villages in Shakargarh Sector. The Battalion was awarded the Battle Honour of Nainakot.

By 8th of December, 22 Punjab had captured Chak Amru after crossing enemy minefields followed by a well contested battle. On the same day 3 Sikh LI captured Parni and 15 Grenadiers attacked Khaira across enemy minefields and the covering forces. Notwithstanding the active enemy tanks and recce and support elements, 15 Grenadiers captured Khaira on 10 December. The next day 1 Mahar captured Harar Kalan which had eluded 1 Horse and 1 Dogra earlier on two occasions. The Battalion was awarded the Battle Honour of Harar Kalan.

The 101 Field Regiment (SP) provided a very effective artillery fire support throughout these Battles. Capt SG Singh, the artillery OP Officer from 101 Field Regiment (SP) was decorated with a VrC for his bravery. In spite of being injured, he had continued to provide effective fire support until he breathed his last. The Regiment was awarded the Battle Honour of Harar Kalan.

Two more villages were captured; Gharota by 14 Raj Rif and Shahazpur by 22 Punjab. 6 Madras captured Masroor before the ceasefire was declared.

BASANTAR

In the Sialkot sector, the Indian Army advanced east of Basantar River from the north to capture Zafarwal and threaten Sialkot. After crossing series of minefields 3 Grenadiers, 6 Madras and 16 Madras, crossed Basantar River at Lagwal-Gazipur and captured Siraj Chak and Laleal Forest at 2030 hours and Jarpal village (Bara Pind) at 2330 hours on 16 December after heavy fighting. The enemy counter-attacked the bridgehead with tanks and infantry four times. Both sides suffered a heavy casualty. With grit and determination, Major Hoshiar Singh, C Company Commander of 3 Grenadiers moved around the company locality in the bridgehead under heavy fire, reorganizing the defences with total disregard to his personal safety in spite of his injury. His presence encouraged his men to stay put and fight to destroy the counter-attacking enemy. In the meantime, tanks of 17 Horse were inducted into the bridgehead and the enemy counter-attacks were defeated causing heavy loss to the enemy.

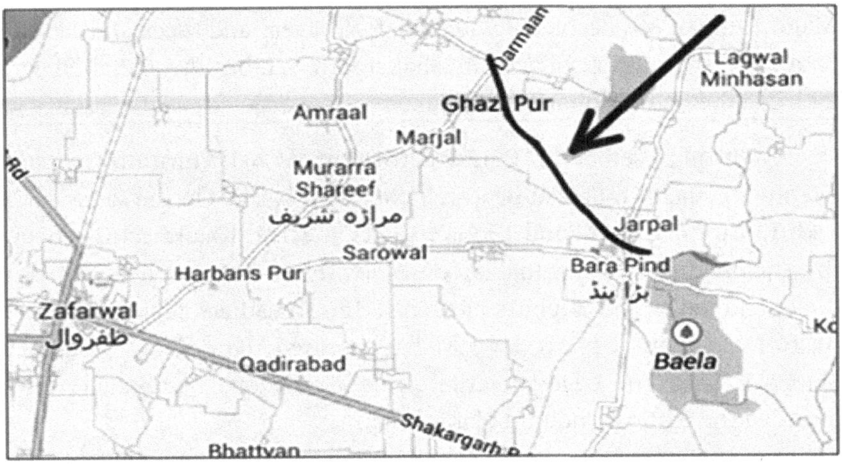

Basantar River- Bara Pind 1971

The Battle for the Bridgehead across the Basantar River was one of the toughest Battles fought by both Infantry and Tanks in the 1971 Indo-Pakistan War. 17 Horse alone destroyed 40 enemy tanks out of a total of 48 enemy tanks destroyed for the loss of their 9 tanks in this battle. 2/Lt Arun Khetrapal was leading his troop of tanks into the bridgehead against the tanks of Pakistani 13 LANCERS who were attacking the bridgehead. 2/Lt

Arun Khetrapal had earlier destroyed two enemy tanks enroute. His tank came under enemy fire twice without suffering any major damage. The third time, while his tank-track was blown off by the enemy fire, the tank-gun was functioning. Pakistani Patton tanks were in close proximity. When he was asked to withdraw from the face of the enemy, he opted to stay in his incapacitated tank to strike the last nail on the coffins of his enemy. At last he and his only opponent were left in the field. Both fired at each other simultaneously. This time the opponent was lucky. 2/Lt Arun Khetrapal died a heroic death in his tank when enemy's fourth shell found its mark. 2/Lt Arun Khetrapal was awarded Param Vir Chakra for his exceptional bravery and sacrifice of his life beyond the call of duty. Not very far from this location, six years earlier in September 1965, the Commanding Officer of the same Regiment; Lt Col AB Tarapore was decorated Param Vir Chakra posthumously for his heroic deeds in 1965 War.

Major Hoshiar Singh PVC

2/Lt Arun Khetrapal PVC (Posthumous)

Major Hoshiar Singh of 3 Grenadiers was decorated with the India's highest bravery award; Param Vir Chakra for his exceptional bravery and outstanding leadership. Before the breakout towards Zafarwal could take place from the bridgehead across Basantar, ceasefire was declared.

CHICKEN NECK

The Border from the north of Shakargarh Bulge takes a sharp turn towards north and runs between Sialkot and Arnia. Thereafter it crosses the Jammu Tawi River west of Jammu city till it reaches south of Akhnoor where it takes a sharp southwestward turn to cross Chenab River and then on to Munawar Tawi River. At the turn south of Akhnoor, the borderline creates a sharp horn which extends into Indian Territory as shown on the sketch below. This intrusion is commonly referred to as Chicken Neck.

The narrowest point of a dagger shaped projection of Pakistan Territory comprising an area of 170 square kms into Indian Territory south of Akhnoor was named as Chicken Neck by one of the Indian Divisional Commanders. (Pakistan calls this piece of ground as Phuklian Salient) A brave general that he was, he declared that the so called projection of dagger will be strangled with a whisk like that of a chicken's neck, and he did it. Thus the name Chicken Neck stuck to it.

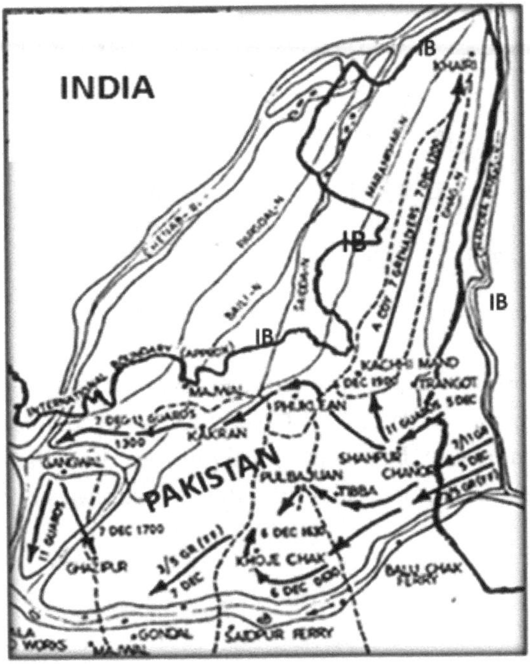

Chicken Neck

The tip of this projection was dangerously close to the strategically important Akhnoor cantonment which is connected to Jammu through a bridge over Chenab River one side and on to Punch Tract to the north on the other side. On the eastern side of the projection is River Chandrabagha, a branch of Chenab River and towards the west and north is Chenab River in some distance. Tanks and other vehicles can cross Chandrabagha River during dry season at a few selected fords. The roads and nalas within the Chicken's neck run in north-south direction and cross Chandrabagha which cuts across the Chicken Neck further south in east-west direction. There were four important ferries on this River. From the east to west they are Saidpur, Gondal, Majwal and Gangwal Ferry. Chandrabagha rejoins with Chenab River at Marala head-works inside Pakistan.

By 5 December 1971, Pakistan had crossed the Border into Indian Territory and made steady progress in Chamb sector. The battle was being fought in the area of Mandiala. If the enemy had progressed further east, Chicken Neck could have played a vital role in the capture of Akhnoor. Therefore, on the night of 5 December, Indian Army crossed the Border and entered into the Chicken Neck and advanced along the northern bank of Chandrabagha River south of Chanor. 7/11 GR captured Tibba which was their first objective by 0330 hours on 5 December. Later, on the 6th they further advanced and captured Pulbajhuan next morning. 11 Guards advanced and captured Chanor against minor opposition. They also captured Shahpur, Puklian and Kakaran. During this period, the ferries at Saidpur and Gondal were secured by Para-Commandos. 7 Grenadiers and the tanks of Central India Horse captured Kachimand. With that, a total of 20 villages and 15 Posts were in the hands of the Indian Army in just three days. The area was provided with combat air patrol by the Indian Air Force.

CHAMB SECTOR

1947

The Chamb Sector is in the northern-most plains of Jammu district from where low hills start rising towards Kalidhar Ranges in the north. It is named after the village Chamb located west of Munawar Tawi River flowing in north south direction before it meets Chenab River in side Pakistan. Munawar Tawi has four crossing places named after the villages located on the river bank.

In spite of entering into a Standstill Agreement with J&K, infiltrators supported by Pakistan had crossed the border at many places in J&K including Chamb on 22 October 1947. In Chamb Sector, Pakistani infiltrators had occupied the area west of the River Manawar Tawi including Chamb village. Due to paucity of resources and higher priority given to the recapture of the areas in Srinagar Valley, areas occupied by the infiltrators in Chamb Sector remained with them till the middle of November 1947.

By the end of November, 15 Punjab (1 Patiala), 3 Garhwal Rifles, 4 Rajput and 2 Jat were tasked to evict the infiltrators from Indian Territory in Chamb Sector. Chamb village was re-captured on 10 December and the infiltrators were evicted from the tactically dominating Kalidhar Ridges north of Chamb. However, the entire intrusion could not be evicted before the ceasefire was declared and enforced on 01 January 1949. At the end of the war, both countries signed an agreement known as Karachi Agreement and accordingly, military operations were frozen. The areas occupied by the rebels were retained by them. The line joining the forward defended localities of both sides was declared as Ceasefire Line (CFL). The area between the original J&K-Pakistan border and CFL became Pakistani Occupied Kashmir (POK). The CFL began in the south at the village of Burejal on the original Pak-J&K boundary line located about 10 kms west of River Munawar Tawi. From there it ran east of the Border and west of Munawar village towards Kalidhar Ranges and further towards Naushera. The CFL and area east of it was held by the units of Indian Army; whereas the IB south of Burejal was held by the Punjab Armed Police. Mattewala, Mandiala and Chamb were some of the large Indian villages west of Munawar Tawi River.

1965

The Chamb Sector witnessed a major battle during 1965 Indo-Pakistan War which was started by Pakistan. Pakistani Razakars of Babur and Gaznavi Forces infiltrated into the Chamb Sector to foment an uprising under the code name of Operation Gibraltar. On 14 August, Pakistani artillery shelled the Indian Post at village Dewa and a gun position nearby. In this shelling, the Commander of 191 Brigade and 10 others were killed and six artillery guns and huge quantity of ammunition were destroyed. The counter-measures taken by the Indian Army against Operation Gibraltar elsewhere in J&K resulted in the loss of Haji Pir Pass in POK which was a major communication centre and logistic base for the maintenance of Pakistani Forces. In desperation, Pakistan launched another offensive operation with regular army code named as Grand Slam in Chamb Sector using infantry and tanks. In this Sector, the Indian troop density holding defences was low to withstand an attack of this magnitude.

Pakistani Army crossed the CFL on 01 September 1965 on a broad-front under the cover of heavy artillery fire from Red Hill in the north, to Burejal in the south. *(Pakistan also attacked simultaneously at Jhangar in Naushera Sector which later proved to be a part of Pakistani deception plan).* Indian tanks from 20 Lancers contested the enemy advance and destroyed many tanks. Against the enemy attacking with a Brigade of infantry supported by Patton tanks on Mandiala and Chamb, Indian units were forced to withdraw to the east of Munawar Tawi River.

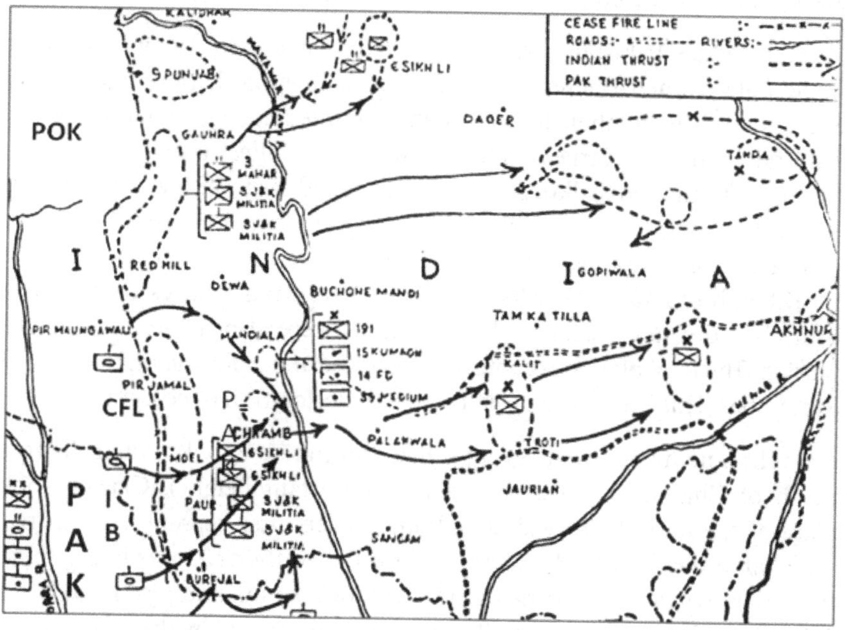

Chamb 1965

The support provided by the Indian Air Force materialized late and proved to be a double edged weapon. It destroyed some of the Indian tanks and ammunition carrying vehicles due to mistaken identity and fluidity of the battle. By the end of the day, Pakistani Army had crossed Munawar Tawi and had consolidated on the eastern bank of the River. The units defending Hill Sector opposite Chamb in the north held on to their positions. Nearly every asset on the west of Munawar Tawi River including Chamb village was lost to the enemy. Pakistani Air Force was active over the battle area and caused considerable damage on the withdrawing units of Indian Army.

Suspecting an imminent threat by the attacking enemy to Akhnoor, the defence there was strengthened. Additional units were rushed to save Akhnoor and reinforced the defences of the bridge on Chenab River. The line joining Jaurian and Kalit was selected to defend and break the enemy momentum. This intermediate position was occupied with infantry and tanks. Pakistan launched another attack on Jaurian village with tanks and infantry on 03 September. Jaurian was vacated after imposing delay on the advancing enemy on the morning of 5 September. Pakistani troops followed the withdrawing Indian Units up to 10 kms west of Akhnoor and occupied a high ground there. The enemy was building up to attack on Akhnoor. Loss of Akhnoor would have isolated Chamb and Punch Tract.

To reduce Pakistani pressure on Akhnoor, Indian Army launched a large-scale counter-offensive in the more vulnerable Lahore and Sialkot Sectors on 6 September. It had its effect immediately on Chamb Sector. Pakistan withdrew a large number of tanks and artillery guns from Chamb Sector to strengthen Sialkot Sector. This depleted the force level of Pakistani Army preparing to attack Akhnoor. Having weakened Pakistani offensive in this Sector, India launched a counter-attack with a view to recapture the Chamb crossings on Munawar Tawi River and villages on the west of it. This did not succeed. Many attempts were also made to recapture Jaurian. The final plan to recapture Jaurian was made for the night of 22/23 September. This did not materialize due to declaration of ceasefire.

The enemy in small groups had infiltrated into Kalidhar Ranges north of Chamb and occupied a few important heights. Clashes took place at the foothills of Kalidhar Ranges even after ceasefire. 1 Madras, 3 Mahar and 6 Sikh LI Battalions were assigned the task of evicting them from Kalidhar Ranges. Most enemy-held localities including Malla, Point 3776, Ring Contour and Twin Pimples were recaptured by these Battalions after difficult climb and tough close-quarter battles. Finally on 5 October, 6 Sikh LI captured Point 3776. The enemy there was decimated and the objective was reoccupied. 6 Sikh LI was awarded four MVCs and three VrCs for bravery. 3 Mahar was awarded one MVC and two Sena Medals. The Battalions were also awarded the Battle Honour of Kalidhar.

At the end of the war, an agreement was signed at Tashkant between India and Pakistan. Accordingly, areas captured during the 1965 Indo-Pakistan War were handed back by both sides. India returned 1,920 square kms of territory mostly in POK including Haji Pir Pass (which remains a subject for debate till date). India got back her 540 square kms of territory in Chamb Sector and a small piece of land at Khem Karan. Once again the CFL between India and Pakistan became the boundary line with the start point at Burejal.

1971

Chamb Sector witnessed another Pakistani Aggression in 1971. On 03 December 1971, Pakistani artillery shelled on the Indian border posts, gun positions and defended localities on both sides of Manawar Tawi River at about 2030 hours. Earlier in the evening, Pakistani Air Force had attacked the air fields at Pathankot, Amritsar and a few other places. Later Pakistani forces crossed the CFL at Burejal, Barsala, Moel, Pir Jamal, Dewa and Lalyali in Chamb Sector. 5 Sikh, 5 ASSAM and 4/1 GR deployed on the west of the River Munawar Tawi withstood heavy attacks by Pakistan tanks, infantry and artillery. Indian tanks had contested and slowed down the enemy advance.

During the day on 04 December, the attack continued with the Pakistani Air Force engaging targets in depth areas. Many attacks were repulsed by the Indian Army Units defending the posts west of the River. However, due to overwhelming numerical superiority in tanks and infantry, Pakistan Army was able to overrun the important village of Mandiala by midday on the 4th. They used the Mandiala Crossing on the river and reached the eastern bank. Many counter-attacks were launched to prevent the enemy from occupying the eastern bank.

Small groups of Pakistanis infiltrated through the gaps and raided Indian gun positions causing damage to the guns and casualty to men. Having realized the seriousness of the situation, Brigadier RT Morlin, one of the defending Brigade commanders, personally led a counter-attack with a company of 9 Jat and tanks. The counter-attack was a success. The enemy was evicted from the east bank of Munawar Tawi and Mandiala Crossing.

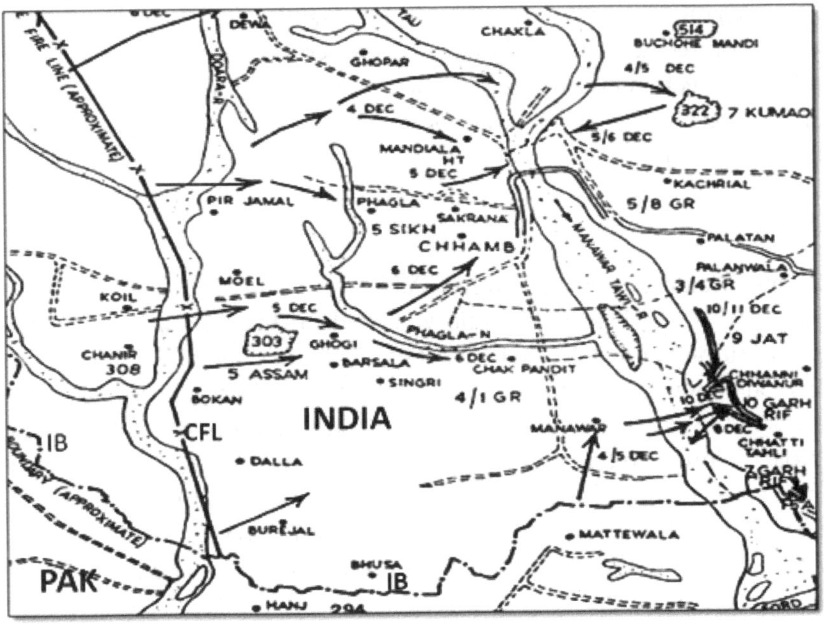

Chamb 1971

The Mandiala Bridge was still in the hands of enemy. A counter-attack was launched to recapture the Bridge from both sides by 5 Sikh and 5/8 GR. The Bridge was successfully recaptured by 1030 hours on the 5th. Simultaneously, all crossings on the River were secured and a few infiltrators who were still lurking in the eastern side of the River were eliminated. Many battles were fought to recapture the villages on the west of the River where the enemy had concentrated armoured and infantry brigades with artillery support. The numerically superior enemy succeeded in capturing and retaining the entire area west of Munawar Tawi River including Chamb village.

On the night of 7/8 December, Pakistani Army attacked the defences of 7 Kumaon along the eastern bank of Munawar Tawi River with tanks and infantry near Mandiala Crossing. The attack was repulsed. Similar attacks took place at the other three crossings as well. Other than on Raipur Crossing, the attacks on the other crossings were repulsed. The enemy foothold at Raipur crossing was counter-attacked and recaptured with heavy casualty to the enemy. Indian Air Force became active in this sector from 8 December. On the next day when Pakistanis once again attempted to cross at Chamb and Darh Crossings, the Indian Air Force engaged them in the open and prevented them from advancing further.

During the night 9/10, the Pakistani infantry units took advantage of the gap in the east bank defences and infiltrated to the depth areas. This enabled the enemy to establish a shallow bridgehead on the East Bank of Munawar Tawi over a front of three and a half kilometres. The defending brigade commander launched a counter-attack on the enemy bridgehead from the north. It was supported by the Air Force and artillery fire. The Artillery created a smokescreen to prevent enemy observation over the River and East Bank. The counter-attack was preceded by air attack and artillery fire on the enemy gun position and tank concentration. By midnight 10/11 December, most of the Indian localities including Sangam and Nathukulian east of Munawar Tawi River were recaptured.

In the north, the Indian localities at Point 707, Lalyali, Dewa and Nathuan da Tibba were held by 8 J&K LI and a company of 5 Rajput. Pakistani Army attacked all these Posts repeatedly with overwhelming numerical superiority. 8 J&K LI held on to these Posts tenaciously and repulsed many attacks. During this attack, one of the Pakistani Air observation Post aircraft was shot down. Finally, by 9 December, Pakistan captured Dewa and it was held by the Pakistani Army till ceasefire on 17 December. The only bridge over Munawar Tawi River near Chamb village was partially demolished.

During 1965 and 1971 Wars, Pakistan took full advantage of the voids in the Indian defences. The terrain was favourable to them hence they captured large areas of Indian territories. While the territory captured by both countries were returned after 1965 War, the territory captured in 1971 War in J&K was retained by the attackers. In both 1965 and 1971 wars India captured more territory in most of the sectors other than Chamb Sector. India's loss was 85 square kms in Chamb Sector. Consequent to this, the alignment of CFL moved further to the east in Chamb Sector. The new alignment started from a Point Middle of Munawar Tawi River near Sangam Post and went northwards through the Riverbed east of Chamb Village and west of Mandiala Crossing.

NAUSHERA-JANGAR

The terrain changes from the riverine plains to hills from the north of Chamb. After the CFL/LOC crosses west of Naushera, low hills rise gradually. Some of the peaks of the ranges are above 8,000 ft from the MSL. Due to the broken nature of the border areas and undergrowth in the forests, the border is not impregnable. Under the cover of darkness small groups can cross the CFL/LOC unnoticed. Further, towards Punch, Uri and Tithwal, the terrain poses greater difficulties. Road communication is poor and vulnerable to adverse weather conditions and enemy interference. The mountains north of Tithwal and east of Gurez are far more challenging. The peaks remain snow covered throughout the year with attendant logistical problems.

When British India was to be divided into India and Pakistan, the Muslims living in the western border districts of J&K rebelled against the Maharaja and openly demanded the merger of Punch district with Pakistan even before Pakistan came into being. Due to geographical isolation of Punch from Srinagar, the Maharaja could not exercise strict control over them. The militants had organized themselves into militia units with the help of World War II experienced local ex-servicemen and Muslim officers and men of the J&K State Forces. They overcame the weak State Security Forces located at Naushera, Jhangar, Mirpur and Kotli by November 1947. Later, with more infiltrators coming from across the Border, they occupied vast areas west of Naushera. The Indian Army was preoccupied in tackling the more serious and urgent situations created by the infiltrators in Kashmir Valley. By the middle of November, additional Indian Army units were ordered to move into J&K and control of the towns in Punch Valley was undertaken.

Naushera is a vital communication centre connecting Jammu, Akhnoor, Punch, Kotli, Jhangar and Mirpur. 50 Parachute Brigade, one of the elite formations of the Indian Army, was ordered to advance and clear Naushera, Jhangar, Mirpur and Kotli. The advance commenced from Akhnoor on 16 November and Naushera was occupied on 18 November after a brief fighting. Moving further to the west, Jhangar was occupied the next day. The next town to be relieved was Kotli in the north which was contested stiffly by the raiders with large number of ambushes and roadblocks enroute. After clearing 47 roadblocks, the Indian Army freed thousands of Hindus and Sikhs at Kotli on 26 November. Due to a long line of maintenance and lack of logistic support, Kotli could not be held for long. Hence it was vacated. However, Jhangar which is a junction connecting Mirpur, Kotli and Naushera by road was held. The local militia who occupied Mirpur massacred Hindus and Sikhs, looted their houses and took many of their women to be sold as slaves. Many died enroute.

Brigadier Mohammad Usman, a World War II experienced senior officer, took over the command of 50 Para Brigade at Naushera during the first week of December 47. On 24 December, the raiders had established a road block between Jhangar and Naushera and attacked Jhangar from three directions. 1/2 Punjab which had organized their defences at Jhangar to cover Kotli and Mirpur approaches, offered stiff resistance. Reinforcement could not be sent due the enemy roadblock between Jhangar and Naushera. Due to numerical superiority of the attackers and inability to reinforce the locality, 1/2 Punjab was forced to withdraw from Jhangar. This was a major setback in the relief of the rest of rebels held areas. Brigadier Usman took a vow to recapture Jhangar at the earliest and until it was achieved, he refused to sleep on a cot.

Continuing their foray, the enemy advanced from Jhangar and attacked Naushera on 26 December which was beaten back. On 4 January once again the enemy attacked Naushera. The attack was broken off with heavy artillery and mortar fire. This was followed by yet another attack with about 5,000 raiders. But they made no progress and withdrew.

Lt Gen KM Carriappa, the newly appointed Army Commander of J&K, visited Naushera Defences. He observed that a massive feature known as Kot in the northeast of Naushera and Pathradi in the southeast were held by the raiders and were overlooking the defences of Naushera. He ordered that those two features be captured at the earliest.

Accordingly, 2/2 Punjab and 3 Maratha LI were tasked to capture Kot and Pathradi. 2/2 Punjab passed through village Kot and attacked the hill features. However, the raiders who were inside the village, realized that the hill feature had been occupied by the Indian Army and they counter-attacked. Additional two companies were send by the Brigade to reinforce 2/2 Punjab. The Raider's counter-attack was beaten back and Kot was captured. 3 Maratha LI captured Pathradi successfully.

Additional units were inducted into Naushera Sector. Naushera defences were reinforced with five Battalions and preparations were afoot to go on the offensive for the recapture of Jhangar. Having got battle indications of an impending attack, the defences of Naushera was readjusted and held in strength in all possible enemy approaches. On 6 February, the enemy launched the anticipated attack with the largest collection of force from three directions on Naushera. Early morning on 6th, Naushera defences were attacked with mortars for about half an hour. Thereafter, Tain Dhar and Kot were attacked in waves of hundreds of raiders. (Later it was estimated that over 11,000 raiders attacked Naushera on that day.)

Tain Dhar was held by 1 Rajput. It was the most important locality, the loss of which would compromise the defence of Naushera. Hence it was reinforced just before the enemy attacked. The attack on 1 Rajput Post Number 2 was intense. This Picket was held by 27 men, of whom 24 were either killed or severely wounded. Yet again, there was another wave of attack coming. The last three men of the Platoon faced it bravely. When the attack was in progress, the reinforcement of 3 Para arrived at Tain Dhar just in time and Tain Dhar was saved. The attackers were decimated. Two of the three men died in the attack.

One of the Section Commanders at Thain Dhar was Naik Jadunath Singh. He was injured in the second attack against his post. He refused to be evacuated and stayed with his section and faced the next attack. With great courage and determination, he came out of the bunker and finally with the Sten-gun, made a most magnificent single-handed charge on the attacking enemy. Taken by surprise, they fled in disorder. Naik Jadunath Singh met his gallant death when two bullets hit him in the head and chest. Brave Jadunath Singh was honoured with the highest bravery award, Param Vir Chakra posthumously for his bravery. In addition, the Battalion was also awarded two MVCs and four VrCs. The enemy withdrew leaving behind thousands of dead bodies. This was the last major battles that the tribals fought. Thereafter Pakistani regular Army took charge of this Sector.

Nk Jadunath Singh, PVC (Posthumous)

Having defeated the enemy at Naushera, Brigadier Usman planned to recapture Jhangar. Pakistan had expected Brigadier Usman to join Pakistan Army during the partition. When he did not migrate to Pakistan, they lured him with promotion and prosperity in Pakistan. Brigadier Usman did not fall prey to the temptations. Having suffered an ignominious defeat at Naushera, Pakistan had announced an offer of Rupees 50,000 on his head. This unethical act did not deter Brigadier Usman from fulfilling his resolve to recapture Jhangar. He went ahead with his preparation for the recapture of Jhangar.

The responsibility to hold Naushera was allotted to another Brigade and Brigadier Usman was given additional resources to advance and capture Jhangar. The operation for the recapture of Jhangar was code-named Vijay and was planned after assessing the strength and disposition of the enemy holding Jhangar carefully. Before launching the attack, two other localities were captured during the preparatory phase of the operation. 50 Para Brigade under Brigadier Usman and 19 Infantry Brigade under Brigadier Yadhu Nath Singh had formed up at Naushera for the attack on Jhangar by the second week of March.

The advance to Jhangar commenced on 14 March. The enemy locality at Pir Thal Naka was contacted by 3 Para. This locality was held by the enemy in strength. 3 Para suffered some casualty including two officers in the initial attack. In spite of the setback, the commanding officer of 3 Para continued the attack. Fresh attack on Phir Thal Naka was launched with 3 Para from the north, 1 Patiala from the south and a diversionary attack from the east with 3 Punjab. Armoured Cars of 7 Cavalry advanced along the road. Artillery, mortars and aircrafts of Indian Air Force had softened the target before physical assault on the enemy. The enemy was surprised by the speed with which the infantry attacked the objective within minutes of the artillery fire lifting from the objective. The defenders ran away without giving a fight. By mid-day Pir Thal Naka was captured. 3 Para did not suffer a single casualty during the final attack. 19 Brigade captured their objective in time on 17 March.

The attack on Jhangar was to be launched on the next day. However, the enemy withdrew from Jhangar without giving any fight. Jhangar was occupied unopposed. Brigadier Usman having achieved his aim and fulfilling his personal vow to recapture Jhangar, asked for a cot to sleep that night. A cot was improvised and this great soldier slept that night on the cot. The enemy counter-attacked Jhangar many times. All were repulsed. Jhangar was very important for Pakistan to maintain their forces at Mirpur and Kotli. Brigadier Usman was determined to hold Jhangar with all forces at his command and capture Sabzkot which was an advance base for the protection of Mirpur.

On 21 May 3 Para and 2 Raj Rif attacked Sabzkot. It did not succeed as the enemy strength and the defence preparation was much larger and stronger than estimated. The attempt to capture Sabzkot was abandoned. On 3 July 1947, Jhangar came under enemy artillery fire. Brigadier Usman was going around talking to the men when there was a pause in firing. The shelling started once again when he was still in the open and he was fatally wounded and died a little later. Before his death, he solicited his men to continue fighting the enemy relentlessly until victory over the enemy was achieved completely.

Thus the Pakistani threat to Naushera was eliminated. Brigadier Usman was the senior most officers to die in battle in the First Kashmir War at the age of 36. His body was flown to Delhi and a state funeral was held at Jamia Milia Islamia. The Governor General of India, Prime Minister and Cabinet Ministers attended the Funeral. He was honoured with a Maha Vir Chakra posthumously. Many memorials have been constructed in memory of this brave soldier. He is affectionately known as the Lion of Naushera by the locals.

1965

In 1965, Pakistan had sent large number of Razakars into J&K under the code name of Operation Gibraltar to create support base for the forthcoming offensive operation to annex J&K. While they did achieve some success in Punch, Mendhar, Rajauri and Chamb sector, nothing much was achieved in Naushera Sector.

RAJAURI

During October-November 1947, local militia and raiders occupied areas between Naushera and Punch. The road connecting Punch with Naushera via Rajauri was dominated by the Pakistani sponsored forces and it remained cut off for normal movement. Rajauri was a Taluk of Punch with mixed Hindu, Muslim and Sikh population. Due to atrocities committed by the Razakars, non-muslims took shelter in the town. By November, the population of Rajauri increased from 5,000 to 40,000.

Captain Rahmatullah Khan who was serving in the J&K State Army at Jhangar had revolted against the Maharaja. He, along with a few more officers, organized large-scale desertion of Muslims from the J&K Army. They killed thousands of Hindus and Sikhs in the area of Rajauri. He appointed Mirza Mohd Hussain; one of the local leaders as the ruler of Rajauri, Darhal, Thana and a few other villages around Rajauri. He raised a militia equivalent to two battalions and controlled the villages between Naushera and Punch.

After capturing Naushera and securing it against the attackers from Pakistan, 19 Infantry Brigade under Brigadier Yadunath Singh along with the tanks of Central India Horse and 37 Assault Field Company Engineers was ordered to advance to Rajauri and secure Rajauri from the Rebels. The 50-kms stretch of road to Rajauri passes through hilly terrain along the bank of Tawi River. The advance commenced along both banks of River on 7 April 1948. Due to large number of roadblocks created by the enemy and minefields, the movement was slow. 4 Dogra which was advancing on the eastern side of the river captured Barwali Ridge held by the raiders after overcoming the enemy in a stiff battle. 4 Dogra won this battle under the command of Captain Bakshi who was the senior most officers officiating as the Commanding Officer of the Battalion. This battle is also known as Captain's Battle.

Due to frequent requirement of clearing roadblocks on the west bank of the river, the advance did not progress well. The CO of Central India Horse decided to leave the road and move on the riverbed to speed up the operation. In spite of random mines found thrown on the riverbed by the enemy, the advance progressed faster. Enroute, Chingas which was a stronghold of the infiltrators was captured on the 10th. 37 Field Company Engineers under 2/Lt RR Rane, demolished many roadblocks, created diversions and cleared minefields tirelessly which resulted in the Brigade reaching Rajauri and capturing it after a multi-directional attack on Rajauri on April 12. The rebels suffered heavy casualties. Leaving behind more than 500 dead bodies, the rebels ran away from the town. According to the locals more than 300 innocent civilians were lined up and were about to be shot dead when the army attacked Rajauri in time and saved them. After independence Rajauri became a tehsil of Punch.

Capt R R Rane, PVC

2/Lt Rama Raghoba Rane was decorated with Param Vir Chakra for his exceptional bravery on the face of the enemy and carrying out the task assigned to his company even after he was seriously injured. Lance Dafdar Waryam Singh of Central India Horse was awarded VrC for saving the CO's tank from an enemy mine by timely action under enemy fire.

PUNCH

1947-48

The Punch Tract west of Pir Panjal Ranges comprises mountainous terrain starting at an altitude of 2,500 feet and progressively increasing northwards. The area is mountainous covered with forests. Punch Valley is connected to Kashmir Valley through a few passes across Pir Panjal Ranges. Punch is the most important town in the area located on the northern bank of the Punch River.

Punch has a long history of being ruled by various invaders beginning with Alexander the Great. It was the largest Muslim majority town west of Pir Panjal Ranges in the Princely State of J&K that was administered directly by the State government officials in 1947. Being geographically isolated from Kashmir Valley, with the locals having closer affinity with their western neighbours, the Muslims of Punch frequently rebelled against the administration and demanded better treatment by the Government.

By the middle of 1947, the Maharaja had sent two battalions of J&K State Forces to be located at Punch to maintain law and order and assist in the collection of taxes. The treatment meted out by the officials was resented by the locals. They organized themselves into insurgent groups. A large segment of the male population was World War II demobilized ex-service men. This helped the insurgents to form cohesive fighting units sooner. Combined with Pakistani raiders, they committed atrocities against the Hindu and Sikh population and attacked the government offices and J&K Army posts. The small number of security elements was ineffective in controlling the rebels against this majority uprising.

The law and order situation deteriorated with the arrival of thousands of tribesmen sent in by the Pakistan Government. They began large-scale disturbances resorting to plunder, murder and rape of non-Muslims in the widely spread out villages in the area adjoining the Rajouri and Punch. By early October 1947, the areas of Bagh and Palandari were under the control of the rebels/infiltrators. On 26 October 1947, Ibrahim Khan, a local rebel leader, declared the formation of Azad Government. Punch city was under siege by the raiders and local militia; armed and controlled by Pakistan Army.

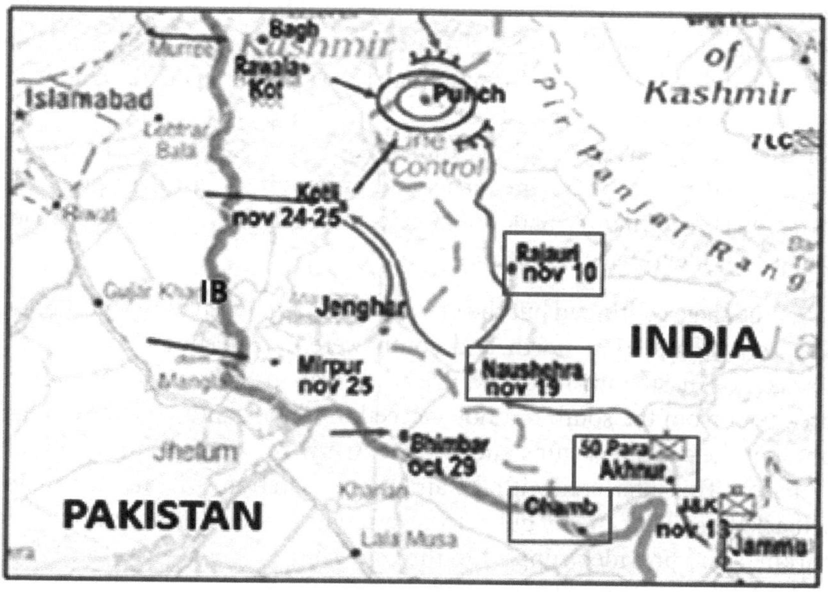

Punch Tract

By the middle of November, the rebels extended their control to Kotli, Mirpur, Rajauri and Mendhar. Punch remained under siege. Thousands of Hindus and Sikhs were killed and many more deserted their villages and took shelter in Rajauri and Punch. The population of Punch swelled from 10,000 to 50,000. There was no means for their sustenance. When the Indian Army was called, they could not advance beyond Naushera before relieving it. This took some time.

The Army advanced from Uri in the north to break the siege and link up with the State Forces at Punch. They were attacked before they could reach Punch. A major bridge was destroyed by the invaders. This prevented the Brigade from advancing further to Punch. However, 1 Kumaon Battalion managed to reach Punch on foot and formed the nucleus of the Punch Garrison. Commanding Officer of 1 Kumaon, Lt Col Pritam Singh was promoted to the rank of Brigadier and appointed as the Garrison Commander. The State Forces were placed under his command. Besides defending Punch, his major challenge was to find food and shelter for 50,000 refugees inside the town.

He was not discouraged by the adverse circumstances. With the help of ex-servicemen and able bodied civilians, he organized the defence of Punch and constructed a temporary runway for landing small aircrafts. Wing Commander Mehar Singh, an outstanding pilot, decided to take calculated risk. He landed piloting a small Harvard aircraft on the temporary runway on 12 December 1947 at Punch. It was a glorious moment both for the Punch Garrison and the Indian Air Force. Later Dakota aircrafts transported ration, medicine, arms and ammunition, artillery guns and personnel of an Infantry Battalion. On its return flight, the aircrafts carried civilians and evacuated casualties.

The siege continued but the Garrison was organized to defend Punch. The approaches from north and south were effectively blocked by the Razakars. An attempt made by Brigadier Pritam Singh in June 1948 to break out from the south did not succeed. In the meantime, Pakistan had brought their artillery guns and regular Army troops closer to the Punch Garrison. This interfered with the air bridge operations which was a major setback. In spite of enemy guns firing, aircrafts landed during the hours of darkness and provided support to the Garrison.

By November a large sized force was assembled at Naushera and Rajauri to break the siege of Punch. This was code-named Operation Easy. It was a large-scale complex operation involving 5, 19 and 268 Brigades with tanks of Central India Horse and artillery units. The operation involved clearing of a large enemy held area of over 2,000 square kms between Rajauri and Punch. The Road connecting the two towns was dominated from the ridges on the east and west of the Road line by the enemy. This had to be cleared before advancing towards Punch. The northern approach from Uri via Haji Pir Pass was in the hands of enemy. In order to achieve the surprise, a deception plan was made to conceal the final approach for the relief of Punch. It involved capturing the massive hill feature known as Pir Badesar which was done successfully. Air Force played an important role in this Operation.

The advance commenced on both sides of the road to Punch from Rajauri. Bhimber Gali and Ramgarh were relieved successfully. Further advance was resumed and the attack was planned on a dominating hill feature known as Point 5372, southeast of Mendhar. This was a strong enemy held locality. To speed up the advance, Brigadier Yadunath Singh decided to contain Point 5372 with one battalion to be cleared later on and the rest of his Brigade bypassed it and continued the advance to Punch from the right. This proved to be a sound decision later.

Before the final assault and linkup with Punch, Point 5982 and Topa Ridge south of Punch were cleared. The final linkup and relief of Punch took place on 20 November. Thousands of Hindus and Sikhs had reunited with mostly their broken family. Due to higher priority given to Punch, other areas such as Bimber, Mirpur and Kotli could not be relieved before the ceasefire was declared on 01 January 1949. Bagh, Sudhanoti and part of Punch District remained under the illegal occupation of Pakistan and formed part of POK. The remaining part of the Punch and Rajouri area became Punch district. As per the Karachi Agreement 1949, Pakistan retained the area occupied during the War. The CFL passed through the west of Punch. Therefore Punch, which was an interior town and a district HQ of J&K State, became an Indian border town and a battlefield in all the subsequent Indo-Pakistan Wars and skirmishes.

1965

In 1965, Pakistan had sent a large number of regular army personnel in the disguise of civilians to foment an uprising in J&K including Punch and Mendhar area under the code name Operation Gibraltar; a name which the Arabs had used to conquer Spain many centuries ago. The infiltrators were part of Gaznabi Force, which was one of the groups of Operation Gibraltar, comprising about 10,000 men. They were to operate in the area of Mendhar, Rajauri, Chingas and Jangar. They infiltrated by the first week of August 1965 and disrupted the Road Akhnoor-Punch by occupying dominating features enroute, establishing roadblocks at many places and ambushing the Indian Army vehicles on the road.

A search and destroy operation was launched against the infiltrators by the units of Indian Army with additional troops inducted into Punch and Rajauri area. 4/5 GR was tasked to clear Topa Top; a dominating feature on Mendhar-Balnoi Road and Gujar Kotha. It was an uphill attack which the Battalion completed successfully after a steep climb and Kukri charge. The road to Balnoi was opened after three month. More attempts were made to capture tactically important Pakistan held features. After the additional Indian Army units launched extensive search and destroy operations, the infiltrators were forced out. The local support to them was drying up. Most of them either gave up fighting or returned to POK in small groups.

In the north, Haji Pir Pass located north of Punch was captured on 28 August by the Indian Army. This was a major setback to Pakistan. With Hajipir Pass in the hands of Indian Army, an attempt was made to open the Punch-Uri Road via Haji Pir. There were two Pakistani Posts located between Punch and Haji Pir Pass known as Raja and Rani. They were held with a company each of Pakistan Army. Both Posts were tasked to be captured by 2 Sikh and 3 Dogra. After an approach march lasting over five hours from Punch, 2 Sikh attacked Raja and 3 Dogra was on Rani Post at 0530 hours on 6 September 1965.

Both Posts had strong defences including wire obstacles and minefields. The reaction from the enemy post at Raja was murderous. The attack was stalled. At this juncture, Lt Col NN Khanna, the Commanding Officer of 2 Sikh climbed on a rock to make him visible to his men and rallied his men to follow him with his Battalion war cry. This electrified his men. He led the attack personally and the entire Battalion followed him. Thereafter, there was no looking back. The Post was captured after a ferocious close quarter fight by 0710 hours. Raja Post was a hard nut to crack; but it was cracked under the inspiring leadership of Lt Col NN Khanna. He was killed when he was leading the assault by a burst of enemy machine gun fire. For his exemplary bravery on the face of enemy and outstanding leadership in battlefield under fire, he was decorated with a MVC posthumously. 2 Sikh lost 39 men and many more were injured. Rani Post was also captured by 3 Dogra simultaneously. The Road Punch-Uri was cleared through Haji Pir Pass. It was here in Punch Sector, the foundation of 9 Para Commando; later 9 Special Service Unit was laid by Major (LT Col) Megh Singh Rathore of 3 Guards.

1971

Raja and Rani Posts were returned to Pakistan as per the Tashkent Agreement in 1965. Again in December 1971, Pakistan launched attack in Punch sector at Gutrian, Langoor, Madari and Shahpur with a battalion against each Post with a view to advance and capture Punch on the night of 3/4. Pakistani attacks on these dominating Posts were repulsed. However, Pakistanis managed to capture Tanpir which was retaken subsequently. In a counter-offensive, Mumtaz Post which frequently interfered with the move of troops within Indian side of the LOC was captured by the Punch Brigade. Pakistani Forces attempted to capture one of the Indian Helipads repeatedly, but without success. On 11 December two important features, Nangi Tekri and Jungle Spur were captured by 21 Punjab.

For the first time, India's Special Forces were launched to raid on enemy targets across the LOC during 1971 Indo-Pakistan War. Six Pakistani 122 mm guns which were deployed near Mandhol village about 19 kms southwest of Punch were interfering with the Indian operations in Punch and Mendhar Sector. After due diligence, it was decided to raid on the gun position and destroy those guns. The task was assigned to 9 Para Commando Battalion. The battalion launched the raid on the night of 13 December 1971 with six officers and over 100 commandos. They waded through the Punch River and reached the Mandhol village. After exact location was identified, the raid was launched and all six guns including one gun loaded with the shell were destroyed. More than 40 Pakistanis were killed and a nearby ammunition dump was destroyed. Two Indian commandos died in the raid and 19 were wounded. The raiding party returned to base by next morning carrying the two dead bodies and evacuated all those who were injured. This raid created panic in the ranks of Pakistan Army. Additional manpower was committed to guarding all gun positions during the rest of the war by the enemy. The destruction of the guns at Mandhol resulted in reduction in the intensity of artillery fire from the enemy in this sector subsequently.

From 1989 onwards Punch area was affected by the Pakistani assisted terrorist activities. Indian Army deployed in and around Punch have undertaken counter-terrorism and anti-infiltration operations and kept the LOC and interior areas under control. The Special Forces also launched surgical strikes on 29 September 2016 on the terrorist launching areas inside POK and the results were made public for the first time.

HAJI PIR PASS

In the entire length of LOC along the Western Border, there are two significant bulges of Pakistan Territory into the east, namely the Shakargarh Bulge and Haji Pir Bulge. Both witnessed major battles in 1965. A bulge in the LOC increases the length of the LOC, resulting in the requirement of deploying more troops to guard the LOC. It impacts both offensive and defensive operations. Haji Pir Pass is the western most passes of Pir Panjal Ranges and connects the Kashmir Valley with Punch Valley. Haji Pir pass is located in the middle of the Bulge. The road connecting Uri in Kashmir Valley with Punch passes through this pass. The Pass is also a trijunction of roads connecting Punch and Uri with Rawalpindi via Bhag. The distance between Punch and Uri via Haji Pir Pass is 56 Kms, whereas presently Haji Pir Pass being with Pakistan, the route taken to travel from Punch to Uri is via Udhampur and Banihal Pass through Kashmir Valley, covering a distance of 282 Kms. This affects the logistics support and troops movement to and from the neighbouring sector.

During the First Kashmir War in 1947, Pakistani raiders used this area to build up supply dumps and it served as a transit point to enter into Kashmir Valley. At the end of the First Kashmir War, the CFL was drawn as per the area held by the Indian Army and the Pakistani raiders. Badori Peak, Pathra, Point 12330, Raja Post, Rani Post and Haji Pir Pass formed part of the Bulge and it remained with Pakistan. Resource constraints at that time did not permit the Indian Army to undertake operations to evict Pakistani Forces from the present POK and Gilgit/Baltistan in the west and north of J&K. Consequently Haji Pir Pass remained with POK and became a vital communication centre and logistic base for the maintenance of Pakistani troops in the entire Haji Pir Bulge and other parts of POK.

In the beginning of 1965, Pakistan made an attempt to divert the attention of Indian strategic planners from J&K to the Rann of Kutch. Though they did not achieve their aim, Pakistan did gain some Indian territory there. Once again in August, Pakistan sent infiltrators under Operation Gibraltar to create a condition conducive to annexation of J&K. Indian Army undertook counter-infiltration operations to evict the infiltrators. After having contained the infiltration, Indian Army resorted to other counter-measures inside POK to destroy their support bases.

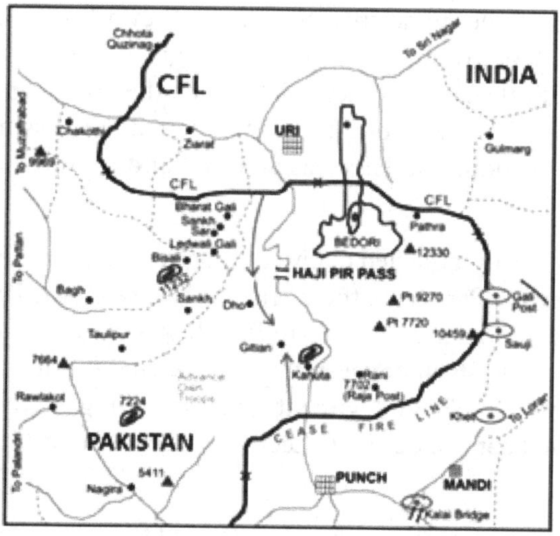

Punch-Haji Pir-Uri with Bulge

One such operation was the capture of Haji Pir Pass with a view to force the invaders to recoil from the Haji Pir Bulge and other part of J&K. 68 Mountain Brigade commanded by Brigadier ZA Bakshi was given the task of capturing the Haji Pir Pass. The Brigade comprised 1 Para, 4 Rajput, 19 Punjab and 164 Field Regiment Artillery. Before launching the attack on 25 August 1965, the enemy's attention was diverted by various deception measures. It rained on the day of attack making the attacker's task tougher.

1 Para attacked the feature known as Sank from the north. This was held by the Pakistani regular forces. Their defences had well constructed bunkers and minefields covered with artillery fire. The initial climb was slippery and tough. The first attack did not succeed. Major Ranjit Dayal, the Second-In-Command of the battalion led the second attack and carried through. The Brigade Commander was with the Battalion during the attack. From Sank the Battalion pressed forward and captured Sur and Lade Wali Gali towards Haji Pir Pass. Thereafter, 4 Rajput was to marry up with 1 Para and advance further towards Haji Pir Pass. However, due to enemy interference, 4 Rajput could not marry up with 1 Para at the appointed time.

The enemy evicted by 1 Para from Sank and Sur were on the run withdrawing towards the Pass. They needed to be pursued relentlessly without breaking contact and prevent the enemy from reinforcing the defences at the Pass. 1 Para, after having fought for 48 hours continuously, was physically tired but their spirit was high and they were willing to walk a few extra miles to destroy the enemy. They asked for permission to undertake the task given to 4 Rajput. It was given. Moving forward, they negotiated vertical cliffs, took detours to reach the objective and overcame the enemy opposition enroute. They approached the Pass from the most unexpected direction. The Pass was attacked and captured at 1030 hours on 28 August 1965.

Pakistani Army launched many counter-attacks to regain the Pass, but failed to dislodge 1 Para from there. The area between the Pass and Punch was captured later on and the road to Punch was opened after the capture of Raja and Rani Posts in between the two. During the attack on the pass, Capt Naidu from 164 Field Regiment Artillery, acting as Observation Post Officer provided continuous and effective artillery support throughout the operation.

Bedori was a large feature which extended from Haji Pir Pass towards the northeast providing depth to the Pass within the Bulge. This was held strongly by the enemy. In order to prevent the enemy from thinning out from there and reinforcing the Pass, a holding attack was launched by 19 Punjab simultaneously. After a tough approach march to the base of that massive feature, the Battalion successfully isolated Bedori and the company commanded by Major Parminder Singh captured their objective in time and prevented any reinforcement of the Pass from Bedori.

Brigadier Bakshi and Major Ranjit Dayal were decorated with MVC for Bravery and outstanding leadership. Capt MD Naidu, the artillery officer, was decorated with VrC. Units were awarded Battle Honour. Nearly after 17 years, Uri was linked with Punch. However, this facility was short lived. As per the Taskent Agreement, Haji Pir Bulge including the Pass was returned to Pakistan.

URI

1947

Uri is a small border town located on the south bank of Jhelum River in J&K. Before the partition in 1947, Muzaffarabad in the west was connected by road with Uri and Srinagar in the east via Baramulla. Uri was also connected to Punch via Haji Pir Pass. The Border outpost was located at Ramkot beyond Muzaffarabad.

Before J&K joined India through the Treaty of Accession on 26 October 1947, Pakistan had sent raiders and local militia to occupy Kashmir Valley. About 6,000 raiders had assembled at Muzaffarabad. Dogra Company of 4 J&K Infantry Battalion offered some resistance to the invaders. However, they were overwhelmed by thousands of raiders and were forced to withdraw. The Muslims of the Battalion joined the raiders. After occupying Muzaffarabad, the raiders led by Pakistani officers advanced towards Uri along the River Jhelum.

On 22 October, the Maharaja of J&K, ordered Brigadier Rajendra Singh, the senior most officer of his Army, to save Uri at all cost. Brigadier Rajendra Singh rushed with about 150 men of 7 J&K Rifles from Srinagar to Uri. The raiders attacked Uri in thousands and captured it. Brigadier Rajendra Singh and his men withdrew to Mahura. While withdrawing, the only bridge on a river between Uri and Baramulla was demolished. This delayed the advancing column of the raiders by two days. Brigadier Rajendra Singh was killed in an encounter with the raiders between Mahura and Baramulla. He was awarded MVC for bravery. The raiders advanced to Baramulla and got busy in pillaging it. This gave enough time to mobilise additional forces for the defence of Srinagar.

Srinagar was saved from the raiders and later they were evicted from Baramulla. 1 Sikh was tasked to recapture Uri and clear the raiders from the hills surrounding it. Uri was recaptured successfully. While clearing the enemy from one of the hills overlooking Uri, a company of 1 Sikh was ambushed by the raiders near Bhatigran. The ambush was defeated and the enemy locality was cleared. In this operation, the Battalion suffered heavy casualty including Jemadar Nand Singh VC who was killed by the enemy automatic fire. Nand Singh VC was awarded MVC for bravery posthumously. Thus, Jemadar Nand Singh became unique in the Indian Army receiving both VC and MVC. Several attempts were made to recapture Dommel west of Uri without success. At the end of the First Kashmir War, Muzaffarabad remained in the hands of the raiders and became part of POK. Uri became the first border town.

1965

In 1965, Pakistani infiltrators entered India across CFL on 30 July as part of Operation Gibraltar. One of the nine groups of infiltrators was Salauddin Force which operated in Uri Sector including Gulmarg and Srinagar areas with approximately six companies. They did not get much support from the locals. The Army hunted them down and they were forced back to Pakistan by 15 August.

1971

Uri Sector maintained a defensive posture in 1971 Indo-Pakistan War. An attempt was made to capture a few tactically important hill features across the CFL, but it did not succeed. As per the Simla Agreement, the CFL became LOC. The area across the LOC in Uri Sector in POK has many insurgent training areas and launch pads. From the late eighties, insurgent activities have increased in the Uri Sector considerably.

(On 18 September 2016, an administrative camp of two Infantry Battalions which was in the process of relieving one of them by the other was attacked by the militants near the Brigade HQ location at Uri. In the attack, 17 men were killed in the camp as a result of militants' lobbing large number of grenades and in the consequent fire which engulfed the camp where the men were living in temporary tented accommodation. Four attackers were killed in the ensuing search operations launched by the Army Units.)

BARAMULLA

1947

Baramulla is the second largest towns in Kashmir Valley. It is a major communication centre connecting Srinagar with Uri, Kupwara and Tithwal. B Company of 4 Kashmir Light Infantry less two platoons was stationed at Kupwara with one platoon at Keran in 1947. A platoon of the garrison police company was holding Tithwal. The raiders reached Baramulla from Uri by 25 October 47. They killed Muslims and non-Muslims, raped and looted the riches including the roofing materials of the houses and hospital. By 26 October 1947, the town was in the hands of the raiders and half of it was either burning or destroyed.

A young Kashmiri named Maqbool Sherwani did not like what he saw at Baramulla. To scare the raiders, he spread a rumour that the Indian Army had landed at Srinagar. The raiders believed it and delayed their move towards Srinagar. When they realized that they were tricked, they killed Maqbool and paraded his body in Baramulla streets. Thus the riches of Baramulla and the trick played by Shaheed Maqbool Sherwani combined, delayed the raiders advance towards Srinagar by four days. This crucial four days made all the differences in the subsequent history of J&K.

After the accession of J&K with India on 26 October 1947, 1 Sikh landed at Srinagar Airfield under the command of Lt Col Ranjit Rai. Leaving behind a few men for the protection of the runway, the unit moved towards Baramulla where the raiders were pillaging the Town. The raiders had to be delayed and prevented from reaching Srinagar so that more units of Indian Army could be inducted into J&K by air and road.

1 Sikh delayed the raiders over the next two days. In one of the battles between Baramulla and Pattan, Lt Col Ranjit Rai was killed fighting the raiders. He was awarded MVC posthumously. He became the first commanding officer to die in the First Kashmir War in Independent India and decorated with MVC. After having delayed the raiders, 1 Sikh joined the Brigade in the Battle at Shalateng. The Brigade with three Infantry Battalions, two troops of armoured cars and air support devastated the advancing raiders. Having suffered a huge loss, the raiders took to heels towards Baramulla leaving behind the dead bodies and hundreds of vehicles. Thus they were prevented from contacting Srinagar and the city was saved from pillage and destruction.

After the devastation suffered at Shalateng, the raiders withdrew to Baramulla. They were pursued relentlessly and evicted from Baramulla. The Indian Army established a Brigade HQ there on 8 November 1947. Baramulla played very important role in the subsequent battles for the liberation of vast areas in the west and north of Baramulla. The HQ of Srinagar Division under Major General Thimayya and an administrative base to support the entire operations was established at Baramulla in due course of time.

TITHWAL

The rugged high mountainous terrain west and north of Baramulla comprising Tithwal, Keran and Gurez is strategically as important for the security of Kashmir Valley as J&K is important for the defence of rest of India. Baramulla is the base for the maintenance of these far-flung areas. Similarly, Muzaffarabad, Balgran, Pakistani Tithwal and Kel are the lifeline of Pakistani forces deployed in POK including Gilgit and Baltistan. The CFL/LOC passes through the gap in between the population centres of India and POK and follows Krisanganga River. The nature of terrain makes it nearly impossible to seal the CFL/LOC; hence this area offers easier avenue for infiltrators from their bases at POK into the Kashmir Valley. Pakistan sent infiltrators through this area in 1947 and 1965 War. Presently the militants in Kashmir also use this region extensively for infiltration.

The Princely State of J&K had a common Border with Afghanistan and China. There is an interesting piece of geography and history in the Afghan side of the border. The Wakhan Corridor in Afghanistan is a narrow strip of rugged high altitude mountains protruding over 200 kms to the east. This separates present day Tajikistan and J&K. It is through the tip of this corridor between two rivers; Afghanistan has a border with China. It was part of Silk Route; presently it is disused. This corridor separated Russia from British India earlier.

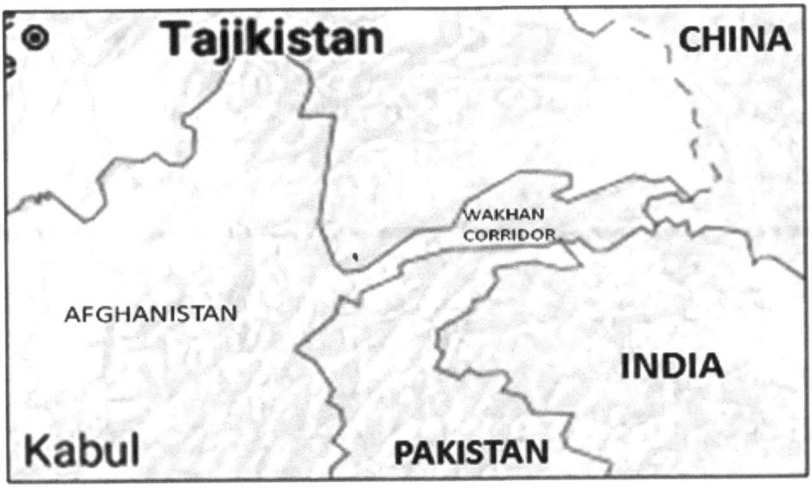

Wakhan Corridor
(India-Afghan Border is now with POK)

The rugged and sparsely populated high altitude areas of Tithwal (Teetwal), Keran and Gurez witnessed many battles in all wars fought between India and Pakistan. The distances from Srinagar in kms are: Baramulla 41, Uri 86, Kupwara 90, Chowkibal 114 and Tithwal 156. Thangdhar, Chowkibal and Nastachun Pass also known as Sharda are located in between Kupwara and Tithwal. In October 1947, two platoons of J&K State Army were deployed in these areas. Subsequently, infiltrators occupied these population centres in large strength.

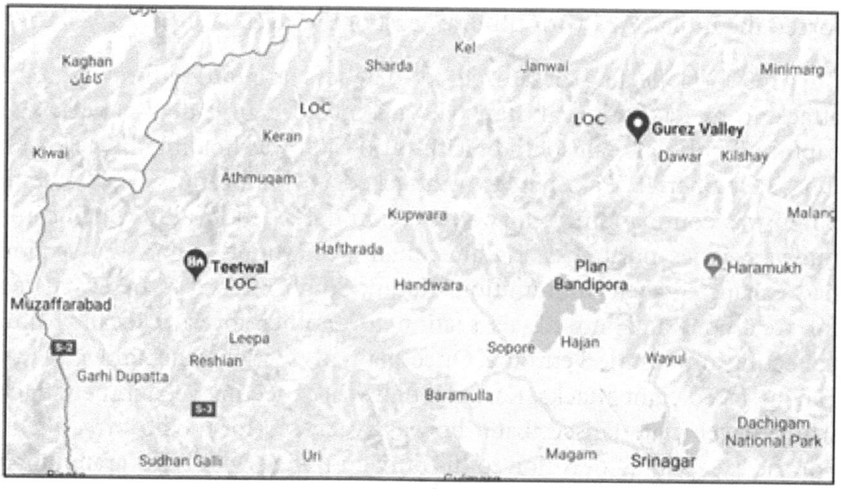

NW Kashmir

1947-48

Having stabilized the crisis situation in the Kashmir Valley, Indian Army focused on building up a viable force to relieve the area west and north of Baramulla. By February 1948, information was received that Trahagam valley including Shulur were being occupied by the Pakistani raiders and militias. This directly threatened Handwara, Baramulla and Sopore and ultimately Srinagar. 1 Sikh was tasked to deal with this threat. The Battalion was given a troop of armoured cars to speed up the operation. The Battalion acted quickly and moved towards Handwara on 8 February. The road was snow covered which slowed down the speed of advance. By 14 February, the area up to Kupwara was cleared.

Muzaffarabad was an important town for both India and Pakistan. More than a brigade worth of Pakistanis were holding Dommel and Muzaffarabad. Major General Thimayya had planned to capture Muzzaffarabad advancing along the road Uri-Muzaffarabad and Kupwara-Tithwal-Muzaffarabad. A large-sized force advanced along the Uri-Muzaffarabad and faced very stiff opposition. The enemy had destroyed all bridges and opposed the advance from vantage points. On the other hand, the advance to Tithwal progressed well with 1 Madras, 1 Sikh and 3 Garhwal. Later 6 Raj Rif and 2 Mahar also joined the offensive operations across Kishanganga River beyond Tithwal. Many close quarter battles were fought to capture the dominating hills including Keran by 3 Garhwal on

09 June. The enemy counter-attacked the area west of Krishnaganga and forced the Indian Army to withdraw east of the river.

163 Brigade had organized its defences around Tithwal to repel attack from Pakistan. Pakistan had assembled a brigade to attack and capture Richhmar Gali south of Tithwal. 1 Sikh was holding the defences. On 13 October 48, Pakistan Army attacked 1 Sikh location. L/NK Karam Singh was commanding a forward section defended locality which came under a series of attacks. Karam Singh was wounded and the section had exhausted their ammunition. Karam Singh refused to be evacuated for treatment and moved his section to another forward locality after collecting ammunition enroute. Once again his section came under attack. Having faced eight attacks, Karam Singh was expecting yet another attack which never materialised. Later he was evacuated for medical treatment. For the exceptional devotion to his duty and bravery, L/NK Karam Singh was awarded PVC. He was the first living recipient of PVC in this war.

L/Nk Karam Singh, PVC

In July 1948, Pakistan had attacked and captured a few hill features on the west of Kishanganga River opposite Tithwal. Ring Contour was one such enemy locality from where the enemy brought down fire frequently. 6 Raj Rif was tasked to capture Ring Contour. The approach to Ring Contour was very narrow. There was no alternative route to the objective. The leading section of Delta Company which led the attack, attempted to cross the narrow defile connecting to the objective. The entire leading section was wiped out by the Pakistani machine gun fire. Piru Singh was the Havildar Major of D Company. He moved at the head of the company and rushed to the enemy machine gun post with his Sten gun firing on the enemy. When he reached the proximity of the enemy machine gun post, he lobbed a grenade and destroyed the machine gun.

CHM Piru Singh, PVC (Posthumous)

He was injured and bleeding profusely. With total disregard to his safety, he crawled further and lobbed another grenade on the second enemy trench. After killing the two occupants, he occupied the trench and fired with his Sten gun on the next enemy's post. He ran out of ammunition and was alone. The other comrades of the leading platoon had either died or were severely wounded. He pulled out the pin from his last grenade and charged towards the last enemy trench and lobbed the grenade into it. The enemy post was destroyed. While charging, this World War II hero was hit by the burst of enemy bullets and died. His company captured the objective and suffered more than 50 percent casualty. Company Havildar Major Piru Singh of 6 Raj Rif was decorated with PVC posthumously for his bravery and self sacrifice beyond the call of duty on 18 July 1948.

1965

In August 1965, Pakistan had sent large number of infiltrators into Gurez, Keren and Tithwal Sectors. They were part from Qasim and Khalid Forces of Operation Gibraltar. They encircled Handwara and Naugam by the second week of August. They also attempted to attack Chowkibal. In all these efforts, the enemy failed miserably. The Gujjars and Bakarwals living with their cattles in the forests informed of the hiding places of the raiders to the security forces and helped the Indian Army units to hunt them down.

The road connecting Muzaffarabad with Kel in POK was the lifeline of Pakistan Army. It was used extensively to maintain their troops deployed along the Border. The Indian Army interfered with the movement of Pakistan Forces on this Road effectively. In turn, Pakistan increased firing across the border. The Indian Army reacted with attack on three Pakistani Posts across the CFL. Later, the area up to southern Bank of Kishanganga was captured.

Once again 1 Sikh was defending Tithwal Sector in 1965. They captured the dominating Pir Sahiba Top. To prevent the Pakistan Army from crossing the Kishanganga River, 1 Sikh was tasked to destroy the bridge at Nauseri. The demolition party approached the bridge when it was lightening and raining. Even before they laid the demolition charges, the bridge exploded when lightning struck the bridge. The demolition party commander sent a radio message stating, 'task accomplished by lightning'. Later it was learnt that the enemy had prepared the bridge for demolition and lightning had detonated it. Besides 1 Sikh, 2 Rajput, 4 Kumaon and 3/8 Gorkhas had undertaken many successful operations in this Sector. The areas captured across the CFL had to be returned to Pakistan as per the Tashkent Agreement.

1971

In 1971, this Sector witnessed a number of small scale operations to gain tactical advantages. After Pakistan attacked across the IB and CFL on 3 December, many pre-planned offensives at lower level were executed. In the north, the BSF had captured a few POK posts. 9 Sikh, 4 Raj Rif, 3 Bihar and 4 Mahar participated in the operations in Tutmar Gali, Kaiyan Bowl and Gasla Top. The most important gain was that these operations forced the Pakistani commanders to move forces from other sectors to reinforce their defences. The tactical gains achieved in this war have improved the defensive posture of this Sector considerably. The areas captured in the 1971 War was not returned.

GUREZ

Gurez/Gurais is a high altitude valley on the northern region of Bandipora in J&K. The village is located on the banks of Kishanganga. It is an important communication centre. The road Srinagar-Gilgit passes through Gurez. During the First Kashmir War, Pakistan occupied a vast area of Gilgit and Baltistan region. The CFL ran along the Kishanganga River. On the Indian side, to the east of Gurez is Sonamarg and Dras in Ladakh and Keran in the west. On the POK side, Skardu is in the northeast, Gilgit in the north and Muzzaffarabad in the west. Gurez is approximately 123 kms from Srinagar.

Road Bandipora-Gurez

As part of Operation Gulmarg, raiders from across the Border had occupied Gurez in October 1947 after Muzzaffarabad fell into their hands. Those raiders who advanced towards Srinagar and were defeated at Shalteng withdrew into Gurez Valley and reinforced Gurez. The raiders held important heights, passes and bridges on Bandipore-Gilgit Road. They could roll down to Sopore/Bandipora area and pose a major threat to Srinagar from the north. Notwithstanding the threat posed by the raiders in this Sector, higher priority was given to recapturing and dominating the main road axis from Muzaffarabad via Uri and Tithwal. Hence, adequate troops could not be found to recapture Gurez until the summer of 1948.

In the last week of May 1948, 1 Grenadiers was assigned the task of capturing Gurez. The raiders were holding Kanzalwan Bridge and Gurez valley in strength. The Commanding Officer of 1 Grenadiers decided to take a longer and difficult approach route to Gurez and achieve surprise. In the meantime, Maj Gen Thimayya visited Tragbal and allotted 2/4 Gorkha Battalion along with the Grenadiers for the task. The operation was code-named Operation Erase. Rajdhani Pass and Tragbal were occupied by 23 June. On the 24th, 2/4 Gorkhas advanced along the Gurez old Caravan road and attacked Char Pathar.

On 25 June, 1 Grenadiers under Lt Col Rajendra Singh advanced along a goat track leaving the well guarded old caravan road. Enroute they faced adverse weather conditions in the form of snow and blizzard while crossing mountains of above 10,000 ft high. A large number of animals, carrying heavy guns and ammunition died enroute. In spite of those challenges, the Battalion contacted Gurez and captured it on 29th. Simultaneously 2/4 Gorkhas captured Char Pathar and Kanzalwan. Pakistan made many attempts to retake Kanzalwan. The Gorkhas and Grenadiers repulsed the attacks. With Uri, Tithwal, Keran and Gurez in the hands of Indian Forces the threat to Kashmir Valley from the northwest was eliminated. The CFL ran west of Uri, Tithwal, Keran and north of Gurez.

In 1965 as part of Operation Gibraltar, Pakistan sent infiltrators of Qasim Force numbering about 500 to destroy a bridge near Kanzalwan. Their attempt was foiled. Helicopters were used extensively to hunt down the infiltrators and most of them were either killed by the Indian Army or they abandoned their mission and returned to POK.

Since 1989, insurgents and foreign militants have used Gurez Sector to infiltrate towards Bandipora and this area has been declared as a disturbed area. The Rashtriya Rifle Units carry out counter insurgency operations to keep the militants away from this area.

Chapter 5

LADAKH -WEST

ZOJILA

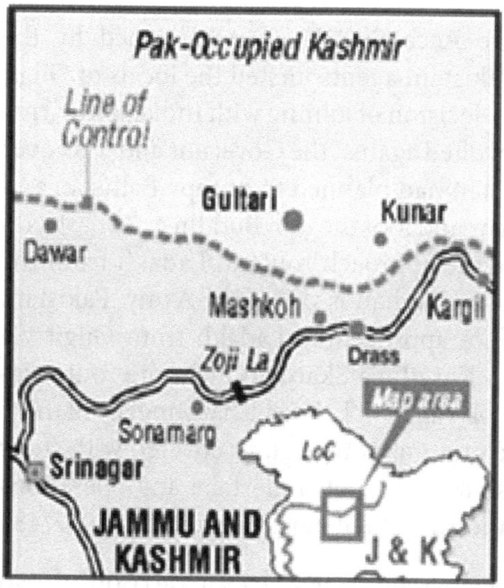

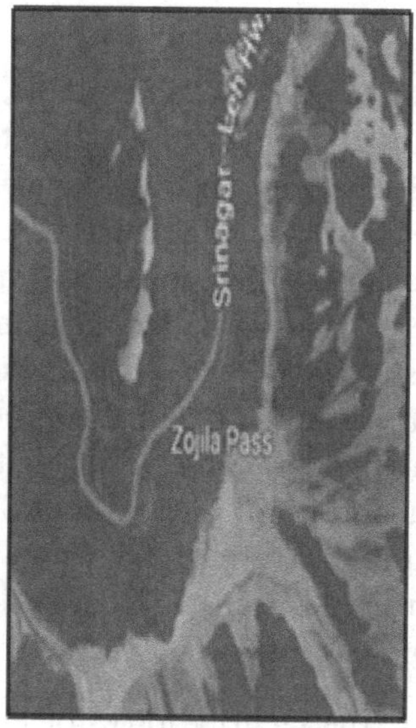

Zojila

Zojila (Zoji Pass/Zoji La) is the gateway to Ladakh from J&K. The Pass is located in between Sonamarg and Dras across the Himalayan Ranges at an altitude of 11575 ft above MSL. In 1947, a mule track connected Sonamarg with Dras-Kargil through Zojila. Zojila gets an average of 20 feet of snow during peak winters and the Pass remains closed. No one is known to have crossed this Pass during the winter before February 1948 when Captain Prithi Chand and a platoon worth of Lahuli/Ladakhi men from 2 Dogra achieved this indomitable feat and made major contributions in saving Ladakh from Pakistan with the help of the local people.

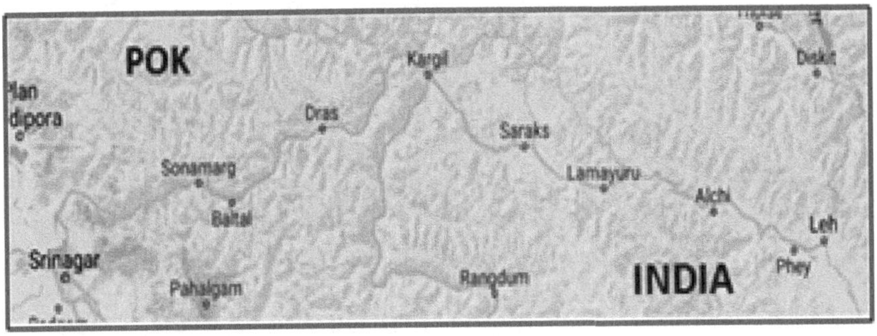

Srinagar-Leh Road Alignment

In October 1947, when the Accession Treaty was signed by the Maharaja of J&K to join India, Pakistani agents incited the locals of Gilgit Baltistan region to rise against the decision of joining with India. J&K Army units that were located at Gilgit revolted against the Governor and took over the control of Gilgit region. Pakistan had planned to occupy Baltistan and Ladakh after the capture of Srinagar and loot the rich Buddhist Monasteries there. That did not happen since the approach route to Ladakh from the west through Srinagar remained in the hands of Indian Army. Pakistani Forces were left with the option of approaching Ladakh from Gilgit via Gurez to Dras and from Gilgit to Kargil via Skardu. One more route was available from Gilgit through Shyok valley to Leh via Khardungla. All these routes pass through high altitude mountainous regions covered with snow during the winter. Hence, Pakistan could not undertake any operations from Gilgit to occupy Baltistan and Ladakh during the winter of 1947/48.

The security forces of Princely State of J&K had a garrison of two battalions of Gilgit Scout at Gilgit. Another battalion, 6 J&K Rifles was deployed at Bunji, Leh, Kargil and Skardu. Muslim officers and men of these J&K forces deserted from the units and joined the rebels. Knowing the importance of Skardu for the defence of Ladakh, the J&K State Army Post at Skardu was reinforced with a company of J&K Rifles from Leh under Lt Col Sher Jung Thapa by the first week of December 1947. Some more troops were added in Skardu later.

Approximately a battalion of rebels comprising erstwhile J&K Army officers and men, local militia, Gilgit Scout and raiders supported by Pakistan Army advanced from Gilgit and attacked Skardu on 10/11 February 48. Lt Col Thapa had organized the defences based on Kharpocho Fort overlooking Skardu town. The attack was repulsed. The attackers had massacred the resident Hindus and Sikhs in the town. With Lt Col Thapa and his men holding the fort, the Pakistanis could not advance towards Kargil from Skardu. The attackers encircled the fort and prevented subsequent attempts made by the J&K Forces to reinforce the fort. Adequate forces were not available to break the siege from within the Fort.

Having failed to advance beyond Skardu towards Kargil, Pakistani infiltrators crossed over Ladakh Ranges and occupied Dras and Zojila. This prevented the use of Zojila-Kargil Track by the Indian Army. Manali-Leh road which is much longer than Srinagar-Leh road was used to bring additional troops and supply to Leh. A small runway was constructed at Leh for Dakota aircrafts. The first Dakota was piloted by Group Captain Mehar Singh. Major General KS Thimayya also travelled in the same aircraft. The aircraft landed safely in spite of many challenges. Subsequently, the Dakotas carried troops and stores regularly and kept the Leh Garrison well supplied. However, with Zojila and Dras in the hands of the rebels, reinforcement and maintenance of Kargil remained a major challenge.

The shoulders of Zojila and hills dominating it were held by the infiltrators with more than battalion strength. Air attacks and artillery fire was not effective against the enemy housed in well-constructed bunkers with overhead protection. Therefore, it was decided to advance along Srinagar Sonamarg road and attack Zojila and clear the enemy from there. 77 Para Brigade was assigned the task. The Brigade advanced from Srinagar and cleared up to Sonamarg. The attack was launched on the right shoulder of Zojila. But the enemy holding the defences of Zojila proved to be a hard nut to crack. The Brigade took up defences and concentrated additional forces to clear the enemy from the Pass.

During a visit to the Brigade, Lt Gen Carriappa suggested to explore the possibility of using tanks for the assault against the enemy bunkers. Tanks had never been used at this altitude anywhere in the world. The challenges were many. The bridges on the road up to the base of the hills, where the enemy had their bunkers, would not take the weight of the tanks. As the saying goes, 'difficult tasks will be done; impossible will be attempted'. The engineers put their heads together and found a solution. Sappers improved the roads and bridges were strengthened. Tanks were dismantled and taken up to the base of the hills in stripped-down condition in two to three vehicle loads and reassembled before launching the assault on top.

The attack was launched on 1 November 1948. Maj Gen Thimayya travelled in one of the leading tanks of 7 Cavalry. The enemy was shocked to see the tanks and left their bunkers and ran away. Their leaders sitting far away refused to believe that Indian tanks could reach this far. 1 Patiala (15 Punjab) followed the tanks and captured the pass on the same day. Further advance to Dras was undertaken the next day and the infiltrators operating between Zojila and Kargil were cleared in due course. 1 Patiala and 7 CAV earned many bravery awards and the Battle Honour of Zojila. After the First Kashmir War, the alignment of CFL between POK and Ladakh from Gurez passed through the high altitude uninhabited mountainous region of Himalayan Ranges, more or less on a straight line in north-eastern direction, south of Kel in POK and north of Zojila and Dras up to Kargil and beyond in Ladakh.

In 1956, a two way road was constructed from Sonamarg to Leh on the alignment of the existing mule track by the Border Road Organisation.

1965

Before the 1965 War, Pakistan launched Operation Gibraltar employing Army officers and Razakars to foment an uprising in J&K. The infiltrators were divided into various forces. The one sent towards Dras and Zojila was the Tariq Force. It was tasked to disrupt the Highway connecting Leh and Srinagar. A group comprising about 100 strong Razakars operated in the area of Zojila–Sonamarg. They headed for important bridges at Sumbal and Hamilton. The Indian Army reacted against these forces immediately and carried out search and destroy operations. A large number of the enemy was killed during the counter infiltration operations and the rest of them were chased across the CFL.

(A 14-kms long tunnel is being constructed at Zojila. When completed, the Pass will remain open to vehicular traffic throughout the year and reduce the travel time by two hours.)

SKARDU

Skardu is located about 100 kms north of Kargil. It was a tehsil of Ladakh. Kargil had better connectivity from Kashmir via Gilgit and Skardu than from Srinagar-Zojila-Dras due to the formidable heights in the area of

Zojila. When Srinagar could not be taken by Pakistan in 1947 and Gilgit fell into the hands of Pakistan supporters, Skardu assumed greater importance for the security of Kargil. The J&K Army was very thin on the ground in Ladakh. To prevent Skardu from falling into the hands of Gilgit Forces, a company of 6 J&K Rifle was sent to Skardu during the winter of 1947 under the command of a brave officer, Lt Col Sher Jang Thapa.

Skardu was attacked with two battalions of rebels from Gilgit Forces on 11 February 1948. The attack was repulsed. The enemy repeated their attacks but failed to capture the fort and failed to resume their advance towards Kargil. Having been frustrated, the enemy laid a siege with part of his forces and the rest crossed over to Dras and Zojila in an attempt to contact Kargil and Leh. Many attempts were made to resupply and reinforce Skardu Garrison. But it could not be done due to enemy interference. In the middle of August 1948, after having exhausted the ration and ammunition, Lt Col Thapa with 35 men surrendered to Pakistanis.

Lt Col Thapa, a tenacious officer was decorated with a MVC for his bravery and leadership while preventing the enemy from contacting Kargil for more than six crucial months for the defence of Ladakh. Due to paucity of troops and severe weather conditions obtaining in this area, Skardu could not be retaken when the First Kashmir War ended in December 1948. Now, it is a thriving tourist town in POK.

KARGIL SECTOR

1947-48

The Kargil Sector extends from Dras to Batalik. Kargil is the second largest town of Ladakh. It is located midway between Srinagar and Leh. Kargil was connected to Gilgit via Skardu till 1948. It was the gateway from Gilgit to Ladakh. The higher reaches of Kargil heights are craggy with steep slopes, narrow gorges and deep ravines. The altitude of higher peaks varies from 15,000 to 17,000 ft. This region is swept by fast and cold winds bringing the average temperature down during summer below freezing point, while in the winter months it drops to minus 25 degrees centigrade. The wind-chill factor combined with solar radiation and other high altitude effects on human being makes this area one of the most challenging terrains for human survival in the world. Roughly, if one platoon is required to attack the enemy on these heights, ten more platoons are required to support them. As the famous saying goes, 'here the mountains eat the troops'.

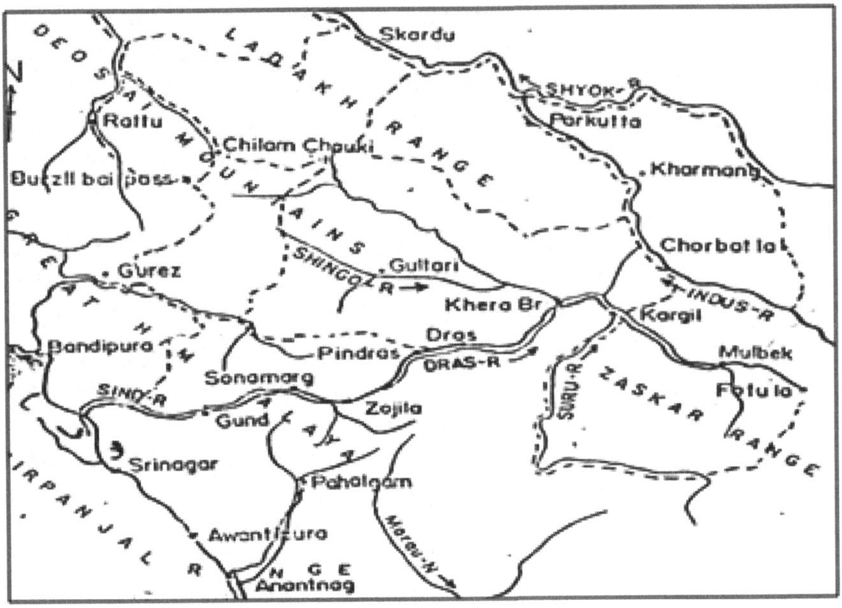

Mountain Ranges in Ladakh

During the First Kashmir War, rebels infiltrated into Kashmir Valley and Ladakh through Gurez and Gilgit Region and occupied Dras and Kargil area. Later, Pakistani Forces from Gilgit attacked Skardu in February 1948. They failed to capture Skardu. Part of the attacking forces crossed over Ladakh Ranges and reinforced the rebel camps in Dras. This base was used by them to operate in Dras, Kargil and Batalik areas. They disrupted the movement of Indian troops and supplies on Sonamarg-Kargil track and created panic among the population.

After Zojila was captured in November 1948, 77 Para Brigade advanced towards Kargil. 1 Patiala captured Dras during the advance. Subsequently, the rebels were cleared from Kargil and Batalik. Another Army column starting from Leh linked up with the Brigade advancing from Zojila at Kargil before ceasefire was declared. At the end of the 1947-48 war, under the Karachi Agreement, the CFL alignment was marked north of Dras, Kargil and Batalik. Gilgit-Baltistan region north of CFL including Skardu was lost to POK.

Dras

Dras is 63 kms from Sonamarg and 56 kms from Kargil. It is the coldest place in India and second coldest in the world. Dras and the NH 1 passing through it are dominated by Tiger Hill and Tololing Peaks located south of CFL. The average altitude of Dras valley is about 11,000 ft above MSL.

On both sides of the CFL, the road communication between Srinagar and Kargil and from Skardu to CFL north of Kargil had improved considerably in late fifties and early sixties. This added to the importance of Kargil as a communication centre for the defence of Ladakh. Srinagar-Leh road passing through Zojila, Dras and Kargil became the lifeline of Indian forces in Ladakh.

1965

Relations between India and Pakistan were at its worst in 1965. After the Rann of Kutch episode in April 1965, notwithstanding the Karachi Agreement, Pakistanis frequently interfered with vehicular traffic in their attempt to capture Kashmir (including Kargil) 17 years after the 1947-48 war.

Point 13620 and Black Rock combined, known as Kargil Heights, was a dominating feature from where Pakistanis could observe a long stretch of NH 1 into the Brigade Sector and the adjoining areas. Pakistan had established a post on the Kargil Heights and was interfering with the movement of vehicles on the Leh-Srinagar Road (between Kargil and Dras where the NH 1 passes closest to the CFL) with artillery fire directed from this vantage points. It was decided to eliminate this threat once and for all by 121 Infantry Brigade which was responsible for the defence of Kargil Sector.

The Brigade tasked 4 Rajput to capture Point 13620 along with Black Rock. The Commanding Officer of the Battalion, Lt Col Sudharsan Singh, decided to attack Point 13620 with Bravo Company. Alpha Company objective was Black Rock which was to be captured by 17 May 1965.

Kargil Height

Major Baljit Singh Randhawa was the Bravo Company Commander. Captain Ranbir Singh Kang, a former company officer of Bravo Company, volunteered to lead the attack with his old Platoon. The CO and Bravo Company commander agreed. The attack involved a steep climb under the nose of the enemy. The approach march commenced at 1900 hours on 16 May. At 0200 hours on 17 May, the leading Platoon contacted the enemy Post which was held by more than a Platoon of Karakoram Scouts. Capt Kang and his men came under heavy fire while negotiating the final vertical height of about 300 feet.

Sensing a possible hesitation on the part of the leading troops due to fatigue, cold and concentrated enemy fire, Major Baljit Singh Randhawa armed with a light machine gun rushed to the front along with the leading men firing his machine gun on the enemy. The men were inspired by this daring action of their Company Commander and followed him. The post was captured. During the mopping up, one of the enemy JCOs fired a full burst on Major Randhawa with his Carbine machine gun and he died after the post was captured. Major Randawa was awarded with MVC (Posthumous) and Capt Kang was decorated with VrC for their bravery. Black Rock was captured by Alpha Company successfully.

Kargil Heights, captured by 4 Rajput, had to be returned on 30 June after the United Nations assured the safety of the Srinagar-Leh road. The assurance did not hold for long as the Pakistanis started firing again from Point 13260 on the NH 1. Once again the Kargil Heights was attacked, this time by 17 Punjab. The Battalion launched a silent attack under Major Balwant Singh on the night of 14/15 August and the objective was captured by early morning of 15 August without suffering any casualty.

Between the first and third week of August 1965, Pakistan infiltrated their Razakars across the CFL surreptitiously through the gaps in the CFL. The Indian Army came to know of the Pakistani plan when two Pakistani Officers caught inside Indian Territory revealed the plan of Operation Gibraltar. Operation Gibraltar was a plan to foment rebellion against Indian Government in J&K including Ladakh. As part of Operation Gibraltar, Pakistani infiltrators of Tariq Group comprising 600 to 1,000 guerrilla-warfare trained men crossed CFL in Ladakh and operated in Dras, Kargil and Leh area in small groups. Some bridges were partially destroyed by them. Traffic on the NH 1 had to be protected with mobile troops.

The Indian Army mounted search operations against the infiltrators immediately. Most infiltrators were either killed or caught before achieving anything substantial mainly due to non-availability of support to them from the locals. The rest withdrew to Pakistan. From the ferocity of counter infiltration operations undertaken by the Indian Army, Pakistan perceived that India may retaliate with an all-out war. To save its population centres from Indian attack, Pakistan pre-empted a possible Indian offensive and attacked with her regular armed forces all along the western border. This in turn forced India to launch counter-offensive against Pakistan including in Kargil Sector to weaken her offensive in Chamb Sector.

As a retaliatory measure, Indian Army crossed the CFL at many points in Kargil Sector, captured many dominating hill features and ensured that the movement of vehicles on NH 1 was unhindered. Thus the second attempt made by Pakistan to capture Kargil and disrupt the lines of communication to the rest of Ladakh ended in a failure. The territory captured in POK was returned after the war according to the Tashkent Agreement.

1971

On 03 December 1971, Pakistanis crossed the western border and made their third attempt to capture Kashmir including Kargil. In Kargil sector, they engaged targets up to NH 1 with artillery fire making it impossible to use the highway during the day. The Indian Army decided to launch a counter-offensive in Kargil Sector across the CFL in response to Pakistani attacks. Indian 121 Brigade under Brigadier ML Whig was ordered to launch an attack into POK and capture the area up to Olthingthang.

In a preliminary operation, Point 13260 and Black Rock, which were handed over to Pakistan as per the Tashkent Agreement after 1965 War, were punished heavily with artillery fire and air attacks. Thereafter, it was recaptured by 2/11 GR. The next day, Indian Army crossed the CFL on both sides of Shingo River with a view to capture the area up to Olthingthang in POK. The main battles were fought at Brachil Pass and Hathimata inside POK. 7 Guards, 16 and 18 Punjab, 9 J&K militia, 5/3 GR and 2/11 GR participated in the offensive.

18 Punjab and 2/11 GR advanced towards the shoulders of 14,000 ft Brachil Pass. Both shoulders were captured by 18 Punjab and 7 Guards on 8 December. Thereafter, advance was resumed to capture Trishul, Point 3985, Wali, Malik and Hathimata. These objectives were captured by 17 December before ceasefire was declared. In the operation lasting 10 days, the Brigade had captured 36 Pakistani Posts along with 116 Sq Kms of territory on both sides of Shingo River. Olthingthang could not be captured during this short war due to heavy snowfall and paucity of time before ceasefire was declared. This time, the area captured by India across the CFL was retained. It enabled straightening of the CFL and improving the defence posture of the Brigade considerably. Brigadier ML Whig was decorated with MVC. The CFL was renamed as LOC and was demarcated up to a point, the map reference of which is GR NJ 9842.

1999

View from NH 1. Dras, Tiger Hill- Tololing

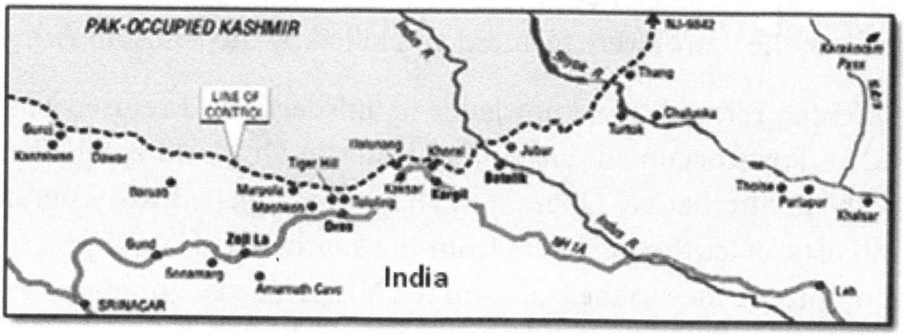

LOC and NH 1 in Kargil Sector after 1972

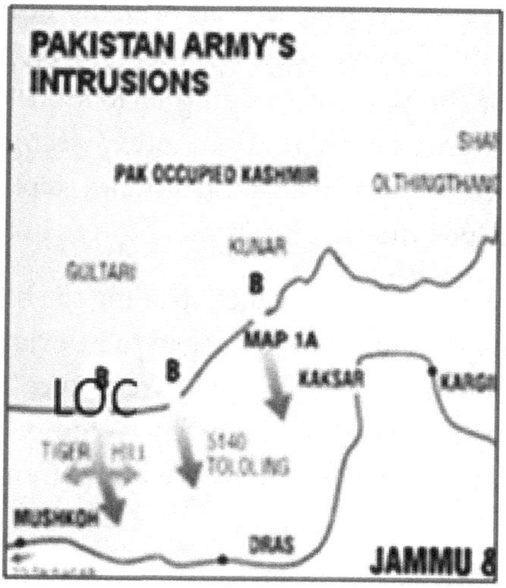

Dras Area

During the winter of 1998-99, Pakistanis crossed the LOC and occupied Point 4590, Point 5060, Point 5100, Point 5140 (Tiger Hill) and Point 5353 (Dras sector) and Juber, Point 4812, Khalubar and Point 5203 south of LOC at heights varying from 14000 to 18000 ft surreptitiously. They stocked these posts with provisions and ammunition for a prolonged stay and had laid mines ahead of these posts on the likely approaches to the posts.

This was not known to the Indian Army units until May 1999. On 15 May 1999, a patrol under Captain Saurab Kalia of 4 Jat was send to their Bajrang Post to ascertain the snow condition of the area. The communication with the patrol broke down, which was not uncommon in this area. The whereabouts of the patrol could not be ascertained. Subsequently, Pakistani Radio announced the capture of the patrol. The members of the patrol were tortured and killed by the Pakistan Army.

Pakistan refused to acknowledge its misdeeds and refused to vacate the Indian Posts occupied during the winter in Dras and Batalik Sectors. Left with no alternative, Operation Vijay was launched to recapture the Indian Posts, evict the intruders from the south of LOC and prevent any threat or interference to the traffic on the NH 1. Two major objectives that were required to be recaptured urgently were the Tololing and Tiger Hill located in Dras area and Khalubar in Batalik area.

The enemy was well entrenched all over the Sector and apparently determined to fight a prolonged war. After having appreciated that it was beyond the capability of the holding formation to evict the enemy, additional forces were moved in from other sectors in record time. The weather and the Border Road Organisation kept the roads in good condition which helped the concentration of forces in a record time.

The initial attacks were aimed at controlling the hills overlooking NH 1. After having achieved this, the enemy had to be evicted from the Indian Territory. Military Commanders decided to recapture Tololing area before Tiger Hill could be attacked. Tololing defences comprise Tololing Height, Knoll, 3 Pimples and Hump. Pakistanis were well entrenched in these posts.

TOLOLING

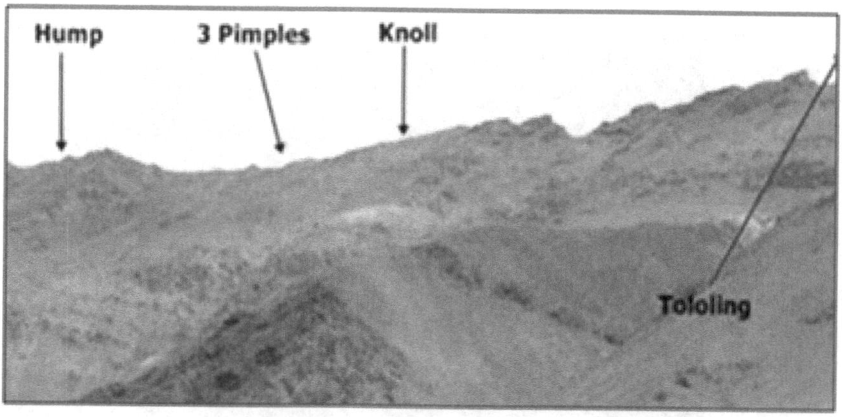

Tololing Ridge Line

8 Sikh, 18 Grenadiers, 2 Raj Rif 1 Naga, and 13 JAK RIF were part of the force assembled to capture the enemy held Posts in Dras Sector. 18 Grenadiers commanded by Col Kushal Thakur was tasked to recapture a part of Tololing. He asked for more time to prepare for the attack and some additional fire power. These demands could not be met. The Battalion launched the attack on 20 May 1999. Two assaults were launched one after the other. In spite of enemy fire, steep climb and adverse high altitude affect, Major Adhikari and his men closed in with the enemy and fought hand to hand. Additional troops could not be sent. The enemy was in large strength and had reinforced the locality during the attack. Hence the attack petered out.

Major Adhikari and four of his men were killed. He was decorated with MVC. Many were wounded. The attackers withdrew from their objective. Yet another fresh attack was launched under the Second-in-Command of the Battalion. This also met the same fate. Repeated failure resulting in heavy casualty forced the higher commanders to change their plan and decided to launch fresh attack with more troops and additional fire power. This took some time.

2 Raj Rif was launched to capture Tololing after a thorough preparation and with additional artillery support. Bofor FH 77B Howitzers were used to softened the targets before physical assault. The second assault was led by

Captain Vijayant. This brave officer and men of 2 Raj Rif captured Tololing on the morning of 13 June 1999. It was a turning point in the Kargil War.

Tololing Top

2 Raj Rif continued the attack on 3 Pimple and Knoll. These localities were well prepared to face the attack and held in strength. 'A' Company under Major P Acharya established foothold on the objective. During the attack both Major Acharya and Captain Vijayant were killed while charging the enemy machine gun which was holding up the advance of the Company. Once the machine gun post was neutralised, the company charged through the enemy and their objective was captured.

Capt Neikezhakuo Kenguruse was commanding a Ghatak team during the attack. He was tasked to neutralise an enemy machine-gun post which was effectively interfering with the attack from the area of Black Rock. He climbed a near vertical cliff under enemy fire with total disregard to his safety and destroyed the enemy with a rocket. While doing so, he was mortally wounded. For his bravery Capt Neikezhakuo Kenguruse was awarded MVC posthumously. During this operation, ten Other Ranks were killed and 42 were wounded. The Battalion was awarded a total of four MVCs, six VrCs and many other decorations for bravery. (Capt Neikezhakuo Kenguruse was commissioned in the Army Service Corps and was attached with 2 Raj Rif).

Having captured Tololing complex, the next objective chosen to reoccupy was Point 5140. It was the most dominating feature in this area located at 1,500 meters from Tololing in the north. The enemy was holding with a company in well-constructed sangars (stone walls) to cover all the likely approaches. It was decided to launch a night attack with 13 JAK RIF under Lt Col Yogesh Kumar Joshi on 19 June. After a thorough preparation, the attack was launched with Bravo and Delta Company at 2000 hours. Both Companies were commanded by young officers; Lt Sanjeev Jamwal and Lt Vikram Batra.

The attack commenced as planned at 2030 hours after blasting the sangars with devastating artillery fire. Bravo Company captured its objective at 0330 hours on 20 June. D Company captured the objective from the rear and captured the top of Point 5140 by 0435 hours. In spite of stiff fight with the enemy not a single man was killed. Batra was wounded. Eight Pakistanis were killed and the rest fled leaving behind their weapons including an anti-aircraft machine gun and huge quantity of ammunition. Lt Col Y K Joshi, Capt SS Jamwal, Nk Dev Parkash and Rfn Mehar Singh were awarded Vir Chakra.

TIGER HILL

After the capture of Tololing, the next major enemy occupied position which was planned to recapture was Tiger Hill (Point 5062). Tiger Hill stands at 16,700 ft above MSL. It is the highest in this Sector. Its top extends about 2000 x 1000 meters. Two spurs, called India Gate and Helmet, run from the highest point to the west. A company of Pakistani 12 Northern Light Infantry was defending Tiger Hill. Their defence was well organized. From there Pakistanis could observe far and wide into Indian Defences and bring down observed fire on NH 1 including the Brigade HQ responsible for recapturing the Tiger Hill.

In May 1999, when Pakistanis occupation of Indian Posts including Tiger Hill inside Indian Territory was confirmed, a hasty attempt was made to evict the intruders. In that, 8 Sikh which was on its way to a field station in J&K, was diverted to Kargil and was tasked to recapture the Tiger Hill. They were in their summer uniform and un-acclimatised for fighting in high altitude area. All the same, the Battalion attacked Tiger Hill on 10 May but it could not be captured. Thereafter, the Battalion was ordered to remain in Kargil Sector and occupy a firm base for the capture of Tiger Hill later.

It was after six weeks that the Battalion was once again ordered to capture Tiger Hill for the second time. By then the Battalion was acclimatised and equipped for the task. 18 Grenadiers and 2 Naga were added to 8 Sikh for the recapture of Tiger Hill along with adequate artillery, engineers and Air Support was provided for the impending task.

The plan was to attack on the night of 3 July at 1930 hours by all three battalions from different directions simultaneously to achieve surprise. The attack commenced as planned. Air Force aircrafts attacked with rockets on the objective accurately and had caused considerable damage. Artillery shelling commenced as the attacking troops closed in with the enemy. Going for the attackers was tough. Lt Balwan Singh of 18 Grenadiers was leading his Ghataks to establish a foothold on the top from the rear. Alpha and Charlie Companies were to launch the attack. 8 Sikh was advancing from the most expected direction; from the front as a deception measure and occupied a firm base. 2 Naga attacked from the left flank.

After twelve hours of climbing, the attackers reached the base. From there contacting the enemy defences involved steep climb. It had to be negotiated with vertical ropes laid before the climbing started. Grenadier Yogendra Singh Yadav volunteered to fix the ropes. Halfway up the cliff, the enemy noticed the movement and opened up using machine gun and grenades. This killed three, including an officer. Yadav was wounded.

Tiger Hill 16,700 ft-Final Assault

Notwithstanding the setback, the Ghataks reached the Top and attacked the enemy sangars. The enemy reacted violently. Suspecting a possible setback, 8 Sikh was ordered to send the reserve company under Major Ravinder Singh to reinforce the Grenadiers. Both Grenadiers and Sikhs attacked the sangars one by one. The enemy came out of the sangars in the open. They were engaged in hand to hand fight in which 10 Pakistanis were killed. 18 Grenadiers suffered six fatal casualties. By first light 4 July Tiger Hill Top was captured.

The enemy kept up their counter-attacks from the west for the next two days. 8 Sikh and 18 Grenadiers retained Tiger Hill top after pitched battles; most of the time at close quarters. Later when the situation stabilized at the top, 8 Sikh was tasked to occupy India Gate and Helmet. 8 Sikh cleared those two localities after a gallant fight against fierce counter-attacks and avenged their loss in the previous attack on Tiger Hill in the second week of May. 2 Naga, attacking from the left flank, captured their objective with heavy casualty of 30 men killed and more than 40 injured. The Tiger Hill complex was finally recaptured on 6 July.

Gren Yogendra Singh Yadav, PVC

Grenadier Yogendra Singh Yadav, who was in the lead on the rope and wounded badly, was awarded with India's highest gallantry award of Param Vir Chakra. Lt Balwan Singh was decorated with MVC for his gallant action as commander of the Ghataks.

POINT 4875 - MUSKOH VALLEY

Even after Tololing and Tiger Hill complexes were recaptured, NH 1 was not safe for convoys moving during the day. The enemy could interfere with the vehicles moving on NH 1 in a stretch of 30 kms from Dras to

Mugulpura from Point 4875 (15990 ft) with accurate artillery fire. Point 4875 complex comprise Whale Back, Point 4875 and Twin Bump. The enemy had occupied these features along with an artillery observation post located at Point 4875. This post also interfered with helicopter operations in Mushkoh Valley. It was the enemy's administrative base. The complex had to be captured to use NH 1 freely and use helicopters unhindered in Mushkoh Valley.

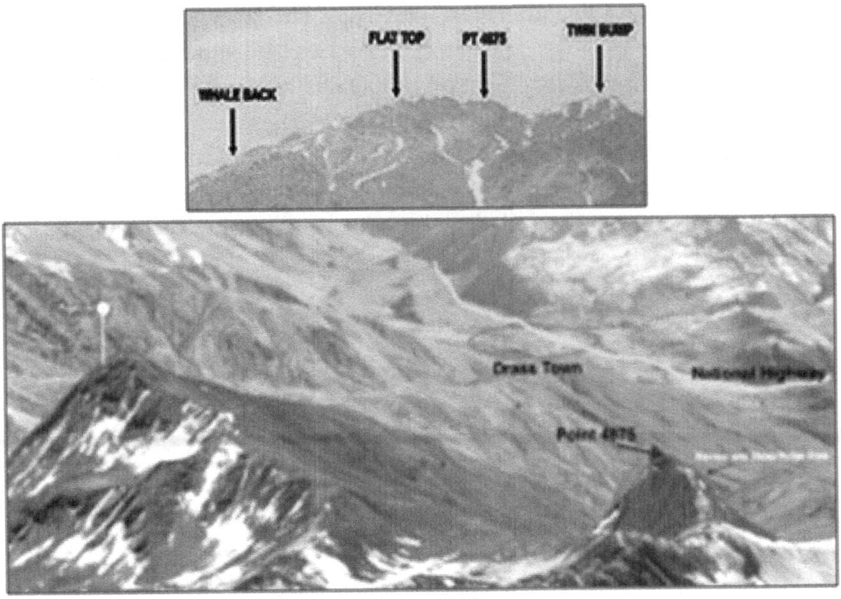

L to R- Tiger Hill, Dras Town, Point 4875 and NH 1 (View from the north)

17 Jat, 2 Naga and 13 JAK Rif were tasked to capture Point 4875, Twin Bump and Whaleback Complexes. On 06 July 1999, Charlie Company 17 Jat, started for Whaleback and Pimple I Complex on the Western Slopes of Point 4875. The attack commenced after a heavy bombardment to neutralise the objectives. Charlie Company negotiated steep slopes and reached the vicinity of their objective. During the advance, the Charlie Company Commander was injured enroute. In spite of this setback, Capt Anuj Nayyar who was leading the Company continued to lead his platoon under heavy enemy fire.

Pakistani infiltrators had constructed a number of sangars on Pimple 1. Capt Nayyar and his assault team captured three sangars. Pakistanis brought down mortar fire and counter-attacked the lost sangars. The counter-attack was repulsed. While tackling the last sangar, Capt Anuj was hit by an enemy rocket and died. The last sangar was cleared and Charlie Company objective was captured at the cost of the life of Capt Anuj Nayyar and his entire assault team. For this exceptional bravery Capt Anuj Nayyar was decorated with MVC (Posthumous). Subsequently, Whaleback and Pimple II were also captured. The Commanding officer and three others including the artillery observation post officer Capt Gildayal were awarded VrCs.

13 JAK Rif after capturing Point 5140 successfully by 20 June was placed under 79 Mountain Brigade in Muskoh Valley. The Battalion was tasked to capture Point 4875 Complex simultaneously with 17 Jat. The Battalion launched the attack and captured area Flat Top which was on the west of Point 4875 on 5 July after a fierce battle. The captured post was held under the command of Capt Nagappa. The enemy had brought down heavy volume of automatic fire from Point 4875 and an unnamed ridge echeloned to the northeast. The existence of enemy sangars on this Ridge was not known to the Battalion. Subsequently, the enemy made many attempts to recapture the Flat Top. In one such attack, Capt Nagappa was wounded seriously. All this while, Capt Vikram Batra, who was wounded while capturing Point 5140 earlier, remained in touch with the progress of the battle at the Flat Top, while lying down with fever and healing his wounds at the Battalion HQ.

When Capt Batra heard that Capt Nagappa was wounded, he went up to the Commanding Officer and volunteered to go to Flat Top to take control of the situation. The Commanding Officer reluctantly agreed to his request. He took 25 men from his company with him (the entire company volunteered to go with Batra) and left for Point 4875. On reaching the Top, Batra wanted to familiarise himself with the ground. He along with Subedar Raghunath Singh and Major Bhat, his artillery observation officer, went around Point 4875 to investigate the enemy fire coming from the close-quarters.

They realised that enemy was holding a ridge northeast of Point 4875 with series of sangars. Batra decided to capture those enemy sangars and eliminate the threat. The ridge was narrow and could not be approached from the flanks. Batra decided to attack frontally. He led the attack firing his AK-47 and reached the entrance of the first sangar after lobbing a grenade. He killed the occupants. In similar assaults, three more sangars which were in echelon were also captured. One more was left. It was a machine gun nest manned by four Pakistanis. Batra charged at them and killed three of them. During the charge, he sustained a burst of fire from enemy machine gun and died on the spot. Point 4875 was secured. For his exceptional bravery and self-sacrifice, Capt Vikram Batra was honoured with PVC posthumously.

Capt Vikram Batra, PVC (Posthumous)

Another important objective which was recaptured by 13 JAK Rif was Flat Top west of Point 4875 Complex. The company commanded by Major Gurpreet was tasked to capture the Flat Top. The leading Scout was Rifleman Sanjay Kumar. The advance on the face of the enemy was difficult and slow. The enemy was well entrenched and had good domination of the area. Having scaled the cliff, the company met with heavy enemy fire. Sanjay was about 150 meters away from the first enemy bunker. With complete disregard to his personal safety, Sanjay crawled up to the bunker and charged. Though he was hit in his chest, he continued the charge and silenced the nearest bunker. Then he picked-up an enemy machine gun and attacked the next enemy bunker. He killed three enemies on the spot. Inspired by his brave act, the rest of his team followed him and captured other bunkers. Taken by surprise, the enemy fled leaving behind their weapons and equipment.

Rfn Sanjay Kumar PVC

For his display of the most conspicuous personal bravery and gallantry of the highest order in the face of the enemy, Rifleman Sanjay Kumar was awarded Nation's highest wartime gallantry award - the PVC. Thus 13 JAK Rif had the distinction of winning two PVC and 8 VrCs in this operation.

2 Naga was deployed in counterinsurgency operations in north Kashmir during 1999 under Colonel Dinesh Kumar Badola. They were rushed to Kargil Sector at the beginning of the crisis. After the capture of Tiger Hill where the Battalion attacked from the left flank on 3/4 July and captured their objective, the battalion was placed under 79 Mountain Brigade in Muskoh Valley and was tasked to capture Twin Bumps east of Point 4875 at an altitude of more than 15,000 ft. 2 Naga captured Twin Bumps by 1200 hours on 6 July in which they lost 14 men and killed more Pakistanis than that.

After having captured their objective the battalion reorganized itself there. While probing further, on 8th July, 2 Naga spotted an enemy mortar position. They planned a raid on that. The assaulting party moved stealthily and closed in with the sentry standing on guard. Sepoy Imliakum Ao crawled up to the sentry and silenced him with his bare hands. Immediately the raid was launched and four more Pakistanis were killed. They captured two 82-mm and three 120-mm mortars along with large quantity of bombs from there. With that the Pakistani interference with accurate mortar fire on NH1 ended. Sepoy Imliakum Ao was decorated with a MVC for his bravery. For the first time, a Pakistani 120-mm mortar was captured by 2 Naga in this war.

BATALIK SECTOR

Batalik Sector is located east of Kargil Sector on either side of Indus River. In 1999, 70 Infantry Brigade was responsible for the defence of this Sector. During the winter of 1998-99, Pakistani personnel of 5 and 8 Northern Light Infantry had infiltrated into this Sector up to 8 to 10 kms south of the LOC and occupied the Posts vacated by the Indian Army at Juber, Point 4812, Khalubar and Point 5203 at altitude varying from 14000 to 18000 ft. By May 1999 the enemy strength was estimated to be between 500 and 600 in Batalik Sector. Units of 70 Infantry Brigade were operating in Kashmir Valley against militants leaving behind a bare minimum number of men in Batalik Sector.

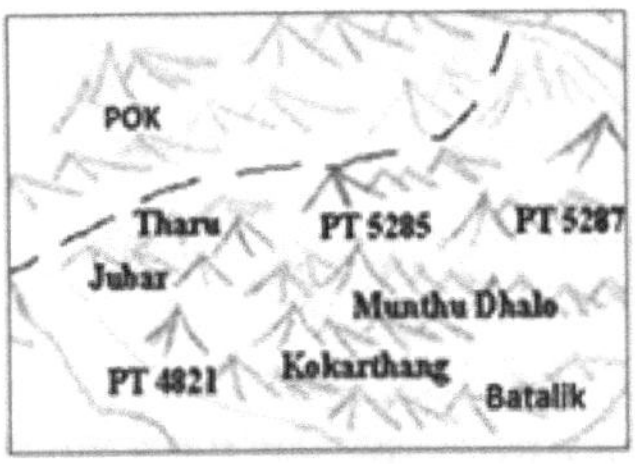

Batalik Sector

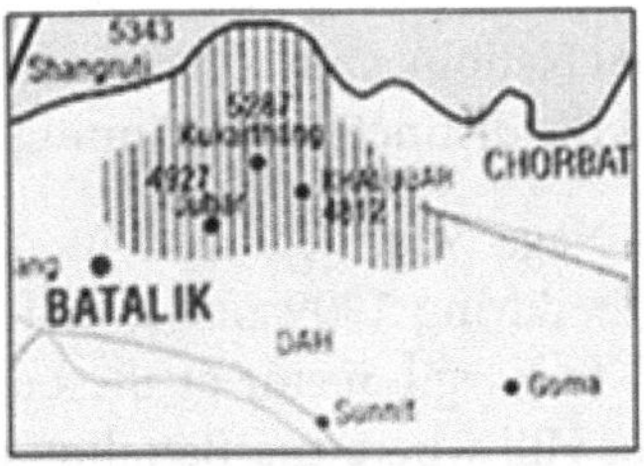

Enemy Infiltrated Area

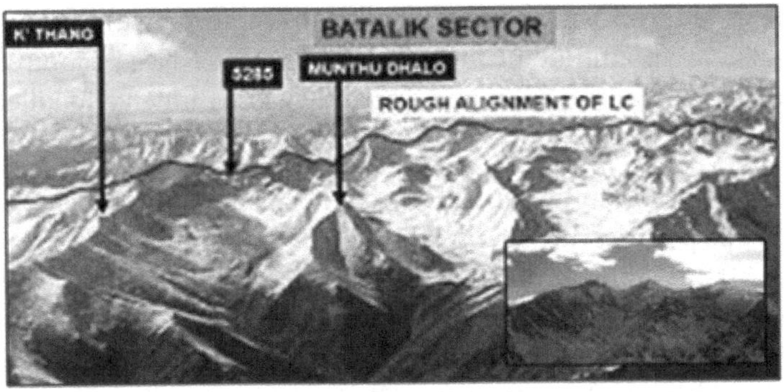

Ridges from LOC, Batalik

Pakistanis having occupied those posts, added sangars and laid mine fields to strengthen the posts. In May 1999, when the troops of 70 Brigade returned, they found their posts were occupied by the Pakistani troops. They decided to recapture their posts with additional resources in conjunction with the operations planned in Kargil Sector to evict the infiltrators. After identifying the extent of enemy threat, the Sector was divided into small sub-sectors and isolated by cutting off the enemy supply routes. The plan to recapture each sub-sector was made carefully optimising the resources available to the full extent. Additional troops including artillery and air supports were added to the Brigade responsible for the defence. Units of Special Forces were employed to cut off the line of communication of the intruders. 12 JAK LI captured Point 5203 on 21 May. With that, the western flank of the area occupied by the enemy was secured. By the last week of May, a wedge was created through enemy-held areas by recapturing some more features.

The Indus Wing of Ladakh Scout was tasked to occupy a ridge leading to Chorbat La to prevent further infiltration through this route. The advance was undertaken under the command of Major Sonam Wangchuk on 30 May. This involved negotiating glaciated areas at a height of 5,500 metres. While crossing a difficult patch of glacier, the enemy ambushed the advancing column with heavy machine gun fire and killed the NCO who was in the lead. Major Wanchuk regrouped his men and attacked the enemy. The enemy machine gun nest was destroyed in the attack and two Pakistani soldiers were killed. The rest of the enemy abandoned the ambush site and ran away leaving behind their heavy machine gun and a universal machine gun. Major Sonam further advanced up to the LOC and ensured the safety of the Batalik Sector's eastern flank. For his exceptionally daring offensive action and completing his task under most testing conditions, Major Sonam was awarded the MVC.

On the night of 30 June 99, 12 JAK Rif was given the task of securing the important peak at Point 4812. In this operation, Lieutenant Keishing Clifford Nongrum was assigned the task of capturing another height ahead of Point 4812. Nongrum chose a difficult route from the southeastern direction to his objective to surprise the enemy. They stealthily crawled over the steep slopes to reach the enemy bunkers at the top. On the peak, Pakistani infiltrators had entrenched themselves in interconnected bunkers made up of boulders which made them immune to artillery fire. On completing their ascent, Lt Nongrum and his men had to face strong enemy opposition in the form of mortar and automatic machine gun fire. Lt Nongrum and his men were pinned down for over two hours. Finally, before the day broke, Nongrum charged the enemy bunkers with grenade and machine gun fire and killed six enemies and established a foothold. This gave enough time for the rest of the Battalion to reach the top and capture Point 4812. During the assault Nongrum was hit by a burst of enemy bullets. He was bleeding profusely but refused to be evacuated.

Finally, when the Battalion successfully captured the objective, Lieutenant Keishing Clifford Nongrum died of his wounds. For this extra ordinary bravery beyond the call of duty and sacrifice of his life, he was decorated with MVC posthumously. The first Pakistan Army Prisoner was taken during this battle.

1/11 GR was tasked to capture the enemy occupied post on Khalubar Ridge on 3 July. The leading company was commanded by Capt Manoj Kumar Pandey. After over five hours of walk and arduous climb when the company was closing in with their objective, the leading platoon came under enemy fire from the flanks. Manoj was with the leading platoon. He moved his platoon to a safer position and planed an attack on the enemy from more than one direction. He was with the platoon attacking from the most dangerous approach. Under enemy fire, Manoj attacked the first enemy position and captured after killing two enemy soldiers.

The second bunker was also secured after killing the enemy occupants. While attacking the third bunker, he was injured by enemy fire. In spite of his injuries, he continued to lead the assault on the fourth enemy position and urged his men to follow him. While he was lobbing grenades on the last bunker, he sustained fatal injury and died. The objective was cleared of the enemy by the rest of his company. The foothold created by Capt Pandey's company facilitated further advance and led to victory in the Battalion attack and capture of vital Khalubar Ridge. Capt Manoj Kumar Pandey was decorated with the Param Vir Chakra (posthumously), the nation's highest award for exceptional bravery and leadership.

Capt Manoj Kumar Pandey, PVC
(Posthumous)

By 8 July, Ladakh Scouts and 17 Garhwal Rifles had captured Kokarthang and other nearby Posts occupied by the enemy. Juber Top was captured by 1 Bihar and 5 Para captured Muntho Dhalo. It was a major breakthrough which turned the tide and forced the enemy to withdraw from the Indian Territory. Most of the regular soldiers of Pakistani Northern Light Infantry units had been cleared from Batalik Sector. On July 23 to July 26, important heights on the LOC were recaptured to ensure domination over areas across the LOC. The fighting ceased on 26 July.

Besides numerous individual bravery awards, six Infantry Battalions were awarded the Battle Honours. Five others were given Unit Citations for their performance. Having lost the war, Pakistan withdrew their forces under political and military compulsions from the Indian Territory. It was a remarkable victory for the Indian Army. 26 July, the day Kargil War 1999 ended, is celebrated as Vijay Diwas every year.

SHYOK VALLEY

From Kargil Sector the CFL/LOC crosses Shingo and Indus Rivers north of Kargil in a northerly direction and crosses Shyok River to reach the Glacier. Shyok River is a tributary of the Indus River. It follows an interesting course in India and enters POK before it joins the Indus River. Shyok originates from Rimo Glacier in the northern Ladakh, flows due south and takes an about turn to northwest. Nubra River from the north joins Shyok River at Diskit. After travelling some distance, it enters POK and joins Indus River at Skardu. From there, the Indus River runs southwards and crosses the LOC into India in Batalik Sector. Shyok Valley, (also known as Turtuk Sector) was the scene of important battles in 1948 and in 1971. Major population centres in the Shyok Valley are Diskit, Hunter, Thoise, Shuru, Udmaru, Bogdang, Chalunkna and Turtuk. From Diskit, Leh is connected through Khardung La.

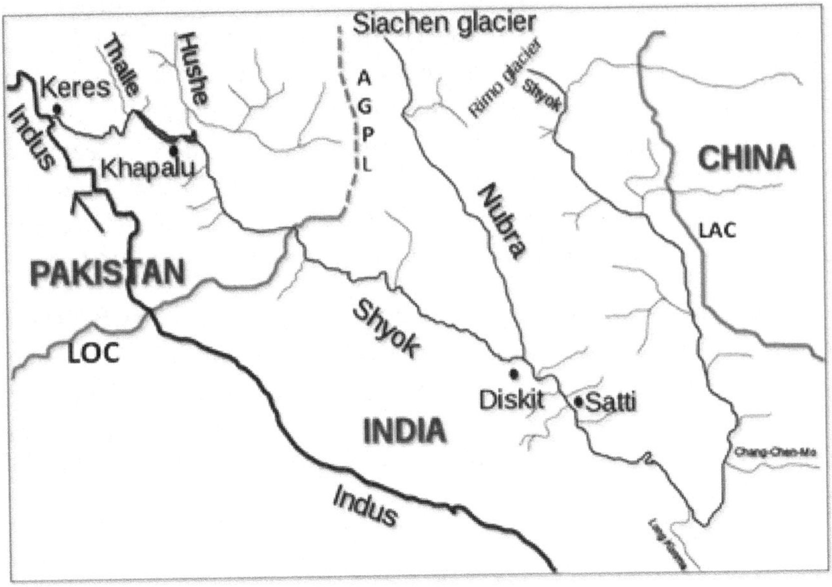

Shyok, Nubra and Indus Rivers

1948

In 1948, Pakistanis were prevented from reaching Leh via Skardu and Kargil by tenacious Lt Col Sher Jung Thapa, who halted them at Skardu. This forced the Gilgit Forces to make an attempt to approach Leh through Shyok Valley. From there, they could have crossed over Khardung La to reach Leh. Besides the capture of the capital city of Ladakh, Pakistanis would have fulfilled their greed of looting and pillaging the rich Buddhist monasteries enroute. The terrain was well known to invaders as they had operated in this area while serving with the J&K Army before the revolt.

By the end of 1947, major part of the plains of Kashmir Valley came under the control of Indian Army. However, northern part of Ladakh and western Punch Valley remained under the Pakistani invaders' control. Lack of requisite force level, poor road communication within J&K including Punch and Ladakh and logistic nightmares in Ladakh were some of the challenges which had to be surmounted by the six-month old Indian Army in lesser known terrain and unfamiliar climatic conditions. The peace-loving Buddhist Ladakhis were about to be converted into war fighting soldiers. A plan emerged in which a training team comprising officers, JCOs and men of Indian Army were to go to Leh and train the locals to defend their motherland. 2 Dogra produced that team. They were despatched under Capt Prithi Chand in the month of February 1948 when Zojila was blocked with more than 20 feet of snow. For the first time, Zojila was crossed in winter and the team reached Leh in the first week of March.

They enrolled 30 young Ladakhi volunteers initially. The young Ladakhis were willing to fight to protect their motherland. Most of them were from Shyok/Nubra Valley. They were trained for two weeks and armed. Thus the Nubra Guard, the forerunner of Ladakh Scout, was born. Under a JCO from 2 Dogra, they were sent to Shyok/Nubra Valley. They knew the area well and were well acclimatised. The youngest of them a school going lad, Chewang Rinchen, aged 17, was their leader. He was from Nubra Valley. La Churuk and Lama House were occupied by the rebels. The Nubra Guards attacked and captured these two enemy Posts. They brought weapons and supplies from there.

The initial victory boosted their morale and strengthened their resolve to save their motherland from the marauders. They frustrated the enemy by preventing attempts made by the Gilgit Scouts to cross Shyok River. Chewan Rinchen was promoted to the rank of Jemadar and decorated with a MVC for his brave deeds at a tender age of 17. He was destined to play far greater roles in the defence of Ladakh in the subsequent battles fought in Ladakh. Though Ladakh was divided between India and POK at the end of the First Kashmir War, major parts of Ladakh District was saved from Pakistani occupation. Gilgit Region and part of Baltistan formed part of POK. The dividing line in J&K including Ladakh was named as CFL.

1971

In 1971, when Pakistan attacked India across the western border, a counter-offensive operation was launched into West Pakistan and POK at vulnerable areas across the CFL. One area selected for launching the counter-offensive was in Shyok Valley. Chalukna and Turtuk are two important small towns in Shyok valley. They were held by the POK forces. Capture of these towns would improve India's defence posture and prevent Pakistan from using the Shyok Valley to infiltrate and occupy vacant areas at Karakoram Ridge including Karakoram Pass. Indian Army decided to capture these two towns with specially organised and trained units of Ladakhis along with Indian Army units including Ladakh Scouts.

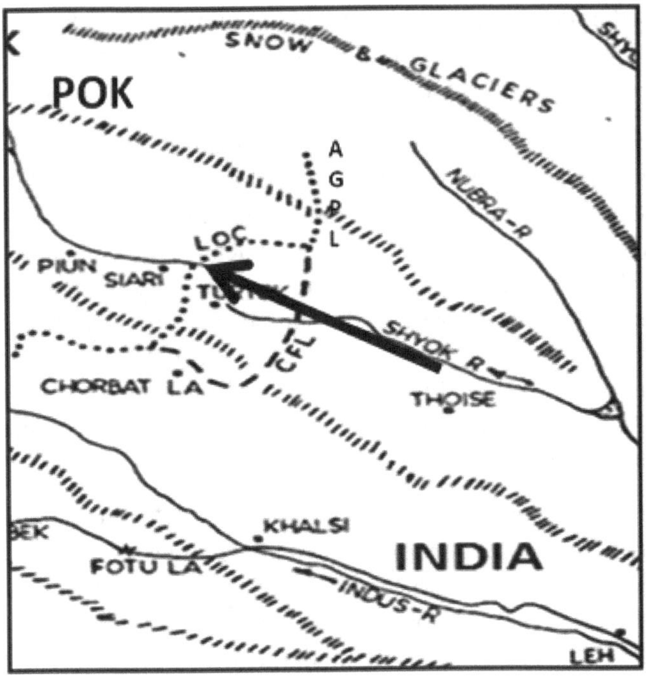

Thoise-Turtuk

By 1971, Chewan Rinchen MVC, SM became an officer in the Indian Army and held the rank of Major. He was one of the commanders of Nubra Guards which was assigned the task of capturing Turtuk. Under him, he had 400 local Ladakhis. He trained his men for the task assigned to him. He selected weapons, clothing and equipment to suit the terrain and weather conditions obtained in his area of operations which were well above 18,000 ft. This operation known as 'Battles on Top of the World' began on 8 December 71. His forces avoided the main track and moved from one objective to the other directly. They advanced 22 kms into POK and captured more than 800 sq kms. Besides Chalunkna and Turtuk, they also captured the world's highest post at Point 18402 and five more villages. This was an achievement beyond expectation. The ceasefire ended the war on 16 December 71. The CFL was converted into LOC with the captured area remaining part of India.

Major Chewan Rinchen Addressing the people of Turtuk-1971

In the words of Major Chewan Rinchen, 'if we had few more days to fight, we could have captured more POK territory and linked up with Kargil'. For his devotion to duty, patriotism and bravery, Major Rinchen was awarded a BAR to his MVC (Second MVC). Turtuk is now a thriving tourist destination in Ladakh.

SIACHEN

In 1949, after the First Kashmir War, the Karachi Agreement was signed by India and Pakistan and both countries had agreed to convert the line joining the forward line of defences held at that time in J&K to be the Ceasefire Line (CFL). It was deemed as the temporary border between POK and India. After the 1962 Chinese Aggression, Pakistan gave away some territory from POK close to the northern border with China in 1963 to settle their border with China. This area forms part of Shaksgam Valley which is rightfully part of J&K.

After 1971 War, according to Simla Agreement of 1972, the CFL was redesignated as the LOC. Although it is not legally an International Border, it became a de-facto boundary. The LOC is recognised by both countries and marked on the map as well as on the ground. Demarcation of LOC ended at a point in the northern part of Ladakh at Grid Reference (GR) NJ 9842. When the CFL/LOC was marked on the ground, the area beyond GR NJ 9842 south of Siachen Glacier could not be surveyed and marked due to very high altitude terrain and inhuman weather conditions. Therefore, the CFL in between GR NJ 9842 and India-China Border in the north was not drawn on the map. A mere mention was made in the Karachi Agreement as 'north to the glacier'.

India interpreted this as an extension of CFL from GR NJ 9842 along the Saltoro Ridge line as per the Water Shed principle of border delineation (line joining the dominating peaks to be the borderline; in this case the highest peaks along the Saltoro Ridge) towards north up to the China Border at Indira Col east of Siakangri which is north of GR NJ 9842. On the other hand, Pakistan has been staking their claim on the entire Siachen glacier from line joining GR NJ 9842 up to Karakorum Pass which is located east of Siachen glaciers as shown on the map below.

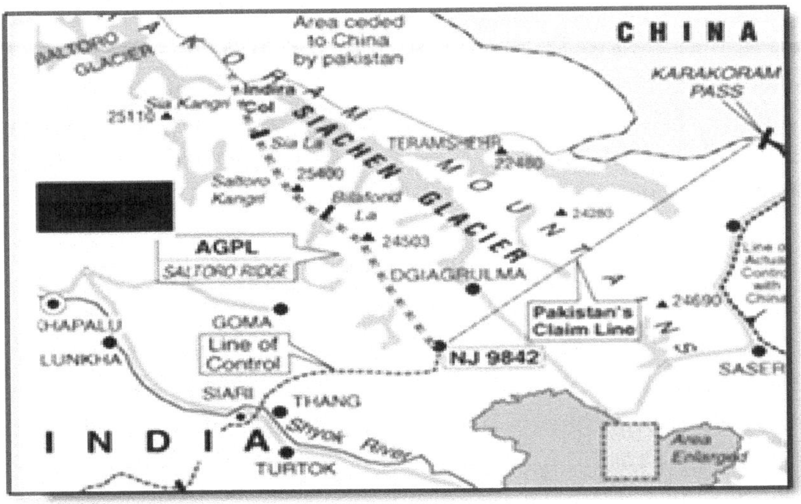

The Claim Lines

The representatives of the two countries met many times to demarcate the LOC beyond GR NJ 9842. Meanwhile, Pakistan had begun giving permission to mountaineers from other countries to climb the peaks within Siachen glacier. Other Pakistani activities indicated that Pakistan

Army could be planning to occupy the dominating heights of important passes on the Saltoro Ridge and present a *fait accompli* to India. To avoid such a situation, India decided to occupy those heights which dominate the three major passes namely Sia La (18336 ft) Bilafond La (17880 ft) and Gyong La (18665 ft) on the Saltoro Ridge.

Operation Megdhoot was launched successfully on 13 April 1984 and the dominating heights were occupied just in time before Pakistan Army could occupy it. Troops of 4 Kumaon and Ladakh Scout reached their objectives by land-routes and by airborne operation successfully under the guidance of Col Narendra Kumar PVSM, KC, AVSM, and FRGS. These Posts were maintained by air. They faced many inhuman conditions. The line joining Point GR NJ 9842 and India China border near Siakangri was named as Actual Ground Position Line (AGPL) as shown on double broken line on the map above.

Security Post in Siachen

Holding posts at these super high altitudes pose many challenges. Acute shortage of oxygen, extreme low temperature, biting cold wind, blizzards, low atmospheric pressure steep gradients, unknown crevasses and avalanches are to name a few. They cause headache, fatigue, dizziness, palpitations, nausea, loss of appetite, insomnia, snow-blindness, and many other maladies/challenges. The human body cannot get acclimatized over 18,000 ft to stay over a long period of time; after a short while, the human body begins to deteriorate.

In Siachen, human beings are at the risk of getting deadly frostbite; a condition resulting from abrupt exposure to extreme cold, that will require amputation of the exposed part (fingers or toes) to save the rest of the body. Those who serve at these altitudes for long, suffer from speech blurring, weight loss, loss of appetite, sleep disorders and memory loss. Life-threatening high altitude diseases occur due to leaky capillaries in the brain and lung known as Cerebral and Pulmonary Oedema.

Under these conditions, security posts, artillery gun positions or store dumps can get buried in a matter of minutes. Cooking/heating pre-cooked food is tedious and time-consuming. Bathing and answering natures call are tiresome. Prefabricated huts require anchoring and careful maintenance. In spite of multi-layered warm clothing that men wear at all times, even a short exposure to ambient weather conditions chill the bones and cause death in extreme cases. Overall, these conditions reduce the human potential to less than 30% of their normal capability. This adversely affects walking, manual work and load carrying capacity. It may take more than an hour to walk one kilometre in plain areas in glacier carrying 30% of average load. Steep hills take much more time. Psychological effects range from men becoming silent and immobile to going berserk.

Machines are also affected by the low temperature and low air density as much as the man behind the machine. Projectiles from weapons travel longer distance away from the target. Freezing of moving parts of the weapons including artillery guns and their recoil mechanism are common occurrence. Fuel and lubricants other than kerosene oil freeze at these temperatures. The average carrying capacity of a helicopter is reduced to either half or one-third.

Having lost the race to Saltoro Ridge, Pakistan had made many attempts to capture the Indian Posts in Siachen. They failed in their attempt. However, Pakistan had occupied a vacant peak on the ridge overlooking the Indian Posts and named it Qaid Post. This Post was interfering with the Indian air maintenance operations. After many attempts, in one of the most challenging operations against the elements and enemy, this Post was captured from Pakistani occupation and renamed as Bana Post after Naib Subedar Bana Singh who was the commander of the final assault team that captured the post. He was awarded PVC for his bravery and leadership.

Nb/Sub Bana Singh PVC

Notwithstanding the fact that maintaining the troops at this altitude is very expensive, Siachen has to be held due to its strategic importance for protecting Ladakh against a possible combined aggression by China and Pakistan. The Chinese Government has maintained that their occupation of Shaksgam Valley will be decided based on the outcome of the Kashmir dispute. Hence it is essential to hold on to the Siachen area and demonstrate our resolve to defend our territory in J&K.

(Demilitarisation of Saltoro Ridge is an option which India can exercise provided Pakistan agrees to mark their present troops holding position on a map, signed by their civil and military leaders and duly witnessed by a representative of a neutral third party such as UNO and attached as part of the De-militarisation Agreement. Pakistan and China have been ambivalent when it comes to demarcating the borders. Hence, the need for such precautions.)

Chapter 6

LADAKH - EAST

India China LAC

The India-China LAC starting at Indira Col till the trijunction of India-China-Burma border is 3,488 kms long. It borders J&K/ Ladakh (1,597 kms), Himachal Pradesh (200 kms), Uttarakhand (345 kms), Sikkim (220 kms) and Arunachal Pradesh (1126 kms). The responsibility of guarding this border during peace time is with the Indo-Tibetan Border Police (ITBP), Sikkim Scouts and Arunachal Scouts. In between, the IB between India and Nepal and India and Bhutan are guarded by the SSB.

In 1947, the British left India leaving behind unsettled borders with China and Tibet. During their rule over Indian sub-continent, they made many attempts since 1865 to demarcate the borderline between China/

Eastern Ladakh

Tibet and India. Nothing concrete could be achieved during their rule. Many borderlines were proposed and a few lines were identified which could have served the boundary. However, as the Chinese changed their claim lines year after year, the lines remained inconclusive and did not become the IB.

The inconclusive lines were named after the head of the British negotiating teams such as Johnson, McCartney McDonald and McMahon. None of those lines were ever demarcated on the ground and there is no evidence to prove that these agreements were enforced on the ground by them. Various borderlines proposed by the British in Aksai Chin are shown on the map below.

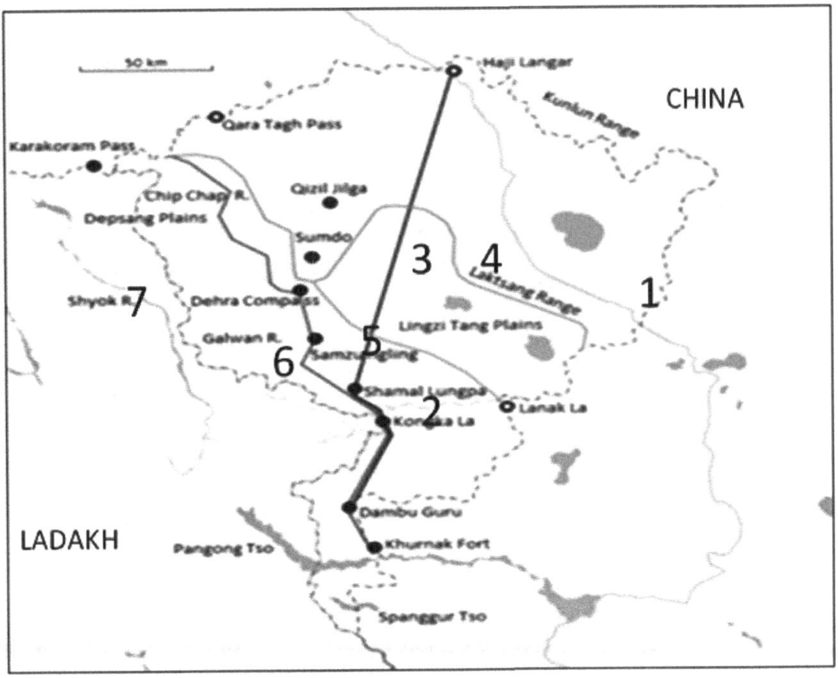

Ladakh-Aksai Chin

1. 1865 Johnson Line.
2. 1873 Traditional Border.
3. 1899 Macartney-MacDolald Line.
4. 1957 Tibet – Xinjiang Road.
5. 1959 Line of Chinese Posts.
6. 1962 Indian and Chinese Post Line.
7. 1962 Chinese Claim Line after War.

Due to harsh high altitude barren rocky terrain, extreme weather conditions obtained in Aksai Chin and lack of resources, Aksai Chin remained inaccessible. Neither the sanctity of the border with China/ Tibet was enforced nor was the region effectively administered both by the Maharaja of J&K and later by the British Indian Government.

China had constructed Western Highway (G219) surreptitiously; linking Xinjiang Province in the north in China to Tibet in the south passing through Aksai Chin after Tibet was annexed by China in the early fifties. Though this strategically important road was constructed earlier, it remained uncontested by India till 1959. In addition to the construction of this road through the disputed territory, China also occupied strategically important localities west of this highway to protect it from the west. Diplomatic efforts made by India to solve the problem did not bear any fruit. China successfully applied the teachings of Sun Zu on the art of winning war by occupying the disputed territory before fighting a war for it. This brought the PLA closer to the line joining Karakoram pass and Pangong Lake in Aksai Chin which is well within the Indian Territory even by Chinese claim.

Having learnt about the aggressive designs of China, India decided to secure the border areas adjoining China and handed over the responsibility of guarding the border to the Indian Army and ordered them to establish military out posts under India's Forward Policy. In the eastern Ladakh, the Indian Army units had occupied isolated military posts in north-south direction from Daulat Beg Oldi (DBO) Sector in the north including Galwan Valley, Chushul and Indus Valley Sector which ends at Demchok in the south. The approaches to these sectors involve crossing Ladakh and Karakoram Ranges. There is no north-south road connectivity within these sectors along the border. There was no motorable road to DBO across Sasirla Ranges in 1962 from Leh (the capital of Ladakh). A few light vehicles were air transported and used for local movement within the DBO Sector. On the Chinese side opposite DBO, well-developed roads existed up to their posts located along their claim lines in 1962.

Daulat Beg Oldi (which means place where Daulat Beg died) is about 20 kms to the east of Karakoram pass. Special Armed Police Force was deployed in this area until the Indian Army moved in. In October 1959, three border clashes took place between Indian security forces and Peoples Liberation Army (PLA) of China; two in the North East Frontier Agency (NEFA) and one in Aksai Chin. The clash in Aksai Chin took place in Changchenmo Valley south of Konga Pass in which eight armed policemen were killed while carrying out routine patrolling.

In March 1959, the Dalai Lama was given asylum in India when he escaped from Tibet. This was considered by the Chinese as an anti-Chinese act and China decided to teach a lesson to India. Based on the indications of Chinese military activities, senior military leaders of the

Indian Armed Forces advised the Government to increase the presence of the security forces in the border areas and prepare the armed forces to face an aggression from China. Those advises were not taken seriously by the Government of India and they continued to believe that China would not use military forces against India. Therefore, till 1962, the entire Ladakh had just one brigade of Indian Army deployed in penny packets.

DAULAT BAIG OLDI

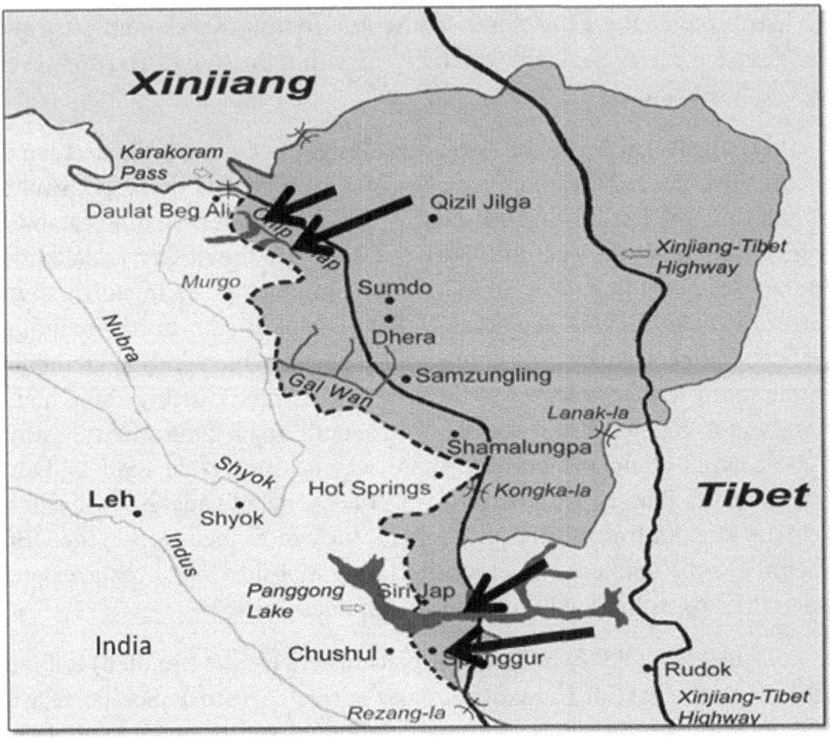

DBO-Aksai Chin-Xinjiang-Tibet Highway

DBO is an uninhabited rocky desert in northern Ladakh located on the ancient Silk Route at an altitude of over 16,600 ft above MSL. It is north of Chip Chap River and eight kms south of the Indo-Chinese border. A military post was established at DBO in 1961 after Major Chewan Rinchen MVC, had carried out reconnaissance and confirmed that the Chinese had intruded into Indian Territory and were preparing permanent defences in DBO area. He also confirmed the suitability of DBO for the construction of a runway for fixed wing aircrafts to operate which was later confirmed by aerial photo reconnaissance. This raised the alarm at higher level in the Indian Army. Subsequently, the Government agreed to the deployment of additional Army units in April 1960. In November 1961, the entire border area with China was transferred to the Army for protection. They were authorised to open fire but only in self defence.

Having failed to convince China of the ownership of Aksai Chin diplomatically and prevent the Chinese Forces from further making inroad into Indian Territory, the Government of India adopted a Forward Policy which entailed Indian Army establishing military posts behind Chinese Posts. In October 1962, deployment of the Indian Army was as follows:

- Daulat Beg Oldi and Chip Chap Sector -14 J &K Militia plus one Company of 5 Jat.
- Galwan Valley- one company of 5 Jat.
- Chang Chenmo Valley - 5 Jat less two companies.
- Chushul – one company less a platoon of 1/8 GR.
- Sirijap Post- One Platoon of 1/8 GR.
- Yalu Posts-One Company of 1/8 GR.
- Spanggur Gap- Two Companies of 1/8 GR.

14 J&K Militia Battalion was the first unit to occupy the posts in DBO Sector. Large number of platoon and section posts was established in this Sector without any mutual support to each other or creating depth localities as firm base which are basic ingredients of defensive warfare. Resources were not available for overhead protection. The Indian Army had a total of four battalions to protect 480 kms long border in the eastern Ladakh which is one of the most difficult terrains on earth. Most of the posts had to be sited to suit administrative conveniences. Additional troops were not given when asked for. One of the most important things that happened at DBO was the creation of a temporary runway on which a Packet Fairchild aircraft piloted by Wing Commander CKS Raja landed at an altitude of 16700 ft. It was a record by itself.

On the opposing side, the Chinese had permanent defences manned by acclimatised and trained troops of approximately one-division strength. Chinese posts were well connected by all-weather roads.

By the middle of October, 5 Jat and 14 J&K Militia had established a total of 21 Posts on both sides of Chip Chap River with the Battalion HQ at DBO. They were incapable of contesting enemy advance in an organised manner. On the 19th of October after the sunset, most of the Indian Posts came under artillery/mortar and automatic machine gun fire. Later when Chinese assaulted those posts, Indian soldiers returned the fire and held on for a while. The Chinese attacked the posts after blocking the defenders route of withdrawal. The fight went on till midday next when most of the defenders were either killed or taken prisoners. Finally, there were only nine men who withdrew on orders and reached the Battalion HQ at DBO next day.

Chandini Post north of DBO was held by 14 J&K Militia. They gave a good fight under the inspiring leadership of Subedar Sonam. The Chinese attacked in strength with superior numerical strength. Many attacks were repulsed. The Post could not be reinforced as it was completely isolated by the Chinese troops. In the end, the Post was overrun with all dead except one Sepoy who was seriously wounded. For the exceptional bravery and self-sacrifice, Sub Sonam and Hav Saroop Singh were decorated with the MVC posthumously and Sepoys Chiring Wangchuk and Phunchok were awarded VrC.

During this period the posts held by 5 Jat came under attack with overwhelming strength. On 20 October Chinese attacked a few more Posts in Chip Chap Valley. Two Posts withdrew after giving a brief fight and another two were overrun by the Chinese. On the night of 21, all Posts were ordered to withdraw to DBO/ Track Junction/ Sultan/ or Galwan Posts. These posts were defendable to some extent.

The defenders in Galwan Valley were better organised compared to posts in the north and fought to the bitter end against well-armed, better equipped and numerically superior enemy. Galwan post, which was held by Subedar Jang Bahadur Thapa and his men since July, was reinforced by a company of 5 Jat led by Major Hasabnis. The Chinese pounded this post with artillery for a full day before overrunning it. By 22 October, most of the small isolated Posts established as part of Forward Policy including Parmodak, Bishan, Chandini and Bhujan were overrun by the Chinese or abandoned by the defenders due to heavy casualties and had became untenable. They could not be reinforced or maintained. Those who could physically move had withdrawn to DBO. Having cleared up to their claim line, the People's Liberation Army halted their advance towards DBO. Similar advance was made in Chushul Sector north of Penggong Lake.

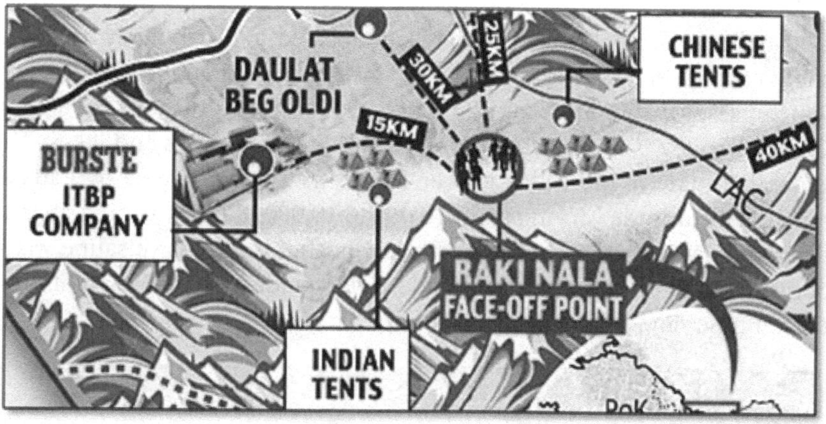

Raki Nala Standoff 2013

Due to un-demarcated border, frequent border crossings became common occurrence in DBN Sector. One of the serious ones was at Raki Nala southeast of DBO in 2013. In spite of an agreement, there is difference in the perception of alignment of the LAC. Even after repeated demand in flag meetings, the Chinese refuse to mark and authenticate the LAC on the map and ground. Of late, with increased proximity of China and Pakistan in political and economic fields, the Chinese intransigent attitude towards India has hardened.

On 15 April 2013, ITBP reported of an intrusion of about 40 PLA men, 30 kms south of DBO near Raki Nala in Depsong Valley in the disputed area Known as Sub Sector north (SSN). The Chinese pitched four tents and established a camp. Landing of helicopters and movement of vehicles were noticed. This indicated that the camp was reinforced and VIPs may have visited the camp. The Indian Army responded by establishing a camp nearly 300 ms away from the Chinese Camp inside Indian Territory. The standoff was followed by negotiations lasting over three weeks. The dispute was resolved on 5 May after India agreed to withdraw from a post nearly 250 kms in the south in Chumar Sector; the post was perceived by the Chinese as violation of a previous agreement.

With the Chinese offensive intents and numerically superior PLA, the border issues remain unsettled. Presently, DBO is held by the ITBP and Ladakh Scout. With the Siachen Glacier and Shyok valley including Haneef Sector firmly in the hands of Indian Army, DBO assumes greater importance in blocking a direct approach route to Chinese from Tibet to POK.

CHUSHUL

Chushul is an important border village located approximately 150 kms south east of Leh and west of Rudok (Tibet). The Xinjiang-Tibet Highway which passes through Rudok is about 50 kms from Chushul. The area of Chushul Valley is rocky interspersed with high mountains and lakes. The general altitude of the valley is over 14,000 ft. It is dominated by Ladakh ranges with altitude varying from 16,000 to 19,000 ft. It has an airstrip. The Panggong Lake, located to the north of Chushul is a massive saline water body of 134 kms long and 5 kms wide at its broadest point. 60% of it is on the Chinese side of the LAC.

Chushul and Spanggur Lake and Gap

The Chushul village and the airstrip are surrounded by mountains with wide gaps in the south and east. There is another smaller lake south of Panggong Lake known as Spanggur Lake. The gap in between the mountains at the western end of the lake is known as Spanggur Gap. This gap is tankable. Chushul is connected with Leh by road. The strategic importance of Chushul lies in its connectivity to Leh, proximity to Rudok and the availability of an advance landing ground for fixed wing aircrafts.

In 1962, Ladakh was held very thinly with a brigade comprising four Battalions. One of the Battalions; 1/8 GR, was located at Chushul. Two platoons of this Battalion held a Post on the northern bank of Pangong Lake at a place known as Srijap. This post was established under the Forward Policy. In the absence of road connectivity with the Battalion HQ, it was maintained by boat only. Other forward Posts along the LAC were manned by the armed police. The rest of 1/8 GR was deployed for the protection of Chushul from southern Bank of Pangong Lake through Gurung Hill, Spanggur Gap and Maggar Hill.

PLA attacked Srijap on 21 October 1962. After shelling heavily, the Chinese assaulted the Post with tanks. The Gorkhas under brave Major Dhan Singh Thapa gave a good account of themselves. However, against numerically superior force and in the absence any scope for reinforcement or possibility of methodical withdrawal, all of them fought till the last. Most of them died and a few including Major Thapa were wounded and taken prisoners. On 22 October, Sirjap was in the hands of Chinese. Major Dhan Singh Thapa was awarded PVC for bravery. After the fall of Srijap, there was a pause in the battle.

Major Dhan Singh Thapa, PVC

During the pause in the battle, additional forces were rushed to Chushul both by road and by Air. Indian Air Force lifted tanks from Chandigarh and landed at Chushul and created a record of landing tanks at such high altitude. Between 22 October and 18 November, a new Division was raised and 114 Brigade under Brigadier TN Raina was moved to Chushul. In addition to 1/8 GR, 13 Kumaon and 1 Jat was inducted into Chushul defences. 13 Kumaon was deployed to defend Rizang La complex, 1/8 GR at Gurung Hill and Spanggur Gap, and 1 Jat south of Chushul. Tanks were moved to cover Spanggur gap along with infantry. Tanks and artillery fire in support of Infantry was coordinated. Minefields were laid in the likely enemy tank runs.

The Chinese attacked Chushul Sector on 18 November commencing with heavy shelling on the entire Brigade Sector and captured part of defences at Rizang La and Gurung Hill. Indian artillery and tanks of 20 Lancers engaged the attacking enemy and caused considerable casualty and damage to the Chinese artillery guns deployed in the Spanggur Gap. The PLA succeeded in capturing the forward localities of Gurung Hill and Maggar Hill with heavy casualty on the Chinese side. Further attack on Rizangla was contested by Charlie Company of 13 Kumaon under Major Shaitan Singh. Rizangla defenders fought 'last man last round' and suffered heavy casualty. Out 124 who were holding Rizangla, 109 including Major Shaitan Singh died fighting on the ground which they were supposed to defend. The rest were seriously injured and were evacuated. Major Shaitan Singh was decorated with PVC posthumously and eight of his men were honoured with VrCs.

Major Shaitan Singh PVC
(Posthumous)

1/8 GR came under attack around 0900 hours. The Gorkhas gave a tough fight. Jamedar Amar Bahadur Gurung was commanding the forward platoon which the Chinese attacked. The Gorkhas inflicted heavy casualty on Chinese. When the Chinese reached the platoon defended locality, the platoon came out of the bunkers and resorted to kukri charge and killed or wounded a large number of PLA men. In the hand to hand fight that ensued, Jamedar Amar Bahadur Gurung was killed. He was decorated with MVC for bravery. The Chinese captured Gurung Hill and Maggar Hill with their numerical superiority and fire power. When PLA occupied Gurung Hill, heavy volume of artillery fire was brought down on them by 2/Lt Goswami of 13 Field Artillery who was the Forward Observation Officer with 1/8 GR. 2/Lt Goswami of 13 Field Regiment Artillery was awarded MVC for bravery.

In spite of high altitude effects on the tanks, 20 Lancers created havoc on the attacking PLA troops by their accurate fire from the tank guns. They used manual mode when the mechanical loading system of the tanks froze in cold. The Chinese suffered heavy casualties and were forced to halt their attack at Gurung Hill and Rizangla. Ceasefire was declared on 21 November. After suffering heavy casualty, the PLA units withdrew from their captured localities from Gurung Hill, Maggar Hill and Rizang La. Peking Radio admitted having suffered large casualty in Chushul Sector.

When Chinese declared ceasefire unilaterally, the Brigade had enough fighting potential left to react to any further offensive by the PLA in spite suffering heavy casualty. The ground of tactical importance of the Brigade including Chushul village and the advance landing ground was held intact. As a defender, Indian Army succeeded in the Battle of Chushul by successfully defending it. The Brigade Commander, Brigadier TN Raina (later COAS) was decorated with a MVC for winning the battle in adverse conditions.

DEMCHOK SECTOR

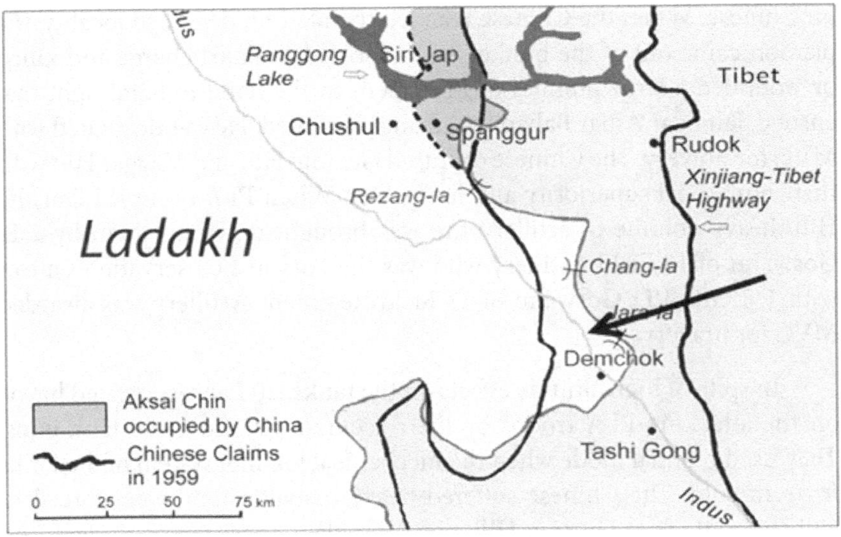

Demchok Sector

Demchok village is located on the LAC about 100 kms south of Chushul in Leh District. It is on the old road linking Ladakh with Tibet. On the Tibetan side is village Tashigong. The road connecting the two villages had been blocked by the PLA. It was a trade and pilgrimage route to Kailash and Manasarovar which is about 300 kms inside Tibet. If this route is opened, the pilgrimage to Kailash Parbat and Manasarovar can be done by the shortest route. Due to good connectivity by road, this sector assumes strategic importance for the defence of Ladakh

During 1962 Chinese aggression, Demchok Sector was held by 7 J&K Militia under 70 Brigade along with Chang La and Jara La. Jemadar Ishe Thundup was commanding the Chang La Post. PLA attacked Demchok Sector including Chang La and Jara La on 22 October. They attempted to encircle Demchok and cut off the route of withdrawal of 7 J&K Militia with a double envelopment. The defenders fought gallantly and delayed the enemy for four hours, but they were hopelessly outnumbered.

Jemadar Ishe Thundup asked his men to withdraw while he himself manned the machine gun and provided covering fire to them. As the planned encirclement of PLA was not completed in time, the defenders found a gap and withdrew unhindered. However, Jemadar Thundup being the last man to vacate the Post was caught in the Chinese assault and was killed. True to the tradition of soldiering, Jemadar Ishe Thundup sacrificed his life to save his men. He was honoured posthumously with an award of MVC for bravery and self-sacrifice in the face of the enemy. Later Chang La and Jarz La were captured by the enemy.

India has made many attempts to open this ancient trade and pilgrim route. However, China has refused. Frequent border patrol clashes on minor issues take place. Recently, China has even objected to constructing a water pipe line to a border village.

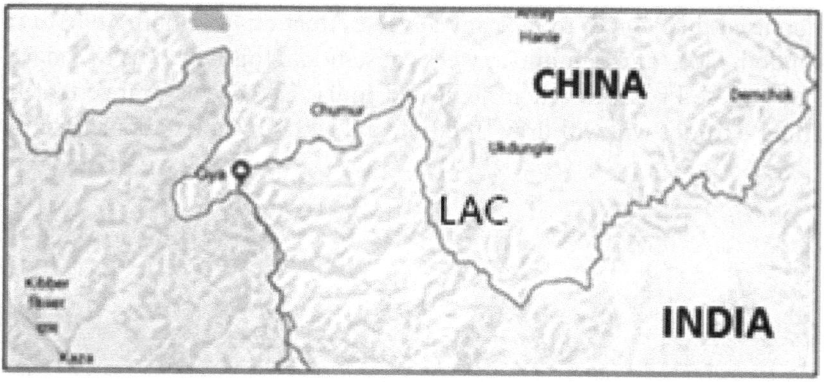

Trijunction Ladakh, Himachal Pradesh and China

Chumar is the last village in Ladakh bordering Himachal Pradesh on the Indian side and Tibet on the Chinese side. The trijunction of borders is located west of Chumar near Zipugi La as shown on the map above. Chumar is neither within the Chinese claim line of 1960 nor it was occupied during 1962 War. Yet it has been a bone of contention, a source of irritation and a bargaining chip. This village is located about 210 kms south of Leh and connected by road. The Chinese neither have any border post opposite Chumar in the vicinity of the LAC on their side nor does any road exist up to the border. Yet, very often Chinese helicopters fly over this area and lodge objections to any civil work done for the development of the village on the Indian side of the border.

During Despong (near DBO) standoff negotiations in 2013, the Chinese objected to the construction of overhead protection on the bunkers at the Indian side of the LAC here. They perceived it as a means of looking deep inside the Chinese Territory. Therefore, as part of the agreement, India had agreed to remove some overhead protection simultaneously when the Chinese vacated from Despong Valley intrusion. A boundary pact of peace and stability was also signed in October 2013 by India and China placing a robust mechanism in place to deal with the boundary disputes between the two countries in the future.

Notwithstanding the Boundary Pact, the Chinese troops intruded into Indian Territory and were constructing road with heavy machinery using their troops on 10 September 2014 near Chumar. The usual Flag meetings took place in an attempt to call off the illegal activities inside the Indian Territory without achieving any result. Meanwhile, both sides mobilised their forces to face any adverse situation developing due to the standoff. Later, after about two weeks of standoff, this issue was raised with the Chinese President when he visited India. He gave assurance that the Chinese troops will withdraw and they did withdraw after about 10 days.

Chapter 7

HIMACHAL, UTTARAKHAND, NEPAL, SIKKIM AND BHUTAN

HIMACHAL PRADESH

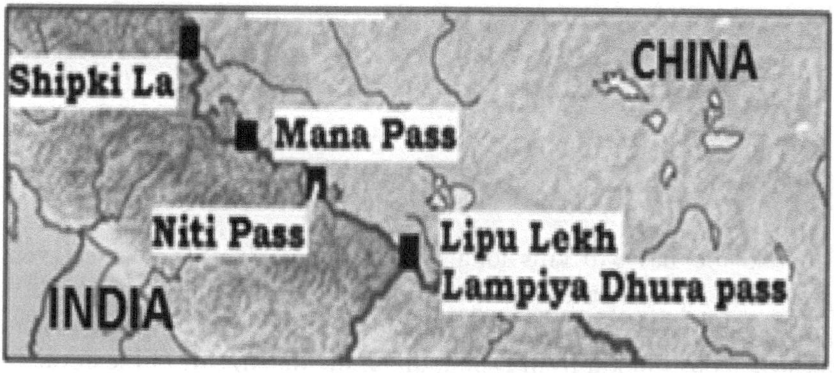

Major Passes-Himachal Pradesh –Tibet

Himachal Pradesh has 260 kms long border on its north-eastern side with China. Kinnaur and Lahaul are two border districts with 140 and 80 kms of their border with Tibet on the Chinese side. Traditionally cross-border trade had been taking place till 1962 War across Shipki La which is located at the boundary at an altitude of 18,599 feet. In addition there are other passes to cross over the border as shown on the map above. Locals have been crossing over to meet their relatives across the border. From 1994, trade was once again resumed after a protocol was signed by both countries.

China has an airfield at Lupsuk, which is nearly 190 kms from Kaurik. Chinese military helicopters are often seen flying close to the border. From the Indian side, ITBP is responsible for guarding the border. They have established 20 Posts and maintain constant vigil. ITBP has a high security camp at Kaurik.

UTTARAKHAND

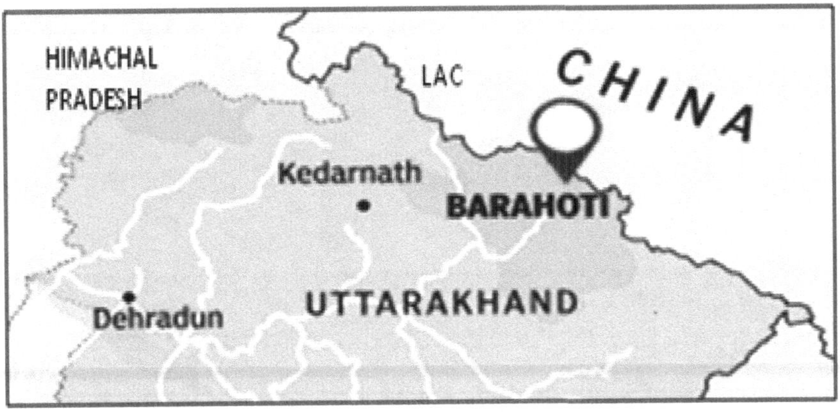

Uttarakhand

Uttarakhand has 370 kms long border with China. There are several passes which connect to Tibet which was used by the locals to trade, cattle grazing and meet their relatives. Barahoti is a 80 sq km disputed pasture located about 140 km from Dehradun on the Indian side of the border. It is connected from Joshimath by road up to Rimkhim and thereafter a track exists up to the border. It was demilitarised as per the Border Agreement of 1958. Both sides had agreed not to carry firearms while entering this zone. Civilians from both sides enter this zone with cattle and ITBP personnel carry out patrolling without weapon. During the standoff at Doklam in Bhutan in July 2017, Chinese entered more than a km into the Barahoti Demilitarised Zone on 22 July. Another intrusion took place a month before. Consequently, the Border Posts were reinforced. However, no engagement took place between the two sides. Such transgressions in the inaccessible areas take place due to varying perceptions of the boundary line on the ground by both sides.

NEPAL

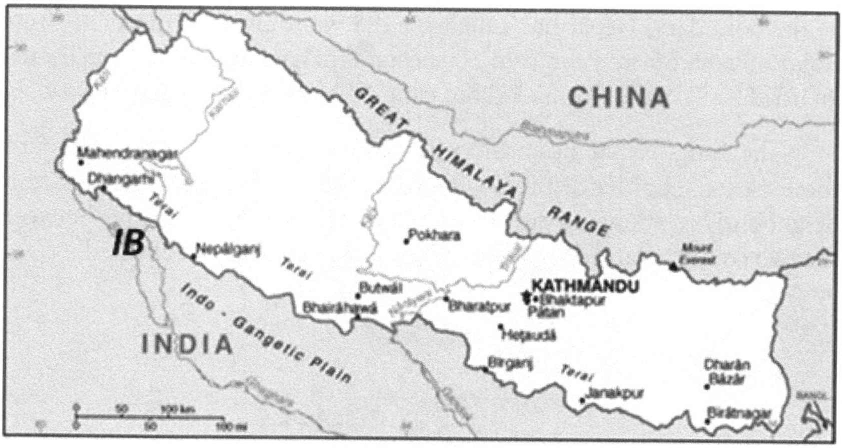

Nepal

The Nepal-India boundary, which runs to the west, south and east of Nepal, is 1,580 kilometers long and dates back to the Anglo-Nepal War of 1814–1816. Nepal's northern border is with China. To the west of Nepal is Uttarakand with Kali River (Sarada after it enters India) as the boundary. To the south are Uttar Pradesh and Bihar. Sikkim is to the east of Nepal. There are five entry points through which the citizens of both countries can enter without passport. The border was marked with 8553 pillars some of which are missing or damaged. Two of the long standing border disputes pertain to the region of Kalapani and Susta. Kalapani is a 35 sq kms territory at India-Nepal-China trijunction in western Nepal. According to Sugauli Treaty signed in 1816 between East India Company and the erstwhile Kingdom of Nepal at the conclusion of Anglo-Nepalese war of 1814-16, the River Mahakali was the boundary between India and Nepal.

The dispute arose regarding the exact alignment of the Kali River and its source which is at Om Parvat. According to India, Kalapani is part of India. Nepal produced a map showing Kalapani within the territory of Nepal. The dispute remains unresolved. In 2015, the Nepalese parliament objected to an agreement between India and China to trade through Lipulekh Pass, a mountainous pass in the disputed Kalapani area, stating that the agreement between India and China to trade through Kalapani violates Nepal's sovereign rights over the territory. The differences have arisen due to different maps that each country possesses and due to the shifting course of the Mahakali River in the area that was earlier accepted as the boundary. Nepal has called for the withdrawal of the ITBP from Kalapani area. Susta is about 14,500 hectares of land in the southern border guarded by Sashatra Seema Bal but claimed by Nepal as their territory.

The India-Nepal Friendship Treaty was signed in 1950. Although there are some border disputes which are required to be solved, the cordial neighbourly relationship due to age-old free movement of people between the two countries and social and cultural ties has not been affected.

SIKKIM

Sikkim

The State of Sikkim which lies sandwiched between Nepal in the west and China and Bhutan in the east is one of the strategically important states of India with 220 sq kms of disputed border with China, both in the north and east. The trijunction, where India, China and Bhutan borders meet is about 150 kms in the north from the 27 kms wide Siliguri corridor of West Bengal. This corridor controls the movement to the North-Eastern States from the rest of India.

A 'V' shaped Chinese territory known as Chumbi Valley separates Bhutan from Sikkim for a larger part in the north. From the trijunction of Nepal, China and Sikkim, the Indo-Chinese border runs due east and turns to the south to meet yet another trijunction of India, China and Bhutan.

Further south is the India-Bhutan border as shown on the map above. Important passes which connect Sikkim with Tibet are Nathu La, Cho La, Jelap La and Dongkha La. Chiwabhanjang La is in the west connecting Nepal with Sikkim. Sikkim was an independent kingdom that had cordial relation with British India. In 1947, the British guarantee of Independence to Sikkim was transferred with special protectorate status for Sikkim. India controlled its external affairs, defence and communication. On 14 April 1975, a referendum was held in which the people of Sikkim voted to merge with the Union of India and Sikkim became the 22nd Indian State.

The India-China border runs north of Sikkim. Indian Army, ITBP and Sikkim Scout are responsible to guard the border areas. Nathu La located about 54 kms from Gangtok at an altitude of 14,140 ft, is designated as a Trading Post and a Meeting Point. In the absence of marking of LAC on ground and the Chinese refusal to recognise the principle of watershed concept for boundary, Chinese claim areas across LAC. This led to many border clashes in this sector. On 16 September 1965, during the Indo-Pakistan war, China issued an ultimatum to India to vacate Nathu La. However, India refused to do so. Between 1965 and 1967, there were many skirmishes at Nathu La, Jelap La and Cho La between the two sides. The borderline at Nathu La passes through the middle of the Pass and it was not marked on ground. Northern shoulder of the Pass is held by the PLA, whereas the southern Shoulder which dominates the northern Shoulder is with the Indian Army.

On 6 September 1967, there was a scuffle between 2 Grenadiers of Indian Army and PLA led by their political commissar regarding the exact location of the border. To prevent such frequent scuffles in the future, India decided to put up a wire fence and mark the boundary on the ground. This was objected by the Chinese. On 11 September, the political commissar asked the Indian Army engineers to stop putting up the wire fence. The Commanding Officer of 2 Grenadiers under whom the work was being done refused. The Chinese opened fire and killed a large number of engineers and infantrymen who were working on the fence. India decided to retaliate and attack the Chinese locality with artillery and Infantry. The skirmish lasted till 15 September in which 2 Grenadiers and 18 Rajput attacked the Chinese post. Both sides suffered casualties.

Since Indian defences were dominating the Chinese Posts and their camp, the PLA suffered heavy casualty and destruction due to accurate artillery fire on them. Having suffered losses, PLA requested for ceasefire. This was a major moral victory to India after the ignominious defeat in the hands of PLA in 1962. There was a clash on 1 October 1967 at Chola, another pass on the Sikkim-Tibet border, a few kilometres north of Nathu La. The Gorkha Battalion guarding Chola asserted their ownership of the Pass and driven the PLA men three kms into their territory. On both occasions, Indian Army fared better than Chinese. The Commanding Officer of 2 Grenadiers, Lt Col Rai Singh was decorated with MVC. Major Harbhajan Singh of 18 Rajput was awarded MVC (posthumous) for bravery. Capt Dagar, Sepoy Gokul Singh and Riflemen RM Limbu and Timjong were awarded VrC.

BHUTAN

Bhutan

British India's 699 kms long border with Bhutan was demarcated in 1865 after the Army of East India Company defeated the Bhutanese in a war in the same year. After India's Independence, the demarcated border remained as Indo-Bhutanese border as shown on the map above. On the Indian side of Bhutan Border are the states of Sikkim, West Bengal, Assam and Arunachal Pradesh. In the north is China with a border of 470 kms long. There are two crossing places on the India-Bhutan Border at Jaigaon and Phuntsholing. SSB is responsible for manning the Indo-Bhutanese border.

In 1949, a Peace and Friendship treaty was signed between India and Bhutan. The boundary was further refined in 1984 between India and Bhutan. There are no major disputes on the alignment of the border between the two countries except a minor territorial adjustment with Arunachal Pradesh.

China offered 495 square-kms of their area to Bhutan in the north in exchange of 269 square-kms area of Bhutanese Territory near the southern tip of Chumbi Valley. Bhutan refused the offer. A series of negotiations were held between China and Bhutan without concluding any agreement. Meanwhile, China had occupied part of the Doklam Plateau inside Bhutan and constructed road to develop the area into a military base. India and Bhutan objected to it and moved their army to persuade PLA to vacate the Bhutanese territory. During the standoff between 16 June 2017 and 28 August 2017, Indian Army asserted its right to be at Doklam and scuffles ensued between PLA and Indian Army personnel. PLA withdrew from Bhutanese territory on 28 August 2017.

Chapter 8

ARUNACHAL PRADESH (NEFA)

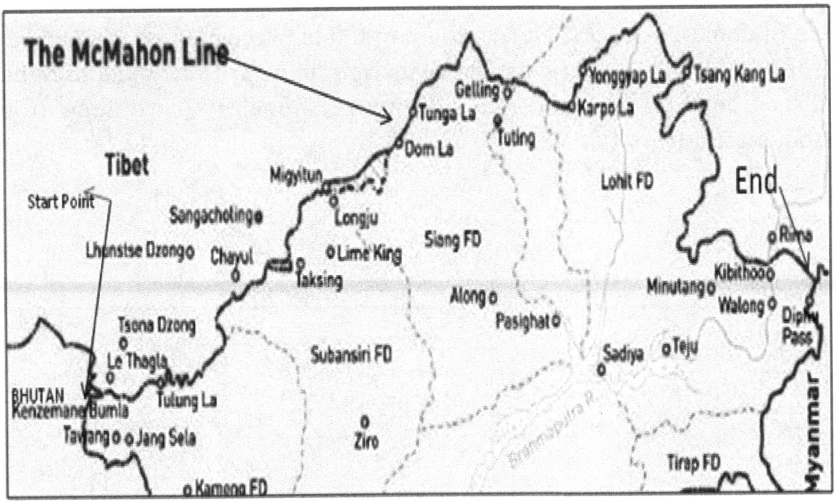

Arunachal Pradesh- LAC

The 1360-kms long Indo-Chinese LAC along the McMahon Line north of Arunachal Pradesh begins at the India-Bhutan China Border trijunction east of Bhutan and runs due east covering the entire State of Arunachal up to the Myanmar border in the east. In the absence of delineation of McMahon Line and the outrageous claim of China to the entire Arunachal Pradesh (NEFA) as part of China was the root-cause of the Chinese aggression in 1962. The McMahon Line passes through high altitude mountains generally along the line joining the highest ridges as per the watershed principle. The two most contentious border areas fall at Thag La Ridge north of Tawang in the west close to Indo-Bhutan border and north of Walong in the area of Kibithu in the east near Myanmar Border.

During the British rule over India, the British Indian Government entered into an agreement on the alignment of Indo-Tibetan Border in 1914 with Tibet. During the meeting, besides British and Tibetan representatives, a Chinese representative was also present. A map marked with the alignment of the Indo-Tibet Border, thereafter known as McMahon Line was initialled by the Chinese representative. However, the Chinese Government refused to recognise the border alignment agreed by the other two. According to this Agreement, Tawang was part of India.

However, Tibet was permitted to administer Tawang and Dirang due to religious connections to these places. In 1938, Assam Rifle posts were established at Dirang and Walong. Tawang remained under Tibetan monastery control. In 1950, People's Republic of China invaded and annexed Tibet with it. In 1951, Tibetan officials were evicted from Tawang by the Assam Rifle under an Indian Political Officer, Major Bob Kathing, without firing a single shot. Subsequently, the border posts with Tibet/China were manned by the personnel of Assam Rifles under the External Affairs Ministry.

TAWANG SECTOR

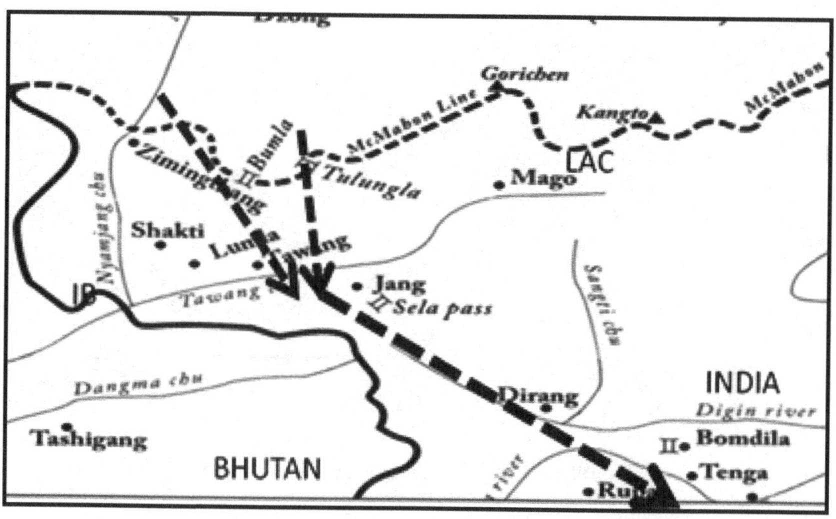

Tawang Sector and Bhutan Border-Western NEFA

In August 1959, the PLA had increased patrolling activities close to the border in Khinzemane and Longju areas in the western NEFA. *(In October, an Indian Police patrol was ambushed by the Chinese in Changchenmo Valley south of Kongka La in Ladakh*). Assam Rifles reacted by increasing their protective measures. The relation between India and China deteriorated at political level due to sympathy shown towards the people of Tibet by India. Anticipating Chinese hostility, the responsibility of the border areas in this sector was handed over to the Indian Army units. From then onwards, the cold war began between the two countries which had earlier declared themselves as brothers.

Indian Army moved its 4 Infantry Division in 1960 to protect both NEFA and Sikkim borders. Assam Rifle and Police Forces manned the border posts established by the Intelligence Bureau under the Army control. A Border Road Organisation was created to develop road communications in the remote undeveloped areas. By 1962, the number of border posts of approximately platoon strength each had increased to 34 under operation code-named Onkar. 7 Infantry Brigade of 4 Infantry Division was moved forward to Tawang.

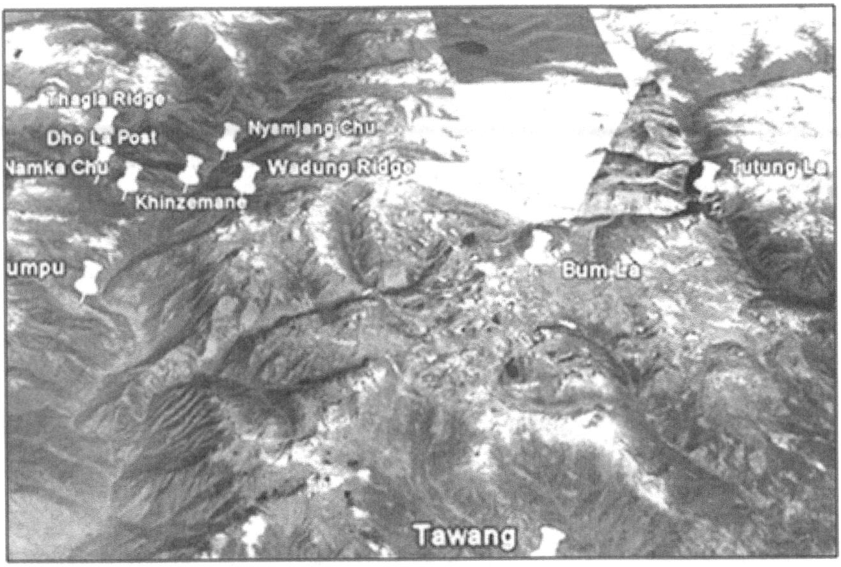

Posts Established in Thagla, Bumla-Tawang area 1962

Indian Army had deployed two brigades (six battalions) in the border areas. They were moved from the plains of India to NEFA, still wearing their cotton uniform which was inadequate to protect against cold weather obtaining in the mountainous region. These Army units were not fully trained to fight a war in the high altitude mountains. On the Chinese side, they had deployed 19 Battalions, armed with latest weapons and equipped and trained in mountain warfare. Opposite Khinzamane, Chinese had two company Posts. They had also occupied Thagla Ridge overlooking Namka Chu River Valley.

According to the Indian perception, McMahon Line was north of Thagla Ridge. Whereas, Chinese claimed and occupied it in strength as they perceived the McMahon line to be in the south of Thagla Ridge. Indian Army launched Operation Leghorn to evict the Chinese from Thagla Ridge. 7 Infantry Brigade was moved to Namka Chu valley from Tawang. The Corps Commander did not approve of it. But he was overruled by the higher ups.

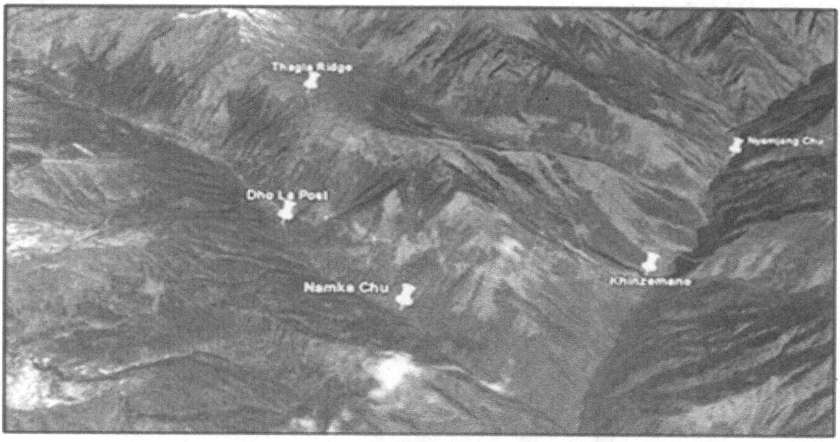

Thagla, Dhola, Namka Chu, Nyamjang Chu

Dhola which is located near the trijunction of Indo-Bhutan Tibet border was one of the Posts occupied under Operation Onkar. The Chinese claimed that Dhola Post was located in their territory and the PLA personnel encircled the Post and were shouting at the Assam Rifle men to vacate the Post. On 18 September 1962, orders were given to the Indian Army to evict the Chinese from Dhola and Thagla Ridge and adopt aggressive posture against Chinese entering into the perceived Indian Territory.

A new Corps HQ was raised with the task of evicting Chinese from Thagla Ridge. The Corps commander ordered 7 Brigade to occupy defences along the Namkha Chu (River) which was being dominated by the Chinese Army from Thagla Ridge. Accordingly, 9 Punjab, 2 Rajput and

1/9 GR occupied the defence guarding the Bridges across Namka Chu and south of it. The Chinese made many provocative moves. Being aware of the numerical superiority and tactical advantages enjoyed by the Chinese, it was decided not to take any offensive action but to hold ground at Namka Chu defences which was unsuitable to fight a successful defensive battle.

By October, when the winter was setting in, casualties of 7 Brigade increased manifold due to cold weather and high altitude diseases. High altitude clothing was not available to issue to troops at Namka Chu Valley. The process of casualty evacuation was very slow. The state of ammunition was unsatisfactory. The Chinese made many attempts to cross Namka Chu. These were thwarted. However, they continued to carry out the reconnaissance of 7 Brigade Defences from the vantage points on the Thagla Ridge.

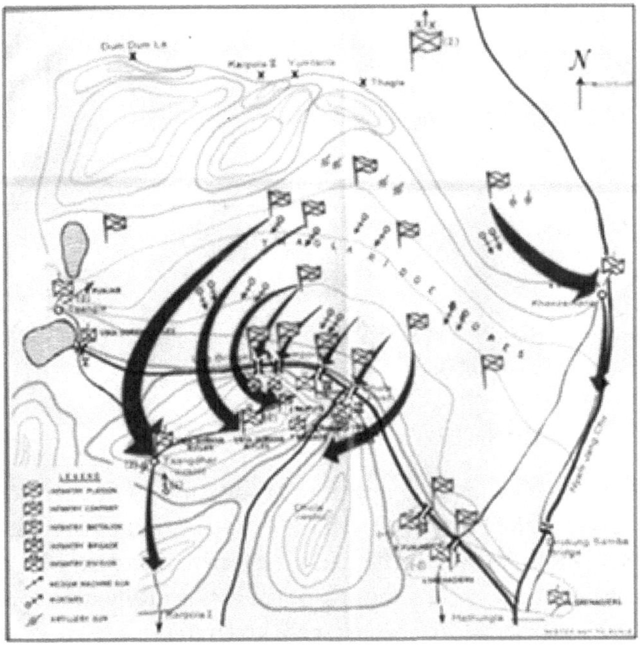

Chinese Attack across Namka Chu

The first coordinated Chinese attack came on 10 October 1962. The PLA attacked and overran the Indian post at Tsenge Jong which had been established on the north bank of the Namka Chu. Ten days later on 20 October 1962 at 5 AM, the Chinese bombarded the entire Brigade Defences including Dhola Post for about an hour. Then they crossed the River at selected places, infiltrated through the gaps in the defences and launched attack from the rear (south). The Brigade Defence was north facing.

The Brigade units were surprised when they faced the assault from their rear. Telephone lines were cut off by the Chinese before launching the attack. Men had to come out of the bunkers and engage the enemy in the open in close quarter battles. Each defended locality fought its own battle. 2 Rajput faced the brunt of major Chinese attack. 282 officers and men were killed in the initial attack. Many more were wounded. The Chinese suffered more. However, the men of 2 Rajput, 9 Punjab and 1/9 GR stood up against the onslaught and wrote their history with their blood. They were tasked to fight the enemy; they fought, killed the attackers and when surmounted, died at the ground they were supposed to defend. Those who were injured and alive were taken prisoners. Others withdrew in small groups to Tawang.

Overwhelmingly superior PLA captured the defences of 7 Brigade by the end of the day. But it was at a heavy cost. The PLA suffered more casualty than Indian Army. The so called debacle of 1962 started only after the battle of Namka Chu but not at Namka Chu where every soldier withstood the rigours of the element and fought the numerically superior enemy when the opportunity afforded. After clearing Namka Chu defences the PLA advanced towards Tawang by infiltrating in small columns and occupied the dominating heights around Tawang.

Tawang was one of the major objectives of the Chinese. The shortest approach from the border to Tawang was along a 26 kms long track from Bumla. It is located at an altitude of 4,492 m from the MSL. Two kms south of Bumla was an inspection bungalow and the track from Bumla is dominated by a Ridge known as IB Ridge. South of IB Ridge was Twin Peak near Tongpeng La. 1 Sikh was tasked to deny Bumla-Tawang axis to the attackers. D Company of 1 Sikh under Lt Haripal Kaushik (Hockey Olympian) occupied the defence at Tongpeng La with a platoon at IB Ridge under Subedar Joginder Singh. Bumla was held by the personnel of Assam Rifle. On 20 October 1962, a large concentration of Chinese soldiers was observed across Bumla. Subedar Joginder Singh had sent one of his sections to reinforce Bumla under Hav Sucha Singh. On 23 October the Chinese attacked Bumla and captured it. The Section under Hav Sucha Singh withdrew to IB Ridge after causing casualties on the enemy.

Subedar Joginder Singh expected an attack on the IB Ridge after Bumla defences were overrun. He was prepared to face the uphill attack by the PLA from the north. Early morning the next day, more than six hundred Chinese attacked the IB Ridge. The first attack was repulsed with effective fire from the IB Ridge. The enemy suffered heavy casualty as they were attacking on a narrow front. After a pause, the Chinese climbed the hill from different directions and attacked the Post in a broad-front. They failed to reach the objective against well controlled accurate fire from the Sikhs. Subedar Joginder was wounded and his platoon was left with only 17 men. Ammunition stock was low. After first aid, Joginder continued encouraging his men to engage the enemy deliberately.

Meanwhile, Subedar Joginder's company commander asked him if he could arrange to bring down own artillery fire on the IB Ridge against the enemy moving in the open. (*This method of fire known as Defensive Fire SOS is resorted to by the higher commanders at critical stage of the battle. It may cause casualty to own men if they are in the open, hence they are warned to take cover before firing starts*). Brave Joginder replied in affirmative. The fire was brought down with devastating effect on the enemy by the artillery observation post officer Capt Gurcharan Singh Gosal. Once the DF SOS was lifted, on the face of vastly superior enemy, Joginder called his men out in the open and resorted to bayonet charge. In the end all but four were left alive. Subedar Joginder who was seriously wounded was taken prisoner. The other three were those who were sent earlier to bring ammunition from the company HQ and could not return in time before the enemy attacked again. Subedar Joginder Singh died in Chinese custody due to his wounds.

From the IB Ridge, the Chinese advanced further and captured Tawang after clearing Tongpeng La. After causing delay, D Company inflicted heavy casualty on the enemy and withdrew to the Battalion HQ at Se La.

Subedar Joginder Singh was decorated with the only Param Vir Chakra (posthumous) in NEFA for his outstanding bravery and leadership. Lt Haripal Kausik was awarded Vir Chakra. The Chinese repatriated the ashes of late Subedar Joginder Singh on May 17 the next year.

Subedar Joginder Singh PVC

(Posthumous)

After the fall of Tawang, the PLA advanced along multiple routes, bypassed Sela defences and reached Bomdila. Against this onslaught, Indian Army had lost its cohesion and command and control collapsed. The Chinese had captured Rupa south of Bomdila and were poised to roll down into the plains of Assam. After the unexpected sweep through NEFA to the foothills of Assam, on 21 November 1962, the Chinese were forced to regain their communication and logistics support. With that, a unilateral ceasefire was declared by the PLA. Thereafter, they withdrew from NEFA back to their starting point gradually.

After the Chinese withdrew from NEFA in 1962/63, both sides stayed away from the Thagla region. In the early eighties, patrolling was started by the Indian troops up to the perceived borderline and in 1984 India had established an observation post north east of the confluence of the Namka Chu and Nyamjiang Chu in the Samdurang Chu Valley. It was manned by the Special Security Bureau during the summer. During the winter, the Post used to be vacated. In the summer of 1986 when 12 ASSAM was tasked to occupy the post, they found it was occupied by the Chinese. Indian Army occupied a nearby post. Both sides claimed the area to be theirs and concentrated large troops leading to tense situation in the region. India launched Operation Chequered Board under which Army and Air Force formations were moved closer to their battle positions.

Representatives of both countries met to negotiate a settlement to the alignment of border in this Sector. A total of nine meetings took place at different levels and finally a settlement was reached in 1993. An agreement was signed at foreign ministers level and the confrontation was avoided by mutually agreeing to relocate their Posts. However, there was no mutually acceptable Line of Actual Control. As of now, the two sides still have their own perception of the McMahon Line on the ground and a 'no war no peace' situation prevails.

WALONG-EASTERN NEFA

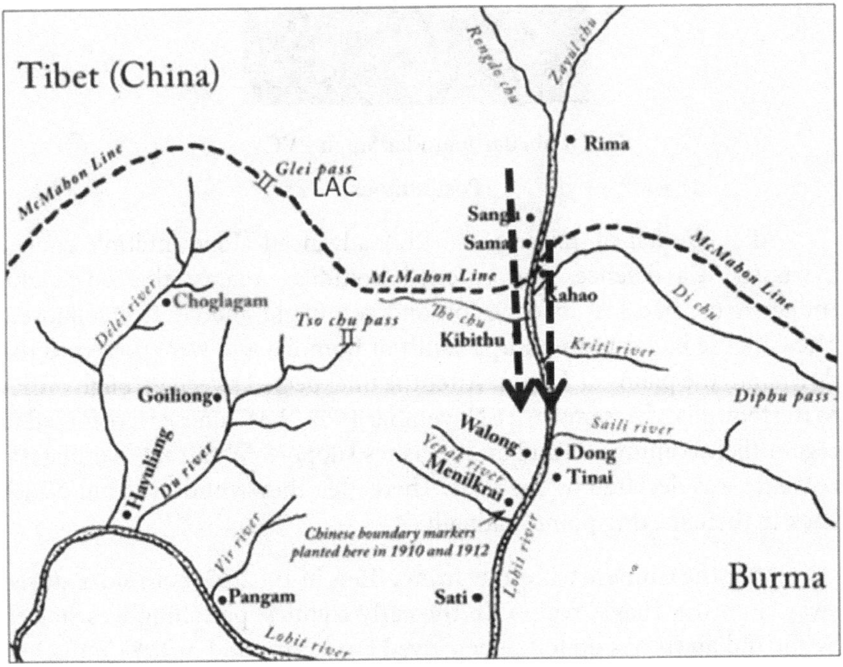

Kibithu-Walong

In 1962, the PLA crossed the McMahon Line in NEFA north of Tawang in the west and north of Walong in the east simultaneously. Walong is located about 50 kms south of India-China-Myanmar (Burma) border trijunction on the banks of Lohit River. It had a runway for operating small fixed wing aircrafts. Walong is dominated by hills with heights varying from 10 to 16 thousand feet above MSL. Lohit River originates from Tibet and passes through east of Kibithu and Walong.

Assam Rifles was deployed for the security of this frontier area before 1962 when responsibility was handed over to the Army. The Army moved a brigade to Walong and deployed a battalion each at Kibithu and Walong. Opposite this sector, China had six battalions in Tibet.

6 Kumaon was deployed in the area of Kibithu with their Battalion HQ at Walong. On 18 October 1962, increased troop activities were observed on the Chinese side of McMahon Line. On the night of 21 October, the PLA attacked on the Company of 6 Kumaon which was deployed at McMahon Ridge south of the border, starting with artillery and machine gun fire. The attack was repulsed. PLA attacked once again. This time it was more violent. Kumaonis repulsed the second attack as well. When PLA was forming up to launch the attack third time with larger strength, it was decided to withdraw the company from the McMahon Ridge and concentrate at Kibithu. Meanwhile, orders were received from HQ 4 Corps HQ to concentrate 6 Kumaon and 4 Sikh at Walong and occupy a Brigade defended Sector. This was done by 23 October. By 3 November, additional troops were inducted into the Walong Sector.

To strengthen the Brigade Defended Sector, the brigade commander, Brigadier NC Rawley had decided to include the dominating areas known as Tri-junction, Yellow and Green Pimple within the brigade defences. The task was given to 6 Kumaon to occupy Yellow Pimple. By the time the unit could launch the attack, the PLA had occupied Yellow Pimple. Therefore, 6 Kumaon launched an attack on 14 November and captured a part of Yellow Pimple. *(During the Indo-China war, this was the only attack the Indian Army launched on a PLA-held area and recaptured it.)* Chinese reacted to the loss of Yellow Pimple violently and counter-attacked with large force and recaptured it the next day. From Yellow Pimple Kumaonese moved to trijunction which was attacked by the PLA. The attack was repulsed. In these two intense engagements, 6 Kumaon lost more than 50% of their officers and men.

Further, the Chinese surrounded Tri-junction making it impossible to reinforce the locality. Even the casualty could not be evacuated. Considering the hopelessness of the situation, 6 Kumaon was ordered to withdraw. In the process of withdrawal, some of the localities had to fight 'last man last round'. The Chinese occupied the Tri-junction by 16 November. PLA continued their attacks relentlessly on 4 Sikh and 3/3 GR. Some of the fiercest battles were fought in the area of Ladders. The Corps and Divisional Commanders witnessed the battles and realised that the Chinese had amassed huge forces for the capture of Walong. Both the banks of Lohit River were under Chinese control. The Corps commander authorised the Brigade Commander to withdraw the Brigade to a better defendable sector in case Walong becomes untenable.

PLA continued their offensive with fresh troops and attacked Walong from three directions. Brigade defences became untenable and was ordered to withdraw to the south in small groups. On 23 November when Brigade was in the process of withdrawing, orders were received for ceasefire. Some of the sub-units which did not get the message continued fighting for a few more days. During the battle of Walong which was spread over a month, the brigade lost more than 50 percent of officers and men. Nearly 400 were taken prisoners. The enemy loss was equally high. As in the other sectors, Chinese withdrew behind the McMahon line after the unilateral ceasefire was declared by them. The Chinese won the War of 1962, but the Indian Army gave a good fight in Ladakh and Walong Sector.

Chapter - 9

MYANMAR, BANGLADESH, SRI LANKA

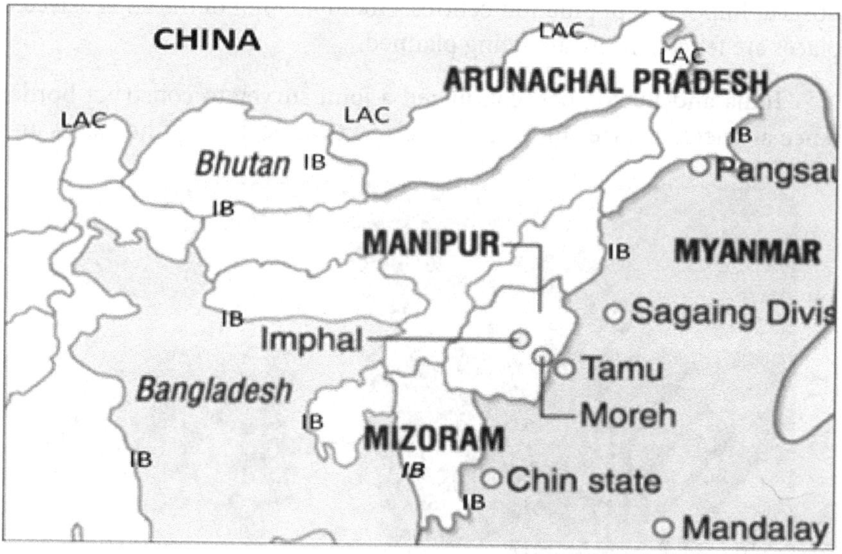

MYANMAR

The IB between India and Burma/Myanmar starts from the trijunction of India-China and Burma. It runs 1,643 km to meet the Bangladesh border in the south of Mizoram. Arunachal Pradesh (520 km), Nagaland (215 km), Manipur (398 km) and Mizoram (510 km) are the Indian states which have IB with Burma. The border area from the north is characterised with ruggered mountains, thick jungles, rivers and deep valleys. The broken nature of varying topography makes it a highly porous IB. The population density on both sides is very low. Due to lack of road communication, the border area on both sides of the IB remained isolated from the rest of the country. The political unrest in the northeastern States of India and militancy across the IB in Burma led to creating a safe haven to insurgents, drug smugglers, human traffickers and other anti-social elements on both sides of the border.

A Land Boundary Agreement was signed between India and Burma in 1967. The India-Myanmar border has the Free Movement Regime which allows the tribes living along the border on both sides to travel up to 16-km across the boundary without visa restrictions. Small scale trade, cultivation and social visits across the IB are freely practiced. To prevent anti-social and insurgency-related activities, Assam Rifle and Army occupy the border posts at important population centres. About 400 km of the IB at selected places are fenced. More are being planned.

India and Burma had conducted a joint survey to construct border fence at selected places in 2003. The project was stalled by the Nagas and

Kukis who live on both sides of the IB. They suspected that the fence will divide their tribe and those living on the Indian side may be isolated from their kith and kin. In 2007, a boundary pillar dispute arose along the Manipur IB regarding some border pillars. Minor disputes are resolved at appropriate levels. Both countries co-operate with each other to maintain peace in the area. The Government of India is considering creating a dedicated Indo-Myanmar Border Force for guarding the IB effectively.

BANGLADESH

Operation Jackpot-Bangladesh

India has a 4,098 km long border with Bangladesh. Bangladesh is surrounded by the Indian states of West Bengal, Assam, Meghalaya, Tripura and Mizoram. The border area is riverine with hilly and jungle terrain. Both sides of the border are thickly populated. Cultivation is done up to the IB in some of the areas.

The British Indian Province of Bengal was partitioned in 1947 by Sir Radcliffe Committee along with partition of Punjab in the west. With its western part remaining with India, eastern parts of Bengal along with Sylhet District of Assam become East Pakistan. The IB was known as Radcliffe Line. The political instability in East Pakistan and atrocities committed on the Bengalis by the Pakistan Army caused a huge refugee problem to the Indian States located around East Pakistan in 1970/71. The Bengalis of East Pakistan began a liberation movement. India decided to provide military support to the freedom fighters to reduce the impact of refugee problems. Finally, India decided to liberate the people of East Pakistan from the tyranny of Pakistan Army by destroying the Pakistan Army in the East.

Accordingly, Indian Army fought their way through and converged on the capital city of Dacca in a quick multipronged advance and completed the task in less than 15 days. East Pakistan was liberated and renamed as Bangladesh. Many bravery awards including a Param Vir Chakra were awarded. The sole PVC recipient was L/NK Albert Ekka.

L/Nk Albert Ekka PVC (Posthumous)

After the creation of Bangladesh with the help of India in 1971, the erstwhile demarcated border with East Pakistan remained unaltered. In 1974, a Land Border Agreement was made to demarcate the land border with Bangladesh and to regulate the enclaves on both side of the border. The enclaves were pockets in which people of one country traditionally lived in the territory of other country. They were neglected by both countries. The agreement was finally signed in 2011 between India and Bangladesh and the status of 111 Indian enclaves and 51 Bangladesh enclaves were changed after due deliberations. Presently there is no illegal occupation of each other's territory. The IB is manned by the BSF.

Border Fencing

The problem of Bangladesh citizens illegally entering India, the insurgents from India taking shelter inside Bangladesh and other illegal trans-border activities persist. Therefore, the BSF which is responsible for the management of the border has constructed border fence with flood lighting at most of the vulnerable areas. Due to the nature of terrain crisscrossed with rivers, it has not been possible to prevent illegal entry across the border entirely.

SRI LANKA

The Maritime Boundary Agreement between India and Sri Lanka was signed on 22 March 1976.

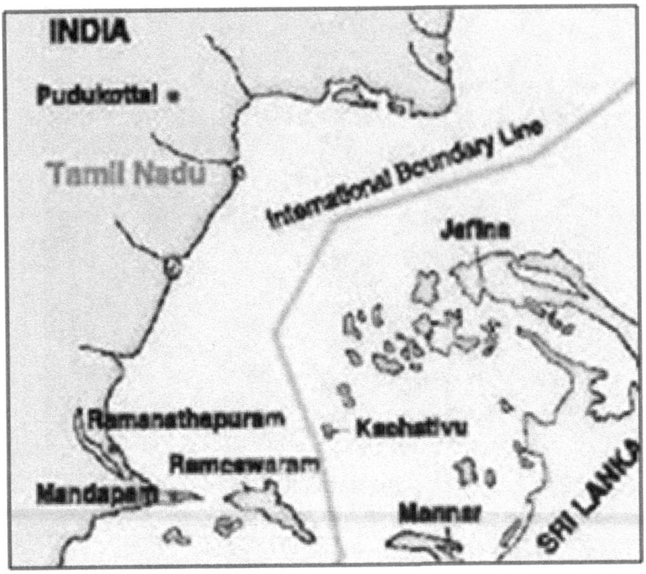

Katchativu

Katchativu is an island of 285-acres of land located on the Srilankan side of the maritime boundary between Tamilnadu in India and Srilanka. In 1974, Katchativu was ceded to Sri Lanka through the Indo-Sri Lankan Maritime Agreement to settle the maritime boundary in the Palk Strait. The area around the island had been used for fishing by both Indian and Srilankan fishermen traditionally. Sri Lankan government strengthened its security at Maritime boundaries. When Indian fishermen crossed boundaries, they were arrested by the Srilankan Navy. In 1991, the Tamil Nadu demanded the retrieval of Katchativu from Srilanka and approached the Indian Courts claiming the ownership of the Island. In 2014, the Central Government informed the Tamilnadu Government that Katchativu belongs to Srilanka and the Indian fishermen do not have the right to engage in fishing activities across the maritime boundary.

CONCLUSION

India's borders with her neighbours pass through variety of geographical regions. In the 72 years since independence, the Indian Armed Forces have fought five major wars and numerous skirmishes against those who dared to cross India's borders. In the process, thousands of our soldiers have made the supreme sacrifice to defend our sovereignty as an independent nation. To ensure that the citizens of India sleep in peace, and that the prosperity of the nation continues, the Indian Armed Forces stand on guard in some of the most inhospitable terrains found anywhere in the world.

Three major aspects of our country will determine the future of border wars with our neighbours; economic prosperity, military might and political clout. These aspects need to be strengthened as the topmost priority of our nation. We need to ensure that suitable talents from across our society are attracted as the sentinels of our frontiers. The best of our youth need to be motivated to join the Armed Forces of India and face challenges in battles that are yet to be fought at our borders. The supreme sacrifices made by selfless heroes of the Indian Armed Forces are a matter of honour and must be remembered and respected. Our youth need to know the tales of sacrifice made by the uniformed forces of India in defending the borders and make them their role models.

China is an economic giant which has an ongoing expansionist policy. Pakistan is an unstable state with internal conflicts and external policy of supporting terrorism. Recent events leading to close ties between these two countries are matter of concern to India. After having fought wars against these two countries, it is safe to presume that in the future, these two countries may jointly or severally wage wars to settle their unjustifiable claims over Indian Territory. India has lost more than 12,000 lives in direct wars against these countries. There is a need for restructuring and strengthening the Indian Armed Forces to meet the perceived future threats. Borderless nations and the concept of a 'global village' are distant dreams.

Geography cannot be altered; neither can we choose our neighbours. The government of the day should continue to make all-out effort to improve our relation with the neighbouring countries and resolve disputes in an honourable manner. Confrontation or war should be the last resort.

In today's world, every nation needs some other nation's support at the time of crisis. Forming alliances with other likeminded nations for show of strength is a key step in the right direction. We need to increase our capability to monitor and dominate our border areas, enhance the fighting potential of our Armed Forces, improve our economic strength and acquire international political clout. The frontiers will remain forever in one form or the other and wars will be fought between countries on territorial disputes and ideological differences. It is up to the Indian leaders to make the future wars less costly to the nation.

Forces guarding the borders should comprise local youths for their knowledge of the terrain and their capability to acclimatise themselves to the battlefields. Modern Command, Control, Communications, Computer, Information, Intelligence, Surveillance and Reconnaissance (C4I2SR) capabilities should be used to supplement border forces in the remote areas. Demarcation of the borders and development of border areas need to be taken up on priority to integrate the people living in our remote border areas with the mainstream India. Forces responsible to regulate the movement across the borders and peace time protection of border areas should be structured and integrated between various agencies.

The Indian Armed Forces personnel have remained dedicated to their cause and are proud of their heritage. Continuing the tradition of their ancestors, they are ready to lay down their life and are proud of their valour and sacrifice. They need to be kept motivated.

यदृच्छया चोपपन्नं स्वर्गद्वारमपावृतम् |

सुखिनः क्षत्रियाः पार्थ लभन्ते युद्धमीदृशम् || ३२ ||

"O Partha, fortunate are the Kshatriyas

when such a righteous battle has unprovoked fallen to their lot;

they find therein an open door to heaven".

– The Bhagavad Gita. Chapter 2, Verse 32.

INDEX

O

P

R

S